CW00953348

The Wild Bunch

Patrick Matthews is a freelance wine writer and has written for *Decanter*, *The Independent*, *The Mail on Sunday*, *Saveur* and *Wine* Magazine. He has also been a regular wine columnist for *Time Out*. He took a Distinction in the Wine and Spirit Education Trust Higher Certificate in 1993 and holds the 'Wines from France 1995 Premier Cru' award for wine writing.

He is also a television producer and director, with credits on BBC2's *Food and Drink*, the Glenfiddich award-winning *Arena Food Night*, Channel Four's *Curry Connection* and numerous other projects.

FABER BOOKS ON WINE

Series Editor: Julian Jeffs

Bordeaux (new edition) by David Peppercorn
Burgundy (new edition) by Anthony Hanson
French Country Wines by Rosemary George
Haut-Brion by Asa Briggs
Italian Wines (new edition) by Philip Dallas
Sauternes by Stephen Brook
Sherry (new edition) by Julian Jeffs
The Wines of Alsace by Tom Stevenson
The Wines of Australia (new edition) by Oliver Mayo
The Wines of Greece by Miles Lambert-Gócs
The Wines of the Loire by Roger Voss
The Wines of New Zealand by Rosemary George
The Wines of the Rhône (new edition) by John Livingstone-Learmonth
The Wines of South Africa by James Seely

SuperBooze by Tom Stevenson

THE WILD BUNCH

Great Wines from Small Producers

———

PATRICK MATTHEWS

———

faber and faber

LONDON · BOSTON

First published in 1997
by Faber and Faber Limited
3 Queen Square London WC1N 3AU

Phototypeset by Intype London Limited
Printed in England by Clays Ltd, St Ives plc

A CIP record for this book
is available from the British Library

ISBN 0–571–19043–X

2 4 6 8 10 9 7 5 3 1

For Claudine, Emma, Luke and Peter

Contents

━━━━

CONTENTS

Acknowledgements

Writers sometimes boast about not doing things which you think would anyway guarantee them a stiffish jail term – i.e.: 'The author has not solicited, nor would he knowingly accept, cash payments in return for favourable publicity in this guide.' Let me instead get down to the nitty-gritty: three nights in Beaujolais, three in Champagne, three in Jerez-de-la-Frontera, two in the Languedoc and five in Sydney on the tab of the relevant growers' organisations. Air flights between London–Sydney, London–Paris and Barcelona–Jerez. About half the wines tasted will have been given me by the importers or producers. The majority of the travel was at my own expense but without some help the book couldn't have appeared in this form. This doesn't mean I subscribe to the view that free trips take no toll of a writer's impartiality. I accepted one further night in a hotel from a *négociant* (wine merchant); the very next day I met a grower who had severed his connections with him for reasons that would have made fascinating reading. You'll look for them in vain in these pages. Sorry.

The following individuals, not mentioned or referred to only briefly in the text, have made important and diverse contributions: Tim Atkin, Alexis Bespaloff, Paddy Biggs, Richard Biggs, Adam Brett-Smith, Sally Brock, Audrey Evans, Harry Eyres, Simon Farr, Aileen Hall, Pam Holt, Julian Jeffs, Alex Kanumanchiri, Prof Ralph Kunkee, David Little, Susan Low, Andrew Lownie, Emily Macdonald, Giles MacDonagh, Catherine Manac'h, Belinda Matthews, Pamela Matthews, Susan Matthews, Paul Merritt, Hazel Murphy, Marcel Orford-Williams, Jane Owen, Francoise Peretti, Bruce Rogers, Susan Shaw, Caroline Stacey, Rosalia Verger, Justine Willett. In general since I first wrote on the subject in 1991 I have met with kindness from too many drinks writers and members of the trade to mention individually.

I would *like* to thank my wife for taking the time to read the typescript and make many useful suggestions . . . actually, she eventually got round to it, winkled out some dire phrases, and throughout helped in her unique way.

The tasting note on page 26 is reproduced by kind permission of Remington Norman, author of *Rhône Renaissance*, Mitchell Beazley, London, 1995. The extract from Max Schubert's diary on page 117 is reproduced from Max Schubert, *Winemaker*, Huon Hooke, by kind permission of Kerr Publishing of Sydney, NSW.

Introduction

The Wild Bunch is an introduction to wines made because of a producer's personal passion or enthusiasm rather than because they conform to the requirements of the British mass market. Most, though not all, come from small-scale growers. One thing they have in common is that they're all different; they enjoy a diversity of character which results from the nearly infinite number of possible permutations of local grapes, local tastes and personal obsessions. Another is that they are relatively inexpensive; mostly priced between £5 and £10 a bottle, they will not attract the attention of the connoisseur of 'fine' wines from classic areas.

The Wild Bunch is in five sections. The first introduces the growers, their enthusiasms, prejudices and how they fit, or fail to fit, into the broader business. The second is about geography and the sense of place: the inspiration growers draw from their vineyard site and the traditions of their surrounding region. The third is about grapes and vines: how growers choose varieties and look after the vineyard. The fourth describes wine-making and distinguishes between techniques which producers adopt because they believe in them and those which just make for an easier life and greater profitability.

Finally I look at the wine trade, the individuals who bring handmade wines into Britain and the obstacles and competition they face.

The book is intended to be read rather than referred to; but to make sense of the narrative, it helps to have an idea of what the wines under discussion are like and where they can be bought. So throughout the text there is guidance on where the wines can be found, together with other suggested producers. This guidance is intended as the starting point for further explorations with the help of the lists of various merchants. It does not attempt to list all the best wines available in Britian from all the best small producers.

Trying to Score

It's dangerous to recommend a wine as 'interesting' if this means spending up to £10 on something you can't see the point of. If a wine is mentioned by name it's because I like it; however I've also tried to indicate if it's likely to have immediate appeal despite being a little unusual – as does, say, a Pinot Blanc from Alsace – or is going to be challenging, like a raspingly sour and salty old dry Amontillado sherry. In order not to arouse false expections I've sporadically given 1 to 5 ratings for 'oddness', meaning non-conformity to fashionable wine styles, and for 'niceness', meaning immediate likeability. I've used numbers rather than letters (i.e. A to E) as it's difficult to remember whether, say, 'D' means 'a lot' or 'not very much'. *The quirk this creates is that a wine I like a lot can still get low scores:* for example a neutralish white Bourgogne Aligoté which is neither very strange nor a real crowd-pleaser.

Unlike many, I rather enjoy reading descriptions of the way a wine tastes, so, for people like me, I've done my best to identify and record my impressions. Wine tasting is not 'bollocks' – the view of one of the characters in Nick Hornby's novel, *High Fidelity*. It's a genuine discipline, using the same skills as are drawn on by tea blenders, say, or perfumiers, and it's one that I have always found very tough. All I can plead for those annoyed by my notes is hard work and the desire to be honest.

I

WINE WITH A HUMAN FACE

In an era when political insurrection is off the agenda in Western countries, British consumers never stop hearing about 'revolutions' – in mobile phones, or satellite television or retailing. A surplus range of agitprop words and images has found new customers, like a successful sell-off of a public utility.

My subject is one of these down-sized revolutions. Within its narrow compass it does have something in common with the spirit of 1789, 1905 and 1917, that was missing, say, in the Watneys Red Revolution of the 1960s. It is a transformation in the wine business and it is mildly revolutionary in having originated not in the marketing department of a big company or from one or two entrepreneurs, but from the bottom up, from the grass-roots producers.

It's unusual to find that people, not technology or capital, can make a difference. But wine is an unusual business, more like showbiz or the media – whose products are one-offs – than car manufacture or microtechnology.

Just as a new film or book has to have something different to say, wine sells on a promise of diversity. This is why supermarkets carry hundreds of different lines, even if the actual contents are often quite similar. If you are looking for differences that are more than skin deep, avoid industrial-scale producers – good though their stuff can often be – and go for the newly emerging independent growers.

Of course, the complexity and variety of wine can simply become mystifying – though some residual mystery is as important as desire and passion are to sex: not indispensable, but otherwise, why bother? Writers try to simplify things by following a single thread, like grape varieties or the geography of the wine regions. Here the starting point, and the subject of the section, is the human face of wine.

I

A Grass-Roots Revolution

There is a lot written about wine, and of the many thousands of words that get into print every year, a large proportion continue to celebrate something called the Wine Revolution. This book is about a different transformation.

The familiar, in fact over-familiar, story is the one telling how flying wine-makers and the supermarkets have made inexpensive wine consistent and reliable. There's a French saying: '*un train peut cacher un autre*' ('one train can conceal another', based on the familiar signs warning drivers against recklessly crashing through level crossing barriers which remain down after a train's gone by). I think that we've been so mesmerized by an endless succession of heavily laden supermarket trolleys that we've missed a much more interesting trend. Year in year out more and more European growers have been setting up as wine-makers in their own right, declaring independence from the big concerns to whom in the past they would have sold their grapes or bulk wine.

From France to Greece, Austria to Portugal, even the most obscure wine regions are acquiring local champions in ever-increasing numbers. And seen from the traditional wine-making countries, this phenomenon is the one that counts – not the Australian veneer being given to cheap wine destined for the British market. The new-wave producers are very successful in their own countries; few of them really need us. But I'd argue that we need them – for their diversity, their roots in hundreds of local cultures and the great range of flavours they conjure up, relying on ripe concentrated grapes rather than on technical manipulation.

Every year more go independent, some destined to become established names, others with a less glorious future. If they feel ready to receive foreign journalists, it's usually a sign that they feel established, so it's especially interesting to meet someone in the make-or-break early years.

Hervé Menard is the sort of young grower who a quarter of a century ago would never have dreamed of making a living by selling his own wine. Even in the 1990s his fellow growers at Bourgueil on the Loire thought it eccentric when he planned to set himself up in business while still in his mid-twenties. He had no prospective clients and hardly any resources.

In 1994, his first year, Hervé owned neither a row of vines nor any equipment more sophisticated than four old wooden open fermenters. Young people who show keenness are often brought into the family wine business and offered access to a small-holding – but Hervé's father, like many local people, works not in wine but in the local nuclear power station at Chinon.

So, lacking any family holdings, Hervé rents his vineyards. He now works 4 hectares, an area the size of two small English fields. The countryside is honeycombed with underground workings created by stone quarrying and this has provided a perfect primitive cellar. By the time of the grape harvest the days are cool; down in the cellar the air is bone-chilling. Far from needing refrigeration equipment, Hervé likes to warm the wine a little after the main fermentation, to provoke the second 'malolactic' fermentation, softening the raw acidity of the wine and leaving it bacterially stable.

Rather than buying a pump he uses his legs to break up the cap of grape skins. This is not the only way in which he's old-fashioned: he's become attached to the wooden fermentation vats he bought on grounds of price. 'Wood makes the wine evolve differently – more quickly.' He refuses to disinfect these vats with chemicals; a rub-down with eau-de-vie keeps them in condition from vintage to vintage.

Hervé has, as it happens, done a wine-making course, but those educated in the squeaky-clean practices of the new world may suspect that anything made in such a technological vacuum must taste pretty earthy. Unfortunately I tried his 1994 Bourgueil in anything but rigorous conditions. Sitting in his underground cellar in November beside a fire of aromatic vine clippings, accompanying a meal of local cheese and charcuterie, it tasted spectacular.

Hervé's Adventures . . .

Hervé Menard's address is L'Echelle, 37140 Bourgueil. Tel: 02 (from UK 00332) 47 97 72 65 and, as he as yet has no importer, the only way to try his wines is to drop in during a trip to the Loire (about two-thirds of a day's drive from Southern England). To find out if you like Bourgueil you could try an example from one of the widely imported growers. There's **P-J Druet** whose wines are regularly listed by Justerini and Brooks, London sw1, and Majestic Wine Warehouses. Both Tesco and Safeway regularly stock a Bourgueil; Tesco follow the **Caslot-Galbrun** family and Safeway the local co-op under the name **Cuvée Les Chevaliers**. They're around the £5 mark and in the hot 1995 vintage can both be recommended.

If he is to make the best wine he can, Hervé has to find discerning and enthusiastic customers. New producers in continental Europe have benefited from changing tastes and aspirations among consumers (as have those involved in making the British 'wine revolution'). In developed countries year in and year out the majority of people have more spending money and they choose to spend a chunk of it on more ambitious food and drink. But the effect of this greater wealth is felt in quite different ways in the markets for wine in Britain and the rest of Europe.

Here wine has provided a sideshow in the unending British class war. Once it was imported only for the benefit of the aristocracy and the older professions. Now it's everywhere and is getting so much cheaper, relatively speaking, that it can only be a matter of time before it competes, as a source of alcohol at a rock-bottom price, with what was till recently called British wine, or premium strength lager.

But across the channel, wine has been the choice of the masses for some considerable time. It's a hundred years or more since wine made on an industrial scale became affordable enough to displace *piquette*, a French mothers' ruin brewed up out of grape skins and sugar. One grower reminded me that until quite recently ordinary people hardly had access to anything else: 'They just didn't drink tea or soft drinks or beer – it was always the most basic 9 degrees wine.' In Continental Europe the change is not that there's more wine about, as in Britain, but that there is a proliferation of new names on the bottles. The effect has been to trigger a flurry of journalistic activity and guide-writing – another kind of parallel with us. From Portugal to Greece, journalists are making names for themselves by taking up the cause of the new wave of producers.

Frequently wine does become a political issue. In Italy, the most useful directory for growers' wines is produced by 'Slow Food'. This is a movement which came into being around local activists who in a British context might have found themselves giving evidence in the McLibel trial: a group who formed, to an extent under Communist leadership, to oppose the proposal in 1989 to open a branch of McDonald's in the Piazza di Spagna in the historic centre of Rome.

Don't all rush . . .

The basic unit of Slow Food is the *convivium* or 'local chapter', which defies the forces of globalist hegemony by getting together to eat and drink. (Someone should build bridges with the similarly-minded Campaign for Real Ale.) To set up or join an existing *convivium* and receive the four annual issues of the English-language newsletter, contact Carmen Wallace at Slow Food's international HQ in the charmingly named town of Bra in Piemonte. Phone Italy 0039 then (0)172 411 273, fax: 421 293. email: info@slow-food.com. The Italian-language wine guide is regularly updated and there's an English version on the World Wide Web: http://www.slow-food.com/

For these people, and many like them, the important qualities of wine are exactly those that make them unlike the transnational offerings of the fast food industry. Apart from its obvious virtues, wine is valued as an authentic, unadulterated product, hand made rather than mass produced and, above all, unique, with roots in a particular place and culture.

Of course it's easy to see why, in Britain, this might feel like someone else's battle. For one thing, when the Europeans have a go at what they call 'globalization' it's to some extent our Anglo-Saxon Anglo-American world they're attacking. McDonald's may be American, but Burger King is owned by our own Grand Met. In our culture we feel quite positive about not having the geographical roots that oblige fashionable white-painted restaurants in Palermo or Barcelona to list only their own regional wines. We have the option of taking a certain defiant pride in even quite nasty new commodities just because they show a clever reading of the mood of the times. As an English drinks writer on a press trip to the Loire, I can remember the pleasurable *frisson* created by enthusing to our shocked hosts about the 'brilliant marketing' involved in the launch of alcoholic lemonade.

Our wine revolution is often presented as an Anglo-Saxon bid to wean backward foreigners off their 'Luddite' methods. But a detailed look at the recent history of the industry does not support this reading of events. For much of the time since World War II, it has been Germany and Austria who have led the way in wine technology. Many of the techniques we think of as typically 'New World' – temperature control, sterile filtration and the use of selected yeasts – originated in Middle Europe and were put to use by the big German and Austrian wine firms. But in the last decade these countries' big firms have been ruined: in the case of Austria by one 'technical adjustment' too many, the so-called 'anti-freeze' glycol scandal, which sent customers in droves to small producers, the only sector whose reputation was not tarnished. In Germany too, technology is too quick to provide chemistry to correct abysmal raw material. The success of German industrial wine followed by the collapse of its price and reputation holds out a cautionary lesson. And far from being more 'modern' in our approach to wine, I'd suggest that the business in Britain is at a stage that many wine-producing countries have left behind.

It is not just the Europeans who have decided that small is beautiful. Even in America and Australia there is a growing tendency to reject the high-tech, highly capital-intensive approach. Science is increasingly seen not as a substitute for the European peasant tradition but as a path to a better understanding of that tradition. California now teems with small wineries that shun herbicides, use wild yeasts and leave their wines unfiltered.

The drawback if you don't enjoy a Californian income is that New World 'boutique' wines can be terribly expensive. These small estates have to sustain the lifestyles to which their owners were accustomed in their previous existences as highly paid West Coast professionals. In the New World it's often better not to look for growers but for the enthusiastic wine-makers who hunt out grapes from long-established vineyards planted with mature vines. The reason their wines can be relatively cheap is that the makers steer clear of the small group of grape varieties that are in the public eye at any one time, such as Chardonnay, Cabernet Sauvignon and Merlot.

In contrast to the New World, European growers' wines are startlingly inexpensive: that is, outside the best-known and most sought-after vineyard areas. David Shiverick, an importer and merchant based in Cleveland, Ohio, can hardly believe the bargains on offer when he goes touring the French regions: 'I guess it's to do with the relative cost of land and the fact that there are these established smallholdings over here for people to inherit.' Another reason is that wine in Europe has less social prestige; to make great wine is not the prerogative of the super-rich. It's a job, not a rich man's (or woman's) hobby.

But even if such hand-made wines are cheap from the perspective of American wine buffs, at around £5–10 a bottle they look dear compared to most of what is on offer in the high-street shops and supermarkets. Since we aren't going to buy them out of local chauvinism – which here is satisfied by regional brewers with different local styles of beer – what exactly are we buying when we pay over the odds?

For one thing, diversity. In Britain this is one of the big attractions of wine: distinguishing between regions, vintages, grape varieties and wine-makers. The exercise was the province of the old-school connoisseur; now it offers a playground for many modern consumers. We love to browse, to dawdle and to make comparisons and in response to this the supermarkets now offer not scores, but hundreds of different bottles. A simple equation holds good: the more different people make the wine, the more different the wines will be from each other.

The supermarkets may like to stock lots of different bottles; this doesn't mean they want to deal with a great crowd of different producers. Instead they operate in a way that favours a manageable number of intermediaries. Many of them rely heavily on the 'flying wine-makers', who work to order anywhere in the world – even if these are criticized for applying an inflexible formula that tends to make all the wine taste similar. If as is likely they concentrate heavily on Australia they will find they do almost all their business with the four big companies who dominate that market. The small growers in contrast are innumerable; it's hard enough to keep track of all the small specialist importers. Perhaps it's surprising that so many, rather than so few, small producers' wines reach British high streets.

This book is biased in favour of diversity: not a controversial-sounding position, even if it means arguing a case for wines which some people may think deserve to be out of the mainstream. It's less easy to explain why, everything else being equal, I would almost always choose a wine from a small grower and would be willing to pay over the odds for it. After all, isn't wine about what's in the bottle rather than what's on the label? In the much-quoted phrase of Deng Xiaoping, what does the colour of the cat matter so long as it catches mice? It doesn't help my case that, from a writer's point of view, I find that small growers tend to be interesting to talk to, so predisposing me to think the best of their wines.

With the experience of a few years of semi-systematic tasting I know that I am likely to prefer the small grower's wine. But it's difficult to make an argument out of an aesthetic response in a subject so lacking in rigour or objective criteria.

It's easy to sound like a Luddite if you use the word 'industrial' about wine in a slighting way. If science and technology can make a good thing available in larger quantities, what's wrong with that?

Wine is only one part of the world of food and drink but it's one in which, because of its privileged (you might say 'fetishized') status, it is considered that in order to have valid opinions you need to have accumulated a huge mound of 'facts'. So in order to talk about general principles it helps to stand back and look at other parts of the food industry, rather than plunging into a region peopled by specialists.

We all depend on the agro-industrial techniques that have made it possible, at least in theory, for the world to support a high population without famine or malnutrition. This revolution – the word here obviously is justified – has created a vast range of new products. Some have become classics: Mars Bars, cornflakes, tomato concentrate, orange juice in cartons . . . others, like shaped and rolled turkey roasts, I find quite easy to resist.

A range of techniques have come into wine-making, many imported from other areas such as the milk industry, brewing or fruit juice processing. The earliest achievement of the modern wine age was to re-invent it as a widely distributed basic commodity, making use of the newly created transport networks in France and other wine-producing countries. More recently technology has created new kinds of wine, such as Liebfraumilch, Beaujolais Nouveau and New Zealand Sauvignon Blanc.

There are good and bad technological wines just as traditional wine-making can be done with varying degrees of success. As a matter of personal taste I think technology works best when it's creating new products rather than ersatz ones: in food, for example, tomato ketchup rather than ready-mixed salad dressing. But what is missing in much modern British wine writing is any attempt to distinguish between the two approaches. An analogy would be if the beer writers regarded all brewers as standard-bearers of a civilizing mission to bring happiness and humanity to all, and thought it disloyal to consider the relative merits of pasteurized keg and live cask conditioned beers.

The pivotal difference between craft-scale and industrial wine-making is that big firms must reduce costs to stay competitive (unless they have a luxury brand which is not price-sensitive). But if they're any good, small producers experience no such pressure. Their chief resource is not capital equipment or microprocessor-based controls but their time, their dexterity and their experience in interpreting their senses of sight, smell and touch – and for these there is, in the words of Loretta Lynn's classic country song on motherhood, 'No Charge'.

Does this make them better? Not necessarily. There are lots of terrible wines from small producers, just as something made at home may be worse than a ready-meal, though fortunately the vigilance of British importers keeps most of them away from these shores. Does it make them different? It tends to, although mass-produced wines are often made using short cuts which try to imitate the results achieved by traditional techniques. To go back to the analogy with food, small producers' wines have something in common with the knobbly outdoor-grown tomatoes from Southern Europe. Their range of odd shapes and sizes may disqualify them from the supermarkets' 'Class I' grade, but does anyone who has tasted them really prefer the immaculate produce of the Dutch greenhouses?

Growers often like to see themselves as pitted against less scrupulous competitors. They see their world divided between the 'good', who ensure the quality of their wine by restricting yields in the vineyard and harvesting at the right time, and the 'others' who try to put a gloss on overcropped and underflavoured raw material with technical manipulations. Such tricks may include the use of oak chips to mimic the effect of barrel ageing; white wine may have been fermented at ultra-cold temperatures and treated with enzymes and a dried yeast strain to boost up the aromas; or it may have been left in contact with the grape skins – a fast route both to the deep colour and to the strong aromas you get from years of ageing in the bottle.

In comparison a hand-made wine may not make the most impact. It will have been designed, not to show up in a comparative tasting, but as something nice to drink, probably with a meal. People talk about 'living wines'. Like people, plants and animals, such wines have the capacity to surprise; they may have nothing much to offer when you pull the cork, then come unexpectedly to life, offering unexpected and unpredictable memories and associations.*

* At a tasting in London in April 1997, Paul Draper of Ridge Vineyards in California, at tasting at Groucho Club in London 23 April 1997, described the two contrasting approaches to wine-making:

> Traditional wine-making is where the pieces of ground have been located over time, and those pieces of ground and the grapes they produce are able to express themselves in the wine. The other major thrust that's dominant in the New World is what I'd call 'industrial wine-making' or 'process wine-making' which is really akin to the processed food industry. Your raw material is grapes and you process that raw material, add acid, take away acid, add sugar to it, do whatever is needed to make it into what you want as a food product.
>
> That second approach is essential if we are to have reasonably priced drinking wines, but where I don't see it as proper is where it's used in the category of finer wines. Some of these wines put together like this by the wine-maker as creator are so appealing; they will have been put together with reference to what they call Consumer Acceptance Panels and their immediate appeal is great.
>
> The only way to see a difference between them and truly fine wine is whether or not there's a centre to the wine . . . whether or not there's a soul. Whether once you've got through the upfront effect of the wine there is something there. Is there something truly distinctive? I'd like to push wine writers into looking for that centre.

Paul Draper's wines make his case for him . . . mostly for upwards of £15 a bottle. They are available in Britain from Adnams of Southwold in Suffolk, 01502 727220, and Morris and Verdin of London SE1 0171 357 8866.

Such wines get their character from the concentration of flavour in the grapes: the quality often called 'fruit'. This doesn't mean a bright single note, like a synthetic strawberry or cherry aroma, but something which reminds you how complex and rich real fruit can taste: red, white or black, barely ripe or verging on rottenness, raw, stewed, dried or candied. It will go on making its presence felt in your mouth, with aftertastes and lingering scents. And it will change and possibly improve with storage, developing when it's exposed to the air rather than rapidly becoming undrinkable.

All this holds good both for 'fine' wines – that you could define as those traded at auction, usually coming from a limited number of properties, mainly in Bordeaux and Burgundy – and for the wines that are the subject of this book and that sell for a fraction of the price. They share complex flavours created, in both cases, by simple means.

Though the techniques used by small producers may be simple, the same does not apply to their motivation. Making delicious wine is a perfectly good end in itself. But when you talk to growers they often reveal separate agendas, environmentalist, with elements of William Morris's brand of Utopian socialism, anti-collectivist and suspicious of state institutions, committed to what Carlos Petrini, the guru of 'Slow Food', has called 'defending territorial patrimony' against universal standardization.[1]

Strange Brews – Growers' Wines in the High Street

Growers and the people who import their wines often prefer to deal with independent wine merchants rather than big chains (see Section Five – Bringing it All Back Home). However some of their stuff ends up in most high streets. Here are a few examples. (To find out how to tell if a wine comes from a small grower, see pages 87–9.)

The North of England-based Booths are the best supermarket for growers' wines, with names like Masía Barril from Priorato in North East Spain (see page 20 onwards), one of North West Spain's sensual pear-flavoured whites from the Albariño grape from **Bodegas Pazo de Barrantes** £9.75 and, above all, Jean Orliac's **Domaine de L'Hortus** £5.99. This is the wine that made the Languedoc famous. Tasted a little over a year after the vintage, the 1995 was about juiciness and elegance rather than bonecrushing weight but ideally needed some bottle age.

Also mainly in the North are Greenalls Wine Cellars; the one unmissable name on their list is that of the legendary pioneer of German red wine (and frustrated would-be saviour of the Egyptian wine industry) **Rainer Lingenfelder**, from the southern Rhine region, the Pfalz. At the time of writing Wine Cellars had his **Riesling** and **Dornfelder** (a delicious juicy red), both from the 1992 vintage, at £5.49 and £6.99 respectively. Recently they've added the same property's **Grande Cuvée** (£9.99 for the 1995 vintage), and also, for £5.49, the 1995 red from the **Domaine Gauby**, one of the best growers of the Roussillon, France's Catalan region (see page 67).

Majestic are packed with riches: **Druet** and the **Domaine des Roches Neuves** for sumptuous Loire Reds; from the superb Domaine name Bott-Geyl in Alsace, the rich brambly flavoured **Costières de Nîmes** from Mas de Bressades (£6.99 Odd: 0/5 Niceness: 5/5); oddities like the sweet red **Recioto della Valpolicella** from Tedeschi and the well-publicized bargain of the last two years; lots of good German growers. A particular favourite is the **Navarra Jardin** from the Guelbenzu family for £4.99. It's from bought-in grapes from the region's old Garnacha vines and is like a southern version of a juicy Burgundy or Beaujolais: paeonies and beetroot flavours, but with the volume turned up (Odd: 2/ 5 Niceness: 4/5).

Oddbins follow Olivier Jullien, a young Turk[2] of the Languedoc. His **Mas Cal Demoura**, Coteaux du Languedoc 94, £6.99. (Oddbins) is dark and brooding with some surprises, like a hint of cooked strawberries. Jullien makes this with grapes grown in his extended family. Odd: 0/5 Niceness: 4/5. Another major name at Oddbins is the only-just-pronounceable **Domaine Schoffit** from Alsace (**Pinot Blanc** at £7.99 is Odd: 1/5 Niceness: 5/5). But despite expectations and exceptions, such as the single estate Germans, and **Gimonnet**, the prince of makers of Chardonnay-based Champagne (if you're looking for affordable growers' wines Oddbins is, currently, a little disappointing).

For the Threshers group (including Wine Rack and Bottoms Up) look for their individual growers' champagnes (see pages 148–9 onwards) and their individual Bordeaux châteaux: **Mercier, Sauvage** and **Suau**. Victoria Wines are good for German wines, with usually some startling bargains in 10-year-old Riesling; they're also now becoming a place to look for southern French growers. Their star listing is the pioneer of the **Faugères** appellation, **Gilbert Alquier** (see page 173); his red wine from the 1995 vintage is

£6.99. Victoria also have a good pair of Southern Rhône reds: the **Château du Diffre, Séguret 1995** and the **Domaine de la Grande Bellane Valréas 1996** at £5.49 and £5.99 respectively. I also like the look of their **Albariño, Lagar de Cervera 1995**, at 6.99. The London-based Fullers chain are more about clean reliable wines for a good price than weird stuff, but they have a local hero from the Loire making the complex sweet Coteaux-du-Layon, **Domaine des Forges** at £8.99 (Odd: 4/5 Niceness: 4/5). They're proud, too, of their exhilaratingly dry **Cuvée Flores 1995** from Vincent Pinaud in Sancerre, at £9.49 (Odd: 0/5 Niceness: 4/5). Plus there's a sweet Muscat de Rivesaltes from the **Domaine de Brial** (£3.99 half bottle) and the rich, dry bitter Amarone from **Tedeschi** (£9.99).

Unwins in London and the South-East recently swallowed up the more quirky and interesting Davisons group. At the time of writing it wasn't clear which Davisons listings would get taken on; Unwins' chief claim to fame is as a supplier of the very good Portuguese grower, Luis Pato: check his 1995 Quinta do Riberinho in red and white at £4.49 and his 1995 Vinhas Velhas ('old vines') for £10.99.

Tesco are becoming quite interesting for growers' wines; one test is the willingness to take on red Loire wines like the Bourgueil from Caslot-Galbrun at £5.49 or the more interesting Saumur Champigny **Domaine des Roches Neuves** (£7.99).

Sainsbury's has what its chief buyer calls a 'dusting'. I like the **Domaine Belle Croix St Bris Aligoté** £5.99 – neutral but concentrated (Odd: 2/5 Niceness: 2/5) and the Sainsbury's **Henri Pellé** Ménétou Salon 95. £5.95. This is one of the great buys of the 1990s and a good introduction to French growers' wines for fans of international Sauvignon. Odd: 0/5. Nice 5/5.

Safeway doesn't make growers' wines a priority, though they have a winner in their grower's Champagne from **Chartogne-Taillet** at £15.99. However their selections from co-operatives are well chosen and they have pioneered organic wines, with the importer Vinceremos/Bottle Green (see page 273). One evergreen favourite is the fresh and frank **Chianti San Vito 1995** from Tenuta San Vito; their Muscadets from the organic grower Guy Bossard whose **Domaine de l'Ecu** (£5.99) is worth putting aside to mature for a few years in ripe years like 1995 and 1996.

Asda: the most unusual wine must be a sweet Soave made from semi-dried grapes: the **Recioto di Soave Castel Cerino 1993** £4.99 a half bottle. Asda also have a good French growers' white, a change if you've overdosed on Chardonnay: the white **Côtes du Rhône** from Château de Trignon (£5.99).

Finally Waitrose: good, though not necessarily for small producers. The great strength is the unending stream of bargains from German producers such as **Robert Eymael** of the **Mönchhof** estate on the Mosel.

Big distributors are best at giving good prices on wines from big producers. The reason to go to a supermarket is to buy cheap sound stuff made by a producer's co-op, or well-made branded wines: sherries and ports, ranges like **Penfolds** from Australia, *Grande Marque* champagne and so on.

1 Quoted by Nicholas Belfrage in *Decanter*, Italian supplement, October 1996.
2 Metaphorically. If you say *un jeune Turque* the French tend to misunderstand, becoming flustered, even racist.

2

Are They Trying to Tell Us Something?

If wines have personalities they get them from the people who make them. An importer once told me: 'It isn't the wine you're looking for, but the person behind the wine.' For years I was tantalized by the fragments of growers' lives glimpsed in wine lists – that soothing literary form which offers some of the pleasure P.G. Wodehouse describes Lord Emsworth as deriving from his endless re-reading of Whipple *On the Care of the Pig*.

But these encounters tend to be reported in a maddeningly sketchy way: '*Herr/Señor/Monsieur* so-and-so has some fascinating opinions which make a visit to his cellars an education in every sense!'

So my first thought in researching this book was to try to meet a cross-section of people who make interesting wines and to try to record what they wanted to say as accurately as my shorthand and my grasp of foreign languages would allow.

Like many English people I have been taught French. This is a reasonable start: the movement for growers to bottle their own wine began in France (starting at the very top, at Château Mouton-Rothschild and working down), France has had a big influence on all other wine-making countries and, out of all the European growers' wines, it is those of France that get imported into Britain in the most significant quantities.

The wine industries of various countries set aside funds to pay for the visits of foreign journalists and if you join such a group there is always someone to interpret. The drawback is that the merchant houses and co-operatives put up the bulk of the money, making it hard for you to insist on spending your time with the producers of your choice. This would have been a principled reason for me to insist on funding my own visits, as urged by pillars of the wine writing profession from Andrew Barr to Robert Parker.

But, in the case of Priorato, a little region in North Eastern Spain, my reason for not asking for money was the strong conviction that the local *consejo regulador* wouldn't give me any. No one there exported to Britain until very recently and even now only a few thousand cases get sent every year. How could it be worth their while?

On the other hand I was determined to visit Masía Barril, a reportedly uncompromisingly grass-roots, artisanal producer. Their wine is in the Booths supermarket chain in the North of England. This is how they were described by another stockist, the mail order Wine Society: 'Masía Barril Típico, Priorato, 1993. Priorato is a beautiful, rugged region producing opaque, dense and massive wines of high alcoholic strength (15 degrees). The blend of garnacha, which lends peppery fruit, and cariñena, which contributes tannin and colour, is most attractive. Try with peppered steak.' To reach Northern Spain meant a drive though the whole of France in the company of a Berlitz Spanish-language tape. Surely I'd get something out of a visit to Masía Barril.

This estate is a long way off the beaten track. I'd assumed that because Priorato isn't near Barcelona it ought, out of fairness, to be virtually on the doorstep of Tarragona, the second city of Catalonia. It doesn't look far, but that's only because the map in Hugh Johnson's *World Atlas of Wine* is on such a small scale that it irons out an endless succession of hairpin bends between Reus and Falset, a particular hazard in a badly maintained car.

Magdalena Barril, small, with long grey hair and a shy smile, was friendly but unsure of the form, and, as it was only a day or so before the harvest, had other things on her mind. I guessed she hadn't always been a wine-grower; indeed if she hadn't been directing her one assistant on how to clean out a fermentation tank I might have placed her as a sculptress or a retired academic.

There was nothing though to suggest a rich person's hobby: no lines of new stainless-steel tanks or oak barrels. Where you might expect sophisticated equipment to circulate the wine in the fermentation tank, Señora Barril opened a hatch – the roof of the concrete tank formed the floor on which we were standing – and showed me how she poked the 'cap' of grape skins with a long pole ending in three little diverging prongs.

As the stress of the drive faded I started to take in my surroundings and their hallucinatory beauty. The farmhouse was on a hill: how did they get water? Was the circular pool a rainwater tank? The reddish land fell away on all sides, rising again in a succession of low ridges outlined with round-headed pine trees. Far-off mountains formed a distant pale blue wall of cliffs. On the other side of the house I looked across a narrower valley to the high dome of a hill with a bare rock face which caught the light as if it had been sculpted like Mount Rushmore. It wasn't like being in a vineyard: instead the ragged-looking vines seemed to colonize strips of land here and there across the whole landscape.

Magdalena opened three bottles. Two were big spicy fruity wines with a strong impression of blackberries. The third was dominated by a frankly faecal smell. She also let me try a glass of *rancio*,[1] which isn't sold in bottle; it was the colour of pale prune juice, dry and acidic, an essence of bay leaves and pine. We tried to chat. Unfortunately there were limitations to my recently acquired Spanish. I am sure that Magdalena told me that the under the *denominacion de origen* rules small producers were only recently allowed to bottle their own wine, and that the property first came into the family in 1931. However, what kind of language snarl-up led me to note down the words 'mother of husband', suggesting that I was in the presence of a bizarrely oedipal family unit?

So in the end I had to go back to the wine trade to interpret what I'd seen. Carlos Reed, who is bilingual, had signed the property up in the late 1980s to Moreno Wines and he told me the Masía Barril story.

'The owner, Rafael Barril, had been one of the top economic advisers to the last socialist government of Spain. He is from Madrid but is in love with the area of Priorato where his father had built the house in 1931. [mother-of-husband = mother-in-law?] He thought that when he retired he'd devote himself to making wine on the property, but now he finds he's in demand as a consultant in the private sector. Now it's his wife who's making the wine and I think she's doing very well. They've only been bottling since 1981 when a writer called Jose Peñín who has a wine club discovered Barril and bought a proportion of that year's vintage in order to bottle it. A lot of their sales have been to people who just turn up – it's a day trip if you live in Barcelona.

'He doesn't make any money out of it but he's just maintained it as a kind of crusade. Because the region's so small he's afraid that making wines of the old-fashioned type with vast alcohol levels is something that's going to get lost as the world becomes more commercial. There are only three or four producers and he's the only one who's not Catalan, yet he's making the most traditional wine. He's an amazing guy when he gets talking; I once went there just for a short visit and I didn't get away for hours.'

This inspired me to have a wrestle with the sheets headed '*INFORMACION SOBRE LA BODEGA MASÍA BARRIL*' that Rafael had sent me through the post from his Madrid offices. Quite soon a sense of the man emerged: a similar blend of radicalism and tradition to that espoused by 'Slow Food' in Italy.

He wrote: 'The object of the family is to maintain and build on the tradition of the celebrated wines of Priorato, which were so appreciated by the Romans under the name of "Tarraco".'

At a symposium in 1987 at Jerez, the home of Sherry, he had presented a paper calling for the creation of a category to be called the World's Oenological Heritage, composed of 'classic historic wines of universal interest'. Masía Barril was a '*bodega cultural*' in opposition to the fashion for '*los vinos* "light"'. His wine was out of step with Spanish fashion in that the vintages were true single vintages, with no blending between years, and did not depend on ageing in wood.

One piece of advice chimed in with my theory that proper wines change with time but don't collapse. 'After its sixth year in bottle it turns into an excellent dry, natural dessert wine without added spirit. Masía Barril suggests the following experiment. Open a bottle while the wine is still young and fruity. Drink half and leave the remainder open for a week. You will find the other half turns into an excellent dessert wine.' I did this back in London, with the results reported in the box over the page. 'Excellent' is putting it rather strongly, but the wine remains drinkable and interesting.

The Wines of Masía Barril

The stockists of these wines, which come in different vintages and (high) alcoholic strengths, like to add disclaimers saying that they are 'food wines' and 'not for the faint-hearted'. I found them alarmingly drinkable on their own, especially in the Siberian weather during which they were tasted. At the time of writing the importers had three variants in stock. Beginning with the least expensive:

Masía Barril Típico 1993 (14 per cent alcohol). Dark and young with a mouth-fuzzing texture, like Turkish coffee. Exotic aromas – tamarind, even a hint of joss-sticks. After being left open for a week, as recommended, the fresh fruit flavours had been replaced by bitter cherries or apricot paste and it smelt like a spice shop in Damascus. Odd: 4/5 Niceness: 3/5

Masía Barril Clasico 1994 (16 per cent alcohol). Thick black and smells as if it comes ready-mulled. Superconcentrated blackberries, cloves and paeony. Worth putting aside for five years. Odd: 4/5 Niceness: 2/5

Masía Barril Típico 1991. These wines are based on Garnacha (Grenache) grapes; this means that for blockbusters they start life relatively smooth but a few years in the bottle make them sumptuous. The 14 per cent alcohol gives this wine the 'hit' of champagne or a stiff gin and tonic combined with a wallow in mature, spicy red fruit. Odd: 4/5 Niceness: 4/5

Stockists: Típico 1993: The Wine Society 01438 741177. Típico 1991 Booths supermarkets 01772 251701, Tanners £8.00. Importers: Moreno Wines 0171 723 6897. If you can't find the 1991 buy a later vintage and wait for two years.

Rafael and Magdalena are a little untypical of professional people who become wine producers. The usual course for those who can afford it is to hire a big-name consultant oenologist, plant a lot of Cabernet Sauvignon and invest in oak and stainless steel. The resulting wine will be a pricey status symbol which for me has all the charm of a wardrobe furnished by Gucci and Hermès – and as much originality.

In contrast the thousands of peasant wine-growers around the Mediterranean who have declared independence from local merchants do have something individual to say. Marcel Richaud is unusual in that he is able to express himself not only in the wine he makes but also in a torrent of words. When he started out in 1974 this small, voluble and impulsive man had almost nothing except a local reputation as someone likely to come a cropper. Yet he now works 40 hectares of vineyards (the Barrils have 30 under vine) and his wines often turn up in Oddbins as well in some of the Conran restaurants.

Richaud is quintessentially European. In Australia conversations tend to begin with marketing: 'We're trying to produce the sort of fruity, easy-drinking style that people want', etc. But he gives the impression that his success came about by accident while he was pursuing his personal passion for his vineyard. His estate has grown to its present moderate size simply to finance his investment in the cellar. He deters customers from spending excessively. While I'm with him a couple of local guys turn up, even though it's Sunday, looking for wine for a wedding party. He asks his wife to let them taste, imploring her to try to keep them to the most basic *cuvée* of Côtes du Rhône: 'For a party it's a waste to get something better – no one will notice it.'

His vineyards are dotted around the hills above Cairanne, interspersed with low-growing evergreen oaks. They are all classified as Côtes du Rhône, but he voluntarily downgrades some sites he regards as inferior to a far less profitable *vin de pays*. And he turns away merchants who assure him that he could made a fortune if he'd agree to use barrels for oak ageing. 'I just wouldn't feel comfortable with it; it's not a technique that I've mastered.'

To stay in business the *négociants* keep up with market trends. Not so Richaud: 'I've got a personal style and approach. It's wrong to try to be in fashion; there's always a different one: carbonic maceration, oakiness, cabernet sauvignon everywhere . . .'

It's not that he works in isolation from his customers. But the point of meeting them is to explain what he can give them, not to ask what they'd like. 'I like to bring them to the cellar door and explain the identity of the south, that dominant spiciness of flavours. The current trend is for wine that's ready for drinking young. No problem. There's a whole range. What we can't change is the location of the vineyards and the impact that has.'

He began with ancient wooden fermenters, and he still uses open fermenters for part of the grape harvest. But wine-making is not his main preoccupation. 'By the time the grapes are harvested the die has already been cast. Eighty per cent of the important decisions have already been made. The wine you make is the result of a year's work in the vineyard; the quality comes from the soil and keeping yields low. It's not about wine-making technique.'

Marcel Richaud is the product of a culture that doesn't have much in common with the business ethos of modern international wine-making. But he doesn't lack motivation. He works partly in order to make delicious wine and give pleasure to people, and partly in pursuit of something entirely personal: something to do with capturing in a bottle the essential nature of the countryside around his home village.

'I'm a man and in time I'll vanish from this earth. But if I can get some recognition for these places I'll have achieved something. My estate can disappear. But the land and the sunshine will still be there.'

The Wines of Marcel Richard

These put some strain on the theory about the similarity of wines and wine-makers. Marcel Richaud is engaging, articulate and passionate – but cool? Somehow though he makes wines which are all about poise and nuance, listed, at the time of writing, at Terence Conran's 'Quaglino's' and equally appreciated, you feel sure, at fashionable places in Avignon and Aix. This was the range available in Britain from Enotria Winecellars (0181 961 4411). For the 1996 vintage and onwards contact Liberty Wines (UK) Ltd, Unit A53 The Food Market, New Covent Garden, London SW8 5EE (0171 720 5350)

Côtes du Rhône 'Les Garrigues' 1995 £4.89. Odd: 0/5 Niceness: 4/5

Côtes du Rhône Villages Cairanne 1995 £5.70. Odd: 0/5 Niceness: 4/5
These were both good with just a year's bottle age and both blend spices and *garrigue* herbs with fruit, red fruit for the Côtes du Rhône, something blacker-tasting for the Cairanne.

Côtes du Rhône Villages Cairanne 'Cuvée l'Ebrescade' 1995 £8.57 Odd: 1/5 Niceness: 3/5

Côtes du Rhône Villages Cairanne 'Cuvée l'Ebrescade' 1993
£8.57 Odd: 0/5 Niceness: 4/5
The single-vineyard wine needs bottle age; after four years the vanilla-like sweetness makes you think it's had been oak aged.

Lesser Southern French *appellations* like the *Côtes du Rhônes Villages* are increasingly appreciated in Britain these days, but the credit is rarely given to the local growers. If good wine comes out of the South of France, according to a widespread consensus, it's because an Englishman or an Australian has shown the locals how to make wine properly. But Australia's reputation, when examined more closely, owes a great deal to people surprisingly like Marcel Richaud.

1 *rancio* wines are those deliberately exposed to the air while they mature, such as Madeira or Oloroso sherry.

3
Outbatck

―――――

'They get everywhere these Australians,' wrote Oz Clarke, greeting the 'flying wine-makers' of the early 1990s, 'and wherever they go the quality of the wine improves.'

Australians love to hear this sort of thing; they especially appreciate it from a Brit, but they'll also happily drink in the same message from a compatriot. I heard the country's best-known wine writer, James Halliday, on song at the annual Maurice O'Shea wine industry dinner in Sydney in June 1996. His eulogy moved seamlessly from the contribution and sacrifices made in two world wars, to the efficiency and reputation of Australian secretaries in 1960s London, the spiritedness of the back-pack generation at large in Europe, separate strands finally united in the resolve of the young wine-makers to overturn centuries of sloth and inertia and give drinkers a fair deal.

'And if you tell them what they've achieved,' he continued, 'they'll probably say there wasn't much to it, mate. Just a little common sense, and some basic hygiene.' By now every eye in the room was misting a little – though the Maurice O'Shea Tokay and cigar smoke may have played their part.

Sydney. Flying wine-makers. Maurice O'Shea. A different world from all those primitive Old World peasants? Not entirely.

Maurice O'Shea, like many of the legends of the Australian wine industry, acted as a human link with the traditions of French wine-making (the most famous in this group being Max Schubert, who created Grange Hermitage, Australia's best known and most expensive red wine, after a visit to Bordeaux in 1950).

Those who went to see O'Shea at work found a setting well

suited to a Burgundian peasant – small open vats, an absence of refrigeration equipment and wild yeasts rather than cultured strains (though it would be an unusual observer who could spot this). He had spent seven years learning viticulture and wine-making in France before persuading his French-born mother to buy a small-holding near Pokolbin in the Hunter Valley. He called it Mount Pleasant after the bosom-shaped twin peaks that rise behind the vineyard.

Don McWilliam is the chairman of the family business that bought up the winery in 1941. Don looks and sounds like a country music legend (perhaps one better known for truck-driving songs than the smoochier productions of his near-namesake). He was sent to Mount Pleasant to learn the ropes from O'Shea, who in 1954 was already ill with the cancer from which he died two years later.

'It was a bloody old tin and wood shed.' McWilliam recalls. 'We didn't get electricity till 1957; everything was done with sore arms and hand presses. It was all hand picked in those days. We didn't use our feet to break up the cap [the mass of skins and stalks which forms on the top of fermenting red wine] but we used wooden plungers.'

But isn't the advantage of feet that you can feel if there are pockets in the wine where the temperature is rising because the fermentation is going too fast? 'We used to stick our arms in and find where the hot spots were. We lived in a little lean-to in the winery with a kerosene cooking stove and a kerosene heater for showers. L'Hermitage it was called; Maurice must have decided on that from his days in France. All that old section's been pulled down now. Morrie was a wonderful cook, a gourmet cook and what he could create on that kerosene stove was unbelievable. When we were eating he'd tell one of the cellar hands, "Get a sample of so and so," so this bloke would go out and draw a jugful of the maturing red wine straight out of the keg – a different one each time. That way we didn't continually have to taste the barrels – we were already doing it on a rotation basis. With Morrie we'd also go and visit our neighbouring wineries and he'd buy bulk wine from the current vintage. He'd an absolute ability to taste a range and determine what the combination of them would do to the finished wine.'

The Mount Pleasant estate was small enough at that time for

O'Shea to run both the vineyard and the cellar, rather than there being a division of responsibilities that's now normal in Australia. Don McWilliam thinks that was all to the good. 'A good wine-maker should have lots of viticultural background. The wine's made in the vineyard – there's no argument about that.'

Primitive as it was, Mount Pleasant made the classic wines on which Australia built its reputation. The English wine writer Remington Norman tasted a selection after Australian wine lovers scoured their cellars for him, coming up with a range including O'Shea bottles from 1951, 1952 and 1939. He reported on them in his book *Rhône Renaissance*. The 1939 Light Dry Red was, he says, 'surprisingly rich and concentrated' with a 'long finish'. On the 1952 Shiraz-based Rhine Castle, he notes a 'deep cherry tone, remarkably youthful; fine rich, silky nose, gloriously complex yet delicate. Very powerful wine, great presence, still with heaps of concentration. Truly magnificent.' (Here even the tasting note has a long finish.)

The brands that O'Shea created and named are still made and sold today. He seems to have been inspired by the royal wedding of 1947 in calling his red wine from Shiraz grapes Philip and his Sémillon-based white Elizabeth. But whereas at that time they were only available in tiny quantities, the McWilliam company turned them into big sellers. In 1980, according to Don, Elizabeth was 'by far the best-known white brand', selling just on 100,000 cases, or more than a million bottles a year (with changing fashions it's slipped back to 36,000 cases).

This expansion has required many changes. Yields of grapes now average 4 and can go as high as 6 tons an acre (68–102 hectolitres of wine per hectare) though the vines dating from 1880 yielding the top 'OP/OH' wines yield a miserly ton an acre (or around 17 hectolitres), and the vineyards are partly mechanized. Some pruning of the vines and most harvesting of the grapes is done mechanically, at night for the whites.

In the new winery (there's a visitors' toilet on the site of Maurice O'Shea's old shack) the wine-makers have tools at their disposal that their predecessor never knew. To keep the grapes from oxidizing they can add ascorbic acid (vitamin C) as well as sulphur. Then they add special enzymes to help get the juice absolutely clear before fermentation. They have tartaric acid to perk up the acid balance and a rotary drum vacuum filter which can make even the sludge at the bottom of a settling tank clear enough to put back in the wine.

'Elizabeth' is still an Australian classic and you shouldn't miss the chance of trying a bottle, but I wouldn't bet that it's the same as in Maurice O'Shea's era.

Australian Sémillon

Sémillon, not Chardonnay, is the original classic Australian white grape. The least interesting form it takes is when it comes as unnamed 'Dry Australian White' or in cheap blends with Chardonnay; the main reason it's there is because there's a lot of it. (At least it is declared, unlike Sultana, the variety planted to make dried fruit.)

Throughout Australia Sémillon is now being used as a fashionable alternative to Chardonnay to make wines on the formula of White Burgundy with oak barrels used either to age the wine or, more authentically, as the fermentation vessels.

The real local speciality is unoaked mature Sémillons, always from the Hunter Valley. These wines should have low alcohol levels, meaning that they were picked rather unripe to retain fresh acidity. There's an alternative approach from Rosemount Estate and the Tesco's own label Hunter Sémillon in which the grapes are picked when riper, quite a bit of tartaric acid added, and oak used to compensate for the youth of the wine. No thanks.

For traditionalists the options are:

Lindeman's Hunter Sémillon. This is just a well-made, neutral dry white, released before it's had time to develop the classic oily, toasty flavours. But it will, if you have the patience to keep it. At the time of writing, the 1995 vintage was available from the northern-based Morrisons chain of supermarkets at £4.99. Buy all you can – Morrisons' head office is on 01924 870000. Lindemans occasionally release older wines, but they're far from cheap. La Vigneronne, South Kensington (0171 589 6113) recently had the 1987 vintage for £17.95. Odd: 2/5 Niceness: 3/5

McWilliam's Mount Pleasant Elizabeth 1989 (Adnams, Suffolk, 01502 727222, £7.95). Odd: 3/5 Niceness: 3/5. McWilliams keep this back till it's a deep yellow with rich nutty flavours. That they do this is a great act of commercial altruism, and it's churlish to recommend paying another £4.50 for a wine I much prefer:

Tyrell's Vat no 1 1990 (£12.50 from Tanners, Shrewsbury, 01743 232400). This too has gone nutty with maturity but has a lot more to offer than a party trick; it's complex, lively and full of interest and has grafted the mature flavours on while keeping the freshness it had when young. Odd: 1/5 Niceness: 4/5

Despite the technical transformation which has taken place since the 1950s, there are increasing numbers of Australians who want to learn from the same school of craft-scale wine-making that inspired O'Shea.[1] Gary Farr looks like a perfectly decent, chunky, bearded, patriotic Australian. So it was a jolt to hear him tell me, in the middle of the country's first industry wine trade and consumer fair, Wine Australia 1996, that the Syrah-based wine Alain Graillot makes at Tain L'Hermitage in the Rhône was better value than the stuff he himself can make at Bannockburn in the state of Victoria. 'I'd rather drink Alain's wine at £8 than mine at £13. We've a very captive market for our wine here.'

But what is to stop Bannockburn scaling up production and hence cutting costs with the aid of the same technologies employed at Mount Pleasant and used by other makers of Hunter Sémillon? Farr thinks that technology often changes wines for the worse. He cites a much praised example from one of Mount Pleasant's neighbours, saying, bluntly: 'It totally loses me. To me it's changed. They were making wine in a much more basic form. Now they've lost it.'

Gary Farr's prices reflect both the fact that he does more hands-on work than is usual in Australia and also the cost of a series of field-trips to Burgundy. He was already the wine-maker at the Bannockburn estate, when he decided he had to visit France. 'The estate's owner had an incredible cellar of Burgundy. I was drinking it and it made me realize that I couldn't make anything like it and I couldn't understand why. So I left for Burgundy, Bordeaux and Alsace. Bordeaux was just boring; it wasn't any different from here. But Burgundy – Burgundy was something else. You had to, you know, jump in the tanks of wine. It was incredible, just unbelievable. I went three years running. To begin with I was only allowed out in the vineyard, helping with the harvest. But by the third year they let me make the wine.'

Back in Victoria, Gary put what he'd seen into practice. The winery had new closed fermentation tanks, but he got out an angle-grinder and sawed off the tops to turn them into open fermenters. After his first trip he made 25 per cent of the wine according to French methods. It added 'far more complexity and character'. Next year the proportion went up to 50 per cent. After the third trip to France they 'went for it head on'.

'Australians are far too clinical and technical. The French rely much more on their feel, their sense of smell and their history. They drink the older stuff and they know what it should taste like. The best wines are still made by pretty basic methods.'

The other big difference Gary finds is the French belief that the quality of the wine is limited by the quantity of the grapes. 'With Australian wine-makers, if they find they can make an agreeable wine at two tons of grapes to the acre then they want to make wine at three tons, four tons, and they go on and on and in the end the quality goes down and down.'

I asked him if these methods enabled him to capture much of the character of the area in which he had his vineyards. 'It's general farming in the region – a lot of sheep. My wines would smell like sheep shit and, yes, some of them do.'

James Halliday praises the estate, finding the Burgundy-like Pinot Noir wines 'supremely idiosyncratic' and requiring bottle age. This may be, though I thought they were relatively rapid-maturing by European standards. Why, I asked Gary. 'Well,' he said, 'I guess it's just a question of our [pause] *terroir*.' *Terroir* is a French word meaning 'country region' (and outside its specialist use in wine has an old-fashioned ring) and is a concept much used by 'Slow Food'. To talk about *terroir* is as much a give-away as it is for a closet Marxist to mention 'historical forces': it shows that you think wine's highest vocation is to encapsulate a sense of place. This is not the accepted view in Australia, and using this word even Gary Farr, the Francophile heretic, showed sufficient feeling to blush.

Farr's mentor has been Jacques Seysses of Domaine Dujac, an 11-hectare estate near the village of Morey-Saint-Denis in Burgundy's Côte de Nuits. Married to an American wife, Seysses, a fluent English speaker, has had an important role in transmitting the art of craft-scale wine-making from Burgundy, its natural home.

1 See the article 'A Handful of Dust' by Max Allen in *Wine* Magazine, July 1996.

4

A Plot in Burgundy

Burgundy is the most famous of all the famous wine names. It is still perhaps most widely understood to mean a robust style of red wine, though this reputation owes almost everything to the blends cooked up by merchants or *négociants* of Beaune, the region's wine capital, and almost nothing to the products of its own vineyards.

When researching this book I found it stood for something quite different, that I'd never read about: an intuitive, empirical approach to wine-making. Jacques Seysses of Domaine Dujac describes it as 'the difference between home cooking and cooking for hundreds of people'. The key feature is the tiny size of the holdings, from which the growers are likely to make a number of different named *appellation* wines.

It's an approach that does not get much publicity – because it has no need of it. Wines made in this way will either be so good that their small quantities will fall short of the demand for them, or, as is perfectly likely, they will be so bad as to be an embarrassment. There are no teachers of this non-technical sort of wine-making, because it can't be passed on except through long apprenticeships.

Like many other English enthusiasts, I came across this world by accident. The first producers I ever visited were the small growers of Southern Burgundy who make relatively inexpensive wine in tiny quantities. They offered a point of view that was quite different – from the then current orthodoxies of British wine writers (though I later found that Americans rather tended to share it).

I first went to visit growers in Southern Burgundy as a way of escaping from my extended family. It was during a stay in my sister's newly bought holiday home; most of the 'rooms' were unconverted and windowless quarters for animals; the few with electricity and windows had too many children under five. My brother-in-law kept going off in the only car on the pretext of looking for charity-shop furniture in the Châlons-sur-Saone branch of *Emmaus* (the French equivalent of Oxfam shops). I brooded and then hit back. I would commandeer the car to visit wine growers under the pretext of research for freelance journalism.

Visiting cellars doesn't have to be thrilling – in fact they can be about as exciting as the gift shop of a stately home. But in this backwoods end of Burgundy I struck lucky first time. Most of the growers in the Mâconnais really are peasants (not a derogatory term in France), with holdings so small they have to do everything themselves, from pruning in the vineyard to making the wine. Though I didn't know much about tasting I was impressed with the people. What's more they were pleased to see me and explain things. In the grander *appellations* of the Côte d'Or, further north, the proprietor would have been less likely to turn out for a casual visitor and in any case that area is so overplanted with vines that it has lost most of its charm.

Areas where wine is integrated into a diverse landscape tend to possess a dream-like beauty. A young wine-maker who'd spent a harvest in the Southern Rhône was accustomed to spectacular landscapes from his childhood in Western Australia; even so, he told me, he'd never seen anywhere as beautiful. The Mâconnais is more lush and less Mediterranean than the Rhône, more like a bigger, grander, hotter, more insect-ridden version of Southern England. That summer was stormy with explosive thunder and hailstorms that rattled the car deafeningly, descending in such dense sheets that you had to stop and wait for visibility to return.

The first grower I met was Olivier Merlin, at the end of a lane rising up from the village of La Roche Vineuse, overlooking the Paris–Lyons TGV line in the valley. He'd bought the cellars and a couple of small vineyards with his wife, Corinne, after a spell working in the Napa Valley in California. The couple personified the romance of wine. They were young 1980s people (something you could tell from Olivier's coloured-framed specs *à la* early Jancis Robinson) and they'd seized the moment. Chardonnay was more fashionable than it would ever be again, and with the opportunity to make a white Burgundy – even if not from the smartest *appellation* – they'd persuaded one of the normally cautious French banks to back them. They were installed above a cellar full of second-hand barrels of maturing wine, living a life to which, lacking wine-making parents, they could ordinarily only have aspired to after decades of work and saving.

And the gamble was working. Robert Parker, the world's most influential wine guru, had given them an all-important high rating (making his familiar bish of listing them as if they were two separate producers, both under the family name and under that of their property, the Domaine de St Sorlin). In Britain they had been taken up by two top Burgundy specialists and were on the wine-lists of some of London's smartest restaurants.

But to the incomprehension of some of their Anglo-Saxon customers, the couple had gone ultra-regional. As well as a Chardonnay-based white, they championed the most traditional local style, a red made from Gamay with an *appellation*, Mâcon Rouge, that has been dismissed out of hand by English writers from Oz Clarke to Hugh Johnson. In most years they refused to take up the cultivated yeast strains then regarded as essential to avoid faulty wines and instead let the wine make itself from the micro-organisms already on the grapes.

But what struck me the most was the practice called *pigeage*. During fermentation they stripped off, as wine-makers in the region had done for thousands of years, to immerse themselves in the red wine as it bubbled away at blood temperature, using their legs to press and circulate the skins and pips. Later I found out that many, perhaps most, small growers in Burgundy still do this, despite the impression given in Hugh Johnson's *Wine Atlas*, which illustrates the practice with a shot of naked men with haircuts placing them in the 1950s at the latest.

Back in England people I told about *pigeage* had mixed reactions. 'Is this what they mean by "coq au vin"?' one friend asked. I found any squeamishness hard to take from people who had at some impressionable stage of their lives considered the dead worm in the bottle of Mescal to be the height of cool. In fact the idea of baptismal immersion in a sacramental liquid had something archetypal and grand about it. Like countless visitors to the region I sensed that I had stumbled on the real thing.

They certainly don't go in for *pigeage* in Bordeaux. This other most famous wine region is dominated by big wine estates making a branded commodity for export and has been ever since its emergence in the seventeenth century. Burgundy by contrast is a patchwork of little holdings created by the sale of the property of the nobility and religious orders at the time of the French revolution. Ever since then the typical holding has been small – frequently less than 10 hectares – a scale which makes it inevitable that the proprietor will be responsible for both looking after the vineyard and making the wine. Bordeaux estates in contrast will have a vineyard manager and a wine-maker. A Bordeaux estate is a business and indeed these days is quite likely to be run by a business, typically a financial services group. A property in Burgundy is a smallholding run by a peasant farmer.

Traditionally the expert wine-makers in Burgundy, as in Champagne, had been the monastic orders, using grapes grown by the region's peasant farmers. But the revolution emptied the great Cistercian monasteries and their lands were auctioned. The eighteenth century had already seen the rise of the merchant houses, the *négociants*, in trading Burgundy wine. However these relied, as they still do, on the skills of the farmers to make the young wine that they blend, age and sell. These skills have always been unequally distributed: buyers always complain about the huge variation in quality between different Burgundy properties. But the best is exceptional.

Bordeaux has led France in technical advances for more than a century. It's where the copper-based Bordeaux mixture was first used against mildew; it's where vines were first grafted on to American vine rootstocks to protect against the destructive phylloxera beetle; it was one of the first regions to use steel tanks with built-in refrigeration; it has high-trained vines to aid mechanical harvesting . . .

In Burgundy, where everything is on a much smaller scale, technology is less important than the skill of the wine-maker in interpreting the information given by his or her senses. Small open vats don't need temperature control; the vineyard plots are so small it's easy to pick everything by hand. Wine-makers, answerable only to themselves rather than a proprietor or shareholders, can give full rein to their experimental instincts when it comes to deciding the best moment to pick, or how long to leave the juice soaking on the skins extracting colour. As a playground for a creative person, a property in Burgundy has something in common with a well-funded research programme in particle physics, a recording contract with a huge advance or a producer's job in an undisturbed corner of the pre-John Birt BBC. There are plenty of possibilities, either to squander your good fortune or to do exceptional work.

Bordeaux's contribution has been more important to many more people than that of Burgundy. Without the work done by its great oenologists, Pascal Ribereau-Gayon and Emile Peynaud, in understanding and countering bacterial spoilage, we would not have the everyday luxury of cheap sound wine. On the other hand, there is also something timely about the Burgundian approach in this era of small firms and self-employment. Now that we are all 'post-Fordian' (to hark back to the 1980s jargon of *Marxism Today*), perfectionist individual craft workers seem less of an anachronistic survival.

To try to describe the spread and influence of craft-scale wine-making is to enter a territory without maps. Consultant oenologists seek publicity to build a marketable reputation. Those who call them in add to it by boasting that they can afford the services of the top people. The firms who sell high-tech wine-making aids likewise have an interest in calling attention to the benefits of their products.

The Burgundian equivalent amounts to no more than chance meetings, word of mouth and the influence exerted by an unusually gifted or charismatic wine-maker. Gary Farr in Victoria learned from Jacques Seysses, a former Parisian biscuit manufacturer, who, in his turn, had sat at the feet of Armand Rousseau in the village of Gevrey Chambertin.

Jules Chauvet was a guru and teacher, but of a very different kind from Professeur Emile Peynaud of Bordeaux University. Chauvet wrote no full-length books, held no chairs in oenology and undertook no lucrative consultancies. He rarely travelled far from La Chapelle de Guinchay, the village just east of the Beaujolais *crus* of Chénas and Moulin-à-Vent where he ran his small *négociant*'s business. But since his death in 1989 at the age of eighty-two his influence has grown and spread.

Kermit Lynch, the Californian wine importer and author who met him during his final illness in 1987, describes a 'gracious guileless man with a poetic streak which he seemed to want to repress'.[1] His message, quoted by his obituarist Evelyne Leard-

Vibout, sums up beliefs I've heard echoed in conversations with scores of growers: 'We have to respect what the natural world has given us. We have to learn to see properly; this world is there in front of us but we don't observe it. The rate of progress is now so rapid, technology has become so sophisticated, yet we can't even make the leaf of a tree from scratch. We have above all to keep intact the precious capital that nature has bestowed on us.'

Chauvet would have a niche in wine history, if for nothing else, for his work as a taster, developing the now familiar comparisons with families of smells: floral, fruit, smoke, animal, spice, presenting his conclusions before meetings of academic oenologists. If he's responsible for the vivid presence of the smells of the countryside in French tasting notes this is no accident given his brief that the right place to assess wine was not in the cellar but out in the open air. Lynch describes tasting Beaujolais Villages in mild drizzle (I suppose Chauvet would have relented had it been an outright rainstorm).

A friend and admirer in his later years was Jean Thévenet who makes white Burgundies in an original and highly concentrated style in the village of Quintaine, fifteen miles to the north of La Chapelle de Guichay. Thévenet is a learned wine-maker, with a small laboratory where he does his own analyses. He has a historian's interest in the region and its wines. You sense he was drawn to Chauvet partly because they shared a certain intellectual rigour; he tells me that Chauvet would have had a purely scientific career if he hadn't been obliged by the death of his father to take up the reins of the family business. (Another wine-maker described Chauvet to me, not as a guru but as a *chercheur*: a researcher.)

'Jules Chauvet had a scientific training and a scientific approach,' says Thévenet. 'What interested him was a search for understanding through incessant hard work.'

Jules Chauvet's Disciples

Bourgueil 1995 Pierre and Catherine Breton (£6.64 RSJ Wine Company 0171 633 0489). This wine even has the paradoxical look – paleish but concentrated – that is shared with wines made by the band of Chauvetist-Neoportists. It's very good: ripe and with a spicy, polished leather quality on top of that Loire red fruit. Odd: 3/5 Niceness: 4/5

Morgon Jean Foillard 1995. This is silky and oozes spicy red fruit. Another two years had given the 1993 extra dimensions: morello cherries, plus liquorice, aniseed and cinnamon. Enotria Winecellars, who'd stocked the 1993, didn't rebuy. Think again, Enotria. The only options left are a trip to Willy's Wine Bar in Paris (00 331 42 96 37 86) or a plea to Vins Fins Ltd of 54 Bath Street, St Helier, Jersey. Odd: 2/5 Niceness: 4/5

Morgon 1995 Marcel Lapierre. On the plus side this, from the doyen of the disciples is concentrated, unctuous and non run-of-the-mill. But tasted early 1997 it's as yet too acidic and unexpressive to give much idea what the fuss is about. £10 (Bibendum Wine Ltd, London NW1, 0171 916 7706). Odd: 3/4 Niceness: 2/4

Dard et Ribo are now being imported by Yapp Brothers of Mere, Wiltshire (01747 860423) who have their red and white 1995 **Crozes Hermitage** and their red **St Joseph** 1995, all at or just under £10. Their white, which has suspended matter in it, is especially uncommercial, but they are a good thing; see page 199. Odd: 4/5 Nice 3/5

Philippe Laurent (see page 198) – Zubair Mohamed of Raeburn Fine Wines in Edinburgh 0131 332 5166 at the time of writing was planning to bring over some of the lesser cuvées, such as the Syrah-based **Côtes du Rhône**, but has doubts about the top wines – with a total absence of sulphur they require special handling. Odd: 2/5 Niceness: (if in condition) 4/5.

Pierre Overnoy. This tiny scale producer of Jura wines has no importer but a big reputation. His address is included for enthusiasts who find themselves in the Jura. Rue du Ploussard, Pupillin, 39600 Arbois Jura phone (0033) (0)384 661460.

Chauvet has cult status and there are already different schools of thought among his disciples. One reason, you feel, that Thévenet is so keen to claim him for science ('he didn't play at being a mystic') is the risk that the conclusions he reached through hard work and an open mind will ossify into dogma. In particular Thévenet, who makes wine using sulphur, wants Chauvet to be remembered as more than an advocate of sulphur-free winemaking.

The point about Jules Chauvet seems to be that his concerns reflected those of many growers who feared that the new range of chemical treatments on offer might constitute a poisoned chalice. Travelling through France it's hard to tell whether you are hearing his views echoed distantly or whether the same circumstances have set up the same responses.

Jean Thévenet says that Chauvet was chiefly worried that chemically based agriculture was cancelling out the influence of *terroir* – the contribution of a geographical site to the taste of wine. With herbicides replacing ploughing, Chauvet argued, vines were no longer forced to drive their roots deep into the subsoil. He urged a return to ploughing and an avoidance of chemicals. This was a theory rather than something he could prove, but Thévenet has been sufficiently convinced to put it into practice on his own 14 hectares of vines.

Mâcon in Together – Jean Thévenet and Friends

Jean Thévenet is no longer an unsung hero and demand is pushing up the prices of his white Burgundies. The reason he is so great is that he has reinvented white Chardonnay in a world which, taking its cue from the styles of Meursault and the Côte d'Or, has been turning it into a formula of toasted oak and butteriness. His version is clean, shimmering, floral, with a greater or less proportion, depending on price, of the honeyed dried-fruit character created by noble rot (see page 118 onwards).

Mâcon-Clessé-Quintaine, Guillemot-Michel 1995 £9.60 Tanners of Shrewsbury, 01743 232400. This is made by Thévenet's cousins and neighbours, working organically. Sniff and you're in an orchard planted in stony soil. Perfect, unless you think white Burgundy has to smell of buttered toast.
Odd: 1/5 Niceness: 4/5.

Henri Goyard 1990 Mâcon-Viré, Domaine de Roally £9.99 (half bottles available) Justerini and Brooks, London SW1, 0171 493 8721; 1993 £9.95 The Wine Society, Stevenage, 01438 741177. Thévenet helped Goyard when he was leaving the co-op. His wines are very good – the highish acidity in his **1993** means that it works better with food than TV. Odd: 2/5 Niceness: 3/5

Jean Thévenet Domaine de la Bongran 92 £12.90 at Justerini and Brooks, **93** £13.60 Adnams, Suffolk (01502 727222). This is

---

the entry-level Thévenet, with a hint of honey and meadow flowers.
Lea and Sandeman, London SW3 (0171 376 4767), are Thévenet
specialists and have the great man's pricey botrytized wines.

The modern world also intervenes in the invisible world of a
vineyard's micro-flora. Chauvet championed the naturally occurring wild yeasts which, especially in Europe, are still widely used
rather than selected commercial strains. Like Louis Pasteur, who
first discovered their role in wine-making, Chauvet believed that
they had a great influence on the taste and quality of wine. The
whole object of his researches was to preserve as far as possible
'this magnificent inheritance of yeasts which goes to make up a
great vineyard site.

Organic cultivation of the vineyard was vital to keep this heritage
intact. Chauvet's tasting experience led him to believe that wild
yeasts produced far more vibrant and complex wines than did
commercial single strains.

So far Chauvet was just holding the line against questionable
modern trends. But when he went on to question the need to put
sugar or sulphur in wine his radicalism extended to the well-
entrenched practices of the day. He told Jean Thévenet that he
began worrying about sulphur after buying a consignment that
was perfect apart from a slight smell of mercaptan; after it had
been bottled this turned into a stink of hydrogen sulphide, the
rotten egg gas.

Today only the tiniest minority of growers, even those who claim
him as their inspiration, avoid all sulphur and sugar. Thévenet,
who makes white wine, uses a little sulphur but doesn't chaptalize;
a group of Beaujolais growers get by without sulphur but do
chaptalize, that is, add sugar to increase levels of alcohol. It's
difficult to be faithful to both aspects of the teaching, according to
Thévenet. To do without sugar you need supermature grapes – but
these will have less of the acidity which secures grape juice against
infection by rogue organisms.

Even after his death Jules Chauvet is still winning converts, and
these do not necessarily come from his own region. Pierre Breton
is a grower of red Cabernet Franc grapes in the Bourgueil *appellation* on the Loire. He started up in 1985, but by the early 1990s
had come to feel dispirited by the escalating levels of chemical

treatments apparently required in his vineyards. The turning point was a visit to the annual wine show in Paris, the *Concours Agricole*, where he was bowled over by the Beaujolais made in Morgon by Marcel Lapierre, one of Chauvet's chief disciples.

Soon afterwards Breton embarked on a series of visits to Beaujolais to learn from Jacques Neoport, a former French language teacher nicknamed *bidasse* (squaddie), who has assumed the role of chief interpreter and communicator of the master's philosophy.

'From 1993 I changed the way I worked in the vineyard. Before then I had ploughed, but I'd used herbicide as well. Now I only plough. I've also gone over to harvesting into very small containers of only 2 kilos each so that the bunches don't squash each other. To try to make wine without sulphur is a total change of philosophy; before I'd followed the Bordeaux attitude of being hyperprotective, not taking the slightest risk, relying on oenologists' products to prevent trouble.'

The repentance of converts may jar on us; there are echoes of cults, evangelism, even show trials. However the new direction in winemaking is a loose set of ideas rather than a movement; there's neither a product to sell, an organization to build or fortunes to be made. Wherever you go you find wine-makers defining what they're doing in terms of the same core principles – but they're unlikely to have received them from Jules Chauvet and his little band of followers.

In California, as at Gary Farr's Bannockburn Estate, Burgundy lovers have learned about wild yeasts, to give just one example, because they wanted to reproduce the techniques used to make their favourite wines. But imitation is not enough. To be Burgundian in spirit you have to find roots in your own *terroir*.

1 Kermit Lynch, *Adventures on the Wine Route*, Farrar, Straus & Giroux, New York, 1988.

5

Terroir International

———

THREE CASE HISTORIES

Hamilton Russell Vineyards, Walker Bay, South Africa

'We don't want our wines to taste like Burgundy.'
This estate, the most southerly in Africa, makes wines that don't remind you of New World Pinot Noir and Chardonnay, Burgundy's red and white grape varieties, but the real thing – Burgundy as made in Burgundy. But don't expect them to be flattered if you ring them up to share this perception with them. For Anthony Hamilton Russell, whose father Tim planted the vineyard in the 1970s with working conditions regarded as a model for South Africa, it simply isn't the point: 'We want them to be an expression of our own *terroir.*'

Ça alors! How do they actually make the wine? Anthony H-R continues as he began, voicing sentiments that could have been scripted in Beaune or Nuits-St-Georges. 'We think wine-making technique is less important than focusing on the vineyard where we have a certain quality potential – that is to say, fully ripe grapes coming from balanced vines.'

It's a funny conversation. I try to talk about Burgundy, but Anthony now moves on to their cellar techniques. And the song is familiar. In 1993 they started fermenting with wild yeasts: they use them a hundred per cent for the Pinot Noir and are steadily increasing the proportion of barrels of Chardonnay they allow to ferment naturally. To allow the yeasts to thrive they are cutting right down on sulphur; they never had to add much anyway as they always hand-harvest intact bunches which don't need this form of chemical protection from the air.

40

It isn't simply that they think the naturally occurring yeasts are better, it's that they come as a cocktail, some starting fermentation and dropping out while others take over as the wine becomes more alcoholic. This makes for more nuances of flavours. 'We drink quite a lot of wine and like anyone who does [I brace myself for a confession] we more and more look for complexity.' It's been trendy for some time to ferment white wines at a very cold temperature to create fruity aromas. This doesn't appeal: 'We're going for slightly warmer fermentations than we used to. We're quite prepared to sacrifice overt fruitiness to create a platform for secondary development in the wine.'

One original aim of Tim Hamilton Russell had been to make a Bordeaux-type wine, but the last of the Merlot has now been pulled out to make way for more Pinot Noir and Chardonnay. Being so far south the 60-hectare vineyards are appropriately cool climate: they're in a coastal valley behind Hermanus, a small town fifty miles east of the Cape of Good Hope.

But Anthony Hamilton Russell denies that his *terroir* amounts to no more than coolish weather. They have been mapping out vineyard parcels to find out whether the lighter shale soils and the heavier clays produce any difference in the wines. They do, apparently. 'You go 150 yards and the wines change completely. It's not that they taste as if they're from different estates, more from different countries.' The lighter soils make a more commercial fruity wine and the clay soils something more minerally, more muscular, more structured. Well, I suggest, the northern Burgundy vineyards of Chablis are on a sort of clay. 'No – it's Kimmeridgean, full of ground-up fossils,' Anthony corrects me (not of course that he's obsessed with Burgundy). I was glad when I found that Hamilton Russell Chardonnay has been a Wine of the Month in France's *Gault-Millau* magazine – it seems only fair.

Hot Buttered Toast

You can make a red Loire wine, claret or Rioja and still feel that your spiritual roots are in Burgundy. There's a more obvious kinship between the buttery, toasty flavoured Chardonnay wines made all over the world and the extortionately priced original model from the village of Meursault in the Côte d'Or. Wine writers get rather sniffy at this mania for imitation: but the results of making

Chardonnay artisanally in far-flung continents can be such as to disarm prejudice. Look for these names:

Argentina: **Catena Agrela Vineyard Chardonnay 1995** £9.00 (Bibendum Wine Ltd, London NW1, 0171 916 7706)

California: **Joseph Swan Wolfspierre Chardonnay 1991** £9.99 Raeburn Fine Wines, Edinburgh (0131 332 5166)

New Zealand: **Dry River Chardonnay 1995** £15.99 Raeburn Fine Wines

South Africa: **Hamilton Russell Chardonnay 1996** £9.58 Averys of Bristol (01275 811100). Also check out the even more refined, elegant and old world-style version made on a neighbouring estate by Hamilton Russell's former wine-maker Peter Finlayson: **Bouchard Finlayson** 1995 £8.95, Waitrose mail order 0800 18881. The '96 vintage may also be at selected Waitrose stores.

Dirk Niepoort, Vila Nova de Gaia, Portugal

'My father thought I was crazy.'
Dirk Niepoort's favourite wine region is Burgundy but everything he's produced, so far, has been in Portugal, his family's adopted country, in an ultra-traditionalist Portuguese style. He made his first table wine as recently as 1990, when he was still in his mid-twenties. Dirk had the advantage of money and security as heir apparent to a Dutch family-owned port house, founded in 1842 in Vila Nova de Gaia, across the river Douro from Oporto. However it didn't save him from a critical trashing – from his own father.

'I did it the way I thought it ought to be done with reduced yields, using only low-yielding, old vines. I did more extraction and made quite big tannic wines but not aggressive, and with quite a bit of alcohol; I liked the fact that the grapes were picked when they were ripe rather than according to an analysis.

'Two months later I did a tasting. Everybody laughed at me and said I was crazy – that the wine was undrinkable. My father too – he thought I was crazy. I made four 'pipes' (500-litre barrels) and left for Australia on my honeymoon. While I was away my

father used three of the four barrels for our workers to drink –
only one was left.

'Because everyone complained so much I changed the style of
the wines in 1991 and 1992 and I like them much less. It was only
in 1995 that I made as good a wine as I did in 1990.'

Time has brought other changes. Dirk Niepoort now basks in
critical approval as he goes about making his ultra-traditional ports
and table wines, with the grapes trodden by foot in old concrete
lagars. His story is strikingly similar to that of the founding father
of modern Australian red wine, Max Schubert, who was also
told that his masterpiece, Grange Hermitage, was undrinkable and
ordered to stop making it.

Another similarity between the two men is that, despite a background outside Europe (Dirk Niepoort studied in California), the
crucial influence on them has been from the Old World. Max
Schubert learned how to make a deep-coloured wine designed for
long wood ageing during his visit to Bordeaux in 1950. Dirk
Niepoort has embraced the classic techniques of Portugal, even
though many of the Portuguese are abandoning them to follow
the example of modern Bordeaux. His crucial experience was his
honeymoon visit to Australia; he was struck by its beauty and by
the people's openness and friendliness, but not by their wines. 'I
didn't like what they were doing at all and I understood it for the
first time. Any two wines from the same area would taste the same
– with their wine-making they all seemed to do the same thing.
And the vineyards: they're planted in the places I'd never dream
of putting a vineyard, the most fertile land.'

What makes Niepoort really excited? 'I think the French make
the best wines in the world. I'm a Burgundy fanatic and a great
lover of German Riesling. Actually only last Friday I committed
myself to Burgundy – I've become a partner in a little property in
Meursault.'

A Lagar Mentality

Dirk Niepoort is working through his Portuguese company Uva and
with the British importer Raymond Reynolds (see page 270) to
defend the traditional style, with foot-treading of the grapes in the
shallow concrete *lagares* and ageing in large chestnut tuns.
Dirk's 1990 experiment was his '**Robustus**', **Quinta do Carril**.

This is a black monster that smells of tar and pine, acidic, almost salty to taste with flavours of small black fruit. Despite all this, and the fact it needs years longer in bottle, it's a stimulating, moreish wine to drink, which would stand up to food with concentrated tomato flavours. This vintage is not on sale, but contact Raymond Reynolds for news of later ones (01663 742230). Odd: 4/5; Niceness: 3/5.

Also from the Uva/Reynolds team:
Gonçalves Faria Bairrada Reserva 1992. Huge warm-smelling medicinal wine – flavours of bay leaves, tamarind and dates. Weird and quite wonderful. Raeburn Fine Wines of Edinburgh (0131 332 5166) have the 1991 at £9.99. Odd: 5/5 Niceness: 4/5 (I think the wine's so strange as to disarm the uninitiated). They also have several vintages of the Bairrada wines of **Casa de Saima** – the younger ones at £5.99, the older vintages at £8.99. Both are amazing – the whites in particular start life with apple-peel, lemon-zest flavours and develop the same sort of oiliness as old Hunter Valley Sémillon.

Bodegas Remelluri, Labastida, Rioja Alavesa, Spain

'Here in Rioja the small producers are despised.'
Telmo Rodriguez feels quite at home in Bordeaux where he studied wine-making in the 1980s (which is why he advised me that it's only a four-hour drive from there to his family's *bodega* – perhaps, but it needs the right car and a Mediterranean turn of speed). But Bordeaux isn't his passion – it's the small-scale, flying-by-the-seat-of-the-pants approach he came across after he left the university there and went to work with Gérard Chave, the current head of a family which has made wine at Hermitage on the northern Rhône since 1481. At Bordeaux, he says, he learned a method that can be applied year in, year out. With Chave, on the other hand, each vintage was like beginning from scratch. Just as the disciples of Jules Chauvet have created their own informal circle, Telmo Rodriguez has his own network with like-minded contacts he met studying at the feet of Chave (one is Laurent Vaillé, despite his youth already hugely successful with his Domaine de la Grange des Pères and its new vineyards on the hill-tops of the Languedoc).

Telmo thinks Rioja has gone in the wrong direction, a conclusion that he's anyway predisposed towards by his background. Remelluri,[1] the family property reached by a dirt road in the middle of vineyards, has always been out of step with the big commercially minded operations in Haro, the capital of the northern Rioja. Telmo's parents Jaime and Amaya, Basques from San Sebastian, bought the old monastic farm in the mid-1960s despite its isolation and lack of mains water or electricity. They started making a novel sort of Rioja, the first to use only the grapes of a single property and the first not to blend different vintages to achieve a consistent style.

'We were the first to try to produce the expression of a *terroir*,' says Telmo, 'but people didn't like the way the wine changed every year. They'd say "it isn't any more Remelluri." The consumer always wants to have the same wine; the trouble is that if you have a bad consumer you'll have a bad wine.'

Rioja couldn't be more removed in spirit from the small producers from the Rhône and Burgundy that Telmo idolises. The region has often been seen as a southern extension of Bordeaux, which is itself founded on the mass plantation of vines. In the 1860s a Frenchman called Cadeache Pinaud imported techniques to turn the light local product into something adapted for barrel maturation and long keeping, creating what he called a '*Médoc Alaves*' or 'Basque Médoc'. A decade later this turned from a local curiosity into something that was in huge demand internationally; the reason was the onslaught of phylloxera on the Bordeaux vineyards: Rioja was able to take up much of the slack in the years before the lethal insects made the journey south and started munching their way through the roots of the Spanish vineyards.

The big *bodegas* made the region's fortune but at a cost which Telmo deplores. 'Here we destroyed that element of the small producer.' Producers with less than a minimum size of vineyard holding were forbidden by the local *consejo regulador* to age their own wine. 'The big companies wanted to have overall control, that is control over the prime material. By refusing to allow the small grower to age his own wine you ensure that he has to sell his grapes to the big companies or the co-operatives. The small growers are despised.'

Telmo fumes at the reception given to another of his friends from the Rhône, Auguste Clape, the leading grower in Cornas, twelve miles south of Hermitage. Clape told him of a visit to Rioja with some other smaller French producers. 'They went to the *consejo regulador* who sent them to see Campo Viejo and Berberana, operations dealing in tens of millions of bottles. Of course they had no idea who Clape was, they just aren't part of the same culture.'

Since the Rodriguez family moved in other single estate *bodegas* have opened up: Bodegas Amezola, SMS and Rodi for example. However some Riojans would perhaps have been just as happy if the family had sat tight in San Sebastian. In an interview with the Scots journalist Dave Broom for *Decanter* magazine Telmo shared his view that the product of some of the 44,000 hectares that make up Rioja would be better distilled for use as gasoline substitute (quite a common fate, in fact, for Europe's wine surpluses; the stuff is sent to Brazil). The president of the *consejo regulador* called him to account; Telmo protested his innocence of any intention to talk down the region: 'In Bordeaux it's well known that only 5 per cent of the production is quality. The rest is sold as very cheap wine.

'For me the right mentality is very simple. Work with the vines. Respect the soil. Make the wine's quality in the vineyard. I don't believe in "top oenologists" or all that rubbish.'

This grumbling and griping sounds a little at odds with loving nature and caring for the environment, but in fact a certain sense of being embattled comes with the territory – or the *terroir*.

Off His Rioja? Rodriguez at Work

As well as his work at Remelluri, Telmo Rodriguez has acted as Spain's domestic flying wine-maker in association with Adnams, making a red Grenache in Navarra called Baso and white in Rueda called Basa.

Basa Rueda Blanca 1995 £4.25 Adnams, Suffolk (01502 727222). Lemony, zippy slightly sweet and nicely concentrated. Odd: 0/5 Niceness: 5/5.

Baso Navarra Garnacha 1995. £4.50 Thresher/Wine Rack/ Bottoms Up, Adnams. This has juicy cherry fruit but lacks the vividness of the similar and more sensational 1995 '**Jardin**' from **Guelbenzu** (imported by Moreno Wines; 0171 723 6897). The problem was that in 1995 Telmo couldn't acquire the product of the vineyards that had made the 1994 so good. At first taste the **1996** seems to be back on top form. Odd: 1/5 Niceness: 4/5

Remelluri Reserva 1993. £9.80 Tanners and Adnams. Not a thin, vanillaey concoction like much Rioja; instead of American oak you hit a thick seam of sweet intense and funky red fruit. Odd: 2/5 (or 0/5 if you're not a conventional Rioja fan) Niceness: 5/5.

Other recommended growers' Riojas: **Amezola Crianza 1989** £7.55 Justerini and Brooks (0171 493 4653); **Valdesano Crianza Rioja Alavesa** Davisons Direct (0181 681 3222).

1 La Granja de Nuestra Señora de Remelluri, to give its full name. The house and winery are on the site of the old winter quarters; in the summer the monks of the Geronimo Order lived in a now-ruined mountain hermitage overlooking the Remelluri vineyards. The property came into secular ownership during the confiscation of church lands of 1837.

6
Lone Wolves

Despite their enthusiasms for natural yeasts, planetary influences (which we'll come to later) and nudity, at least during *pigeage*, and their dislike of herbicides, rules and big corporations, small growers are no late flowering of the Woodstock generation. The talented ones lack the benevolent sloppiness of true hippies; they may live in rural communities but they're singled out by a perfectionism their neighbours do not share and are likely to resent. Cussedness abounds, though to see it elevated to a near-poetic dimension you have to do as I did and go and visit the Domergues.

When I mentioned that I was going to visit this couple my interlocutor in the Southern French village of Siran was interested but wary: 'Madame Domergue is very determined – not at all like the people from around here.'

In fact in a part of the world teeming with former Algerian colonists and Australian flying wine-makers, the Domergues are hardly exotic. He is originally from Toulouse, only sixty miles away, and teaches wine-making and vineyard management at nearby Béziers; Patricia, the second Mme Domergue and a former viticulture student, is at least half a Southerner by birth. In 1990 the couple bought the Clos des Centeilles, set among a Mediterranean landscape of low hills so classic it seems to require a Madonna with child in the foreground to look compositionally correct.

Apart from making wine, the couple's chief form of relaxation appears to be puncturing conventional wisdom. She is a tough, handsome blonde; Daniel is wiry, with the intensity of manner which gets teachers labelled as 'inspirational'. He takes a Socratic delight in showing up the shaky foundations of people's beliefs – even when these beliefs correspond precisely with his own wine-making practices.

At Clos des Centeilles they let the fermentations start spontaneously rather than using commercial yeast strains. 'But many excellent wines do use dried yeasts,' Daniel insists. They don't filter, thus conforming to the current American view of good winemaking practice. 'But when people ask me why I don't filter I just tell them, "Because I don't own a filter." It doesn't mean I belong to the sect of non-filterers. We're living through a *fin-de-siècle*. People in such times always want simple certainties – to have discovered a new religion.'

This sort of thing makes the Domergues very stimulating to be with – until they take the knives to a dogma in which you have a personal stake. The couple believe, and it sounds perfectly likely, that they have given offence to Michel Bettane, a wine journalist almost as influential in France as Robert Parker is in the Anglo-Saxon world. Daniel pulled him up on two issues of vineyard management: the correct density of planting in dry areas and the use of clonal, or genetically identical vines.

'Bettane is against clones. He is an eminent Latin and Greek scholar. Well, good for him and I respect him for it – better that than he should have nothing in his head. But how does that qualify him to pronounce . . . on clones? He says they remove complexity. But no one has done any work on this. That would involve a programme of comparing otherwise identical wines, which might take twenty years. In fact no one knows what causes what – which doesn't stop people saying any old thing.' Daniel Domergue, as you might have guessed, does not in fact use clones in his own vineyards.

The misconception that most irks the Domergues is that serious wines, the kind that will repay keeping, have to be brooding tannic beasts, oozing with the aromas of new oak barrels: 'That word "structured",' says Daniel with distaste. 'As I get older I find what I require is sensuality, smoothness, enjoyment, and that's what I want in a wine,' smoulders his spouse.

This view is one reason they aren't joining the campaign to upgrade the local area, called La Livinière, to *cru* status. As they are the only growers of major repute in the *cru* boundaries this must come as something of a body blow to the campaign.

It isn't that Daniel is stand-offish. In the 1960s he was a strong supporter of the virtually insurrectionary growers' movement to demand cash support from the government after the market for cheap blending wine collapsed. The problem is with the grape varieties that the new *cru* of La Livinière would make mandatory. When the Domergues bought the estate they found it heavily planted with the unfashionable Cinsault. The oenologist at their local producers' co-operative advised them: 'If you have Cinsault sell the wine quickly – it turns to vinegar.' They made wine with it, more out of curiosity than anything else, and were bowled over by the results, as have been the critics.

For their neighbours in the *appellation*, quality these days means only one thing: Syrah, the dark, aromatic and currently ultra-fashionable variety from the Rhône, 150 miles to the north-east. With this grape variety it's easier to make the intense deep-coloured style championed by Parker and Bettane.

Patricia is exasperated by the dogmatism of the late converts. 'They're insisting on 40 per cent of Syrah grapes. Twenty years ago my husband was planting Syrah and Mourvèdre and they said he was a lunatic. It's our misfortune that we're always out of step with fashion.' All the couple's 17 hectares of vines fall within the proposed new *cru*. However, should it come into being they will continue to sell their wine simply as Minervois.

The fact is that people buy wines from the best single estates because of the reputation of the producer, not of the *appellation*. And the best producers display what appears to some a slighting lack of reverence for the way the rules are framed. The Domergues use a technicality to sidestep the requirement of the Minervois *appellation* for a proportion of Carignan, a variety for which they feel some disdain. 'You can make an attractive, soft wine from Carignan,' states Patricia, 'but keep it for ten years and it'll turn bitter as gall.'

They continue to grow it but bottle it separately, keeping it out of the blends for which they have higher ambitions. The Domergues' Carignan wine, called Cuvée Carignanissime, was first created on the suggestion of Simon Loftus of Adnams, an English wine-merchant who likes to encourage loose cannons. For years the main customer was the Oddbins chain, the smaller proportion going to Adnams. When I visited the Domergues they were reeling from Oddbins' decision to delist Carignanissime on the puzzling grounds that the chief buyer Steve Daniel found it 'too hard'. As Patricia Domergue says, 'Whatever criticism you might make you can't say it's too hard. It's as soft as baby food.'

Bruce Kendrick of Haughton Agencies, who works in partner-ship with Adnams, blames the couple's pricing – 'It's a wine that works at £4.99, not at over £6.00' – and their 'typically arrogant attitude – and you can quote me on that' – but at the time of writing was confident that it would be eased back into Oddbins with the help of a weaker franc. He sighed for the Australians and their responsiveness to his suggestions. 'With the French the atti-tude is that if you can't sell their wines it's because you're not a good agent.'

The Minervois – the Domergues and their Rivals

'Cuvée Capitelle' 1991 £9.70 Adnams 01502 727222. This is the 100 per cent Cinsault that put the Domergues on the map. In a class of its own – further discussed on page 175. Odd: 4/5 Nice-ness: 5/5

'Clos des Centeilles' 1990 Adnams. This has some Syrah, as used everywhere to give impact to Southern French wines. In this case it just adds a black fruit note in a wine that's smooth, sump-tuous and complex, with notes of mace and almonds.

Guigniers de Centeille, Côtes du Brian 1992, £9.75 Adnams. This tests the theory that the Pinot Noir of Burgundy is an ancient variety of the Languedoc. But after four years in bottle is there life in this Brian? While it will never make waves in a blind tasting, it's fine, concentrated and delicious. Odd: 4/5 Niceness: 3/5

Other growers' Minervois:
Château de Violet, Cuvée Clovis, 1994, Thresher £5.39 – also from Raeburn Fine Wines, Edinburgh, 0131 332 5166. Dark, toasty and truffle-oily. A success in a different style for the wine-maker Helene Serrano. Odd: 1/5 Niceness: 4/5.

Also: **Domaine Piccinini 1994** £4.95 Justerini and Brooks; **Domaine St Eulalie 1994** £5.10 Tanners

---

Despite the hiccup with Oddbins, the Domergues win a certain respect from their neighbours for their ability to sell Minervois for forty francs rather than fifteen francs a bottle. It isn't a universal truth that the better wine growers have to fall out with their less ambitious neighbours, but when you keep hearing different versions of the same story you begin to suspect that, as conspiracy theorists put it, 'It's no coincidence.'

Partly it's a problem of personalities. Henri Goyard, who makes intense white wines from a postage-stamp-sized holding in the Mâconnais, told me that he could never have survived as a member of his local co-op: 'I just couldn't have fitted. I'd have been endlessly victimized. They'd have picked on me.' Thierry Germain left Bordeaux to become a hotshot at Saumur-Champigny in the Loire because he couldn't stand the conformist social ambiance of that somewhat stuffy region.

There can be something stifling about rural European communities. Long before there were *appellations* or co-operatives, growers got together in mutual aid societies, or *confréries*. I was invited to the launch of a new *confrérie*, an all-female body, called into being frankly as a marketing ploy under the name of '*Les Demoiselles de Chiroubles*', Chiroubles being one of the Beaujolais *cru* villages entitled to use its name in its *appellation*.

The ceremony took place in a marquee on a rainy April day and involved two other uniformed groups: *Les Compagnons du Beaujolais* and *Les Dames des Arts de la Table*. At its climax the ladies filed in revealing their purpose-designed costumes (capes and big white bows) and their president thanked the many other speakers in a speech proclaiming her group's vocation to be 'feminine, but *not* feminist'.

You could argue that the only thing more absurd than religious ritual is its secular equivalent and take this kind of gathering as your text. But it was also quite moving. As at end of term performances, the participants gave off a mixture of stage fright and delight at being the centre of attention. And the audience, like that at a school concert, willingly suspended a sense of irony. Perhaps a third of the men present had handlebar moustaches: these serve as a badge of Beaujolais's regional identity and source of masculine pride, proclaiming the wearer to be a bit of a character. A further third were presidents of some body or other. France is the land of associations. If other than in a nightmare you were called on to speak at a formal gathering in France you could safely address the company as '*messieurs les présidents*'. The point is: everybody is somebody.

Beaujolais is made up of smallholdings and turning out with the *confrérie* is a mark of solidarity. But the French everywhere are hooked on dressing up in silly clothes. Bordeaux, which must compete with Champagne as the least democratic wine region, is also in thrall to this addiction.

The association of the producers of the Médoc, the region which can boast Latour and Mouton-Rothschild, puts together an annual magazine. It's in French but has an English parallel text; confident in the excellence of their secondary education system, the publishers have seen no need to check this translation work with a native English speaker.

My eye was caught by a headline worded 'A Simple Fête in Good Taste' over the byline of Jean-Michel Cazes, the proprietor of Chateau Lynch-Bages. His article described the festival of the annual proclamation of the harvest, the *ban des vendanges*. This was illustrated with a photo of the British and Japanese ambassadors, each dressed in what looked like purple velvet dressing gowns topped with high collars as favoured by the contemporaries of Queen Elizabeth I and both, to judge from their expressions, so numb with boredom they could have undergone extensive dental work without anaesthetics.

Between them was a lady called Marie-Louise Pelegrin, also sporting more purple velvet than Jimi Hendrix in his heyday.

In his text, M. Cazes explained her role: 'Bent on a simple fête in good taste, Marie-Claire Pelegrin made herself readily available and brought boundless goodwill to its organization.' He continued, under the cross-heading 'The Hundred Years War'. 'The tents erected on the lawn in front of the château presented a huge setting against which Eric le Collen recreated, stage by stage, the Hundred Years War. And what a spectacle! the artillery, the cavalry and the infantry, not forgetting a fantastic pack of hounds.'

And, what a victory too for the hostess's love of simplicity and good taste.

You do find good producers who are leading lights of their local *confréries* and *cru* committees. Many though have neither the inclination to fraternize, nor the time. 'Agriculture is a hard life,' says Olivier Merlin, 'and this is the hardest form of agriculture. The work just never stops.' And it is the most dedicated growers who have the least spare time; for one thing they don't rely on the mechanical and chemical aids that make things easier for their neighbours.

In *Burgundy* Anthony Hanson describes how, after the war, Pierre Guillot, a producer at the northern end of the Mâcon *appellation*, found that sulphur, the wine-maker's all-purpose disinfectant and anti-oxidant, gave him heartburn and headaches. He resolved to do without it as far as possible, together with the potassium ferrocyanide used at that date to eliminate traces of iron.

The result, according to his son Alain, was that Guillot was expelled from the local co-operative, denied access to local wine laboratories, and schoolfriends would cross the street so that their parents would not have to meet this ostracized family. As Hanson comments: 'It cannot have been much fun.'

Alain, incidentally, is now president of the National Agrobiological Viticultural Committee and an established producer. So is his brother Jean-Gérard, whose wines adorn the lists of such top London restaurants as Bibendum in the Fulham Road.

To this day a heavy hand with the sulphur appears to be the route to acceptance in parts of the Mâconnais. The best wine in Pouilly-Vinzelles near Mâcon, made by Gérard Valette was discovered by his UK importer despite a lack of recognition from his local *cru* committee. Jasper Morris of the London importers Morris and Verdin went to the village a few years ago when it hosted the annual *Grands Jours de Bourgogne* event. This is a sort of travelling circus when the world descends on a single Burgundy village. The wives will have put in weeks of work on the decorations, stringing wreaths of real or plastic flowers from house to house and over the branches of the plane trees. The producers fling open their cellars, panic at the horde that descends and try to weed out freeloaders without losing the chance of impressing a journalist or wholesaler.

'There was a terrible Pouilly Fouissé session,' recalls Morris. 'The village committee had preselected the wines and it was obviously, you know, the good old boys. All the wines were faulty: oxidized, over-sulphured – just clumsy wine-making.

'Later there was a separate session of Pouilly-Vinzelles and Pouilly-Loché, done slightly differently, with about a dozen wines each introduced by the producer. They were each allowed two sentences and everyone else said: "I am so and so and I hope you like my wine." When it was the turn of Valette's son he got up and said: "This wine is made from low yields and the grapes were hand picked." '

This short declaration of principles told Morris that he was looking at the best producer (and if he'd used the French wine guides as a shortcut he'd have found his judgement confirmed). The Valettes, father and son, are recognized as being among the very best growers of these *appellations*. They make lovely concentrated wines, honeyed and floral in the style of the best Chardonnay white wines of southern Burgundy.

So why had they failed to make the shortlist? When I met Gérard it emerged that nearly twenty years earlier he had been the first to leave the Chaintré co-op to make his own wine. Later a further eighteen growers had followed him. The issue was the quality of the co-op's wine-making. 'We had wonderful vineyards and they weren't resulting in wonderful wines. It had been a difficult period,' he said.

But Jasper Morris thinks he was left off simply through the honest preferences of his neighbours. 'I don't think it was a case of fear of a young Turk; I just think they *like* bad, sulphured oxidized wine.'

At least you can't accuse them of that in Beaujolais. Thanks to the marketing skills of the super-*négociant* Georges Duboeuf, everyone knows what the product is supposed to be like, even if it's very little to the taste of Kermit Lynch or the disciples of Jules Chauvet. The northern part of the region has a reputation for wines that will keep, though these are eclipsed in the public imagination by the hype around Beaujolais Nouveau, and producers sometimes make wine in separate batches, with vinifications to produce both a lighter and a more concentrated style.

In the less well-regarded south of the region nearer Lyons they mainly stick to Beaujolais Nouveau and a single vinification; except for Jean-Paul Brun, another Adnams supplier, who does *eight*.

J-P B provokes strong reactions, and not just because he unpatriotically declines to deck out his upper lip *à la* Jimmy Edwards. (He's clean shaven, with the grizzled, close-cropped look favoured by metropolitan types like the architect Richard Rogers.) Writing for English readers it's hard to convey the seriousness of his offence. He makes untypical Beaujolais.

Driving through the imposing red-soiled hills of Southern Beaujolais following a tasting session with Jean-Paul I tried to tease Anne Mathon, the region's elegant publicity officer, out of the sulk into which she'd plunged following an obviously traumatic experience. 'Honestly, you're reacting as if this wine-maker is some sort of national threat – *la patrie en danger*.' 'I think that puts it very well,' she replied, unthawed.

A few weeks later in London I ran into Catherine Manac'h, the leading light of the French agricultural export body, Sopexa, and one of the people who's done most to make wine an everyday part of life in Britain. Catherine is kindness personified, but there are limits to tolerance. When I explained that Brun was making an *appellation controllée* Beaujolais from Pinot Noir, the Burgundian grape variety, I heard a sharp intake of breath, the sound a head teacher might make on being told that a known paedophile had been seen hanging around the school gates. 'I think I should look into that,' she said, not panicking but visibly concerned.

But Jean-Paul Brun has studied the *appellation* rules and knows that the law is powerless. By some quirk of history Pinot Noir is a permitted variety in Beaujolais. There is also no way of stopping his offensive practice of making a *cuvée* using the proper variety, Gamay, but the wrong fermentation technique: destemming, open fermenters and *piégage* rather than whole bunches and semi-carbonic maceration. The essential argument had been played out for my benefit in his tasting cellars, illustrated and accompanied by glasses of the offending wines.

The punch-up started with a red Beaujolais Jean-Paul calls his Cuvée à l'Ancienne. This is the Gamay fermented like a red Burgundy. I apparently thought it was 'serious and brooding with cassis/black fruit and pepper on the nose'. While I was honing my wine-speak Anne interjected that there was nothing on the nose – which, in comparison to the usual style of Beaujolais, there wasn't – then changed tack and condemned it for *un odeur bizarre*.

Next the infamous Pinot. This wasn't my favourite of the range, and the two-year-old version seemed too oaky and old before its time. The objection Anne voiced was: 'This simply isn't Beaujolais. It's a disastrous piece of marketing; this sort of thing stops Beaujolais having a coherent identity.'

Jean-Paul gave, in a measured manner, as good as he got. The rules were excessively restrictive. They were framed by an older generation at the Institut National des Appellations d'Origine with the effect of inhibiting the creativity of younger wine-makers. 'To make Beaujolais you're supposed to follow a standard method out of a book – do that, do that, do that. All I'm trying to do is to make the best wine that can be made from my soils.'

The rules for describing and guaranteeing a wine's origin were originally drawn up to protect both the customers from fraud and the growers from being undercut by cheap imitations. Today though they are equally likely to cause the better producers unending grief.

7

In a Class of their Own?

───────

When growers ask what this book's about I'm apt to feel like a bearer of bad news. My spiel begins on an upbeat note: 'It's a guide to producers I admire . . .' and their faces brighten ' . . . whose wines sell for moderate prices in the UK,' I continue, and their shoulders slump and they sigh, hurt at being reminded that the sums don't add up as they'd like.

Their misfortune, and the consumers' good fortune, is that they make wine in a region that does not have a sufficient reputation to guarantee a high price. If you own a vineyard in the delimited area for Barolo or if your address contains the words Pauillac, Pomerol or Puligny you are a winner in life's lottery and I will be unlikely to be able to buy much of your wine. On the other hand, if you are legally entitled to call what you produce Coteaux du Languedoc or Toro or Bairrada you may possess a certain local cachet, but little or no advantage in world markets.

But what hurts most is to have the use of a name which might be, or has once been, worth something, but which has lost its value – like coming into an inherited fortune and discovering it is made up entirely of pre-revolutionary Russian government bonds.

Sometimes a name is devalued because of a simple shift in fashion, like the one that has made Sherry so underrated. This can't be helped. But in other cases the conscientious producers feel that they have been robbed of their good name by the lazy and unambitious who ask only what the *appellation* can do for them, not what they can do for the *appellation*.

What develops is a tussle between the many and the few. For the majority the *appellation* name enables them to get a better price than if they were simply selling table wine. For a minority it pulls the price down. Unless they can establish a reputation for themselves, their attempts to charge more are always vulnerable to the reply: 'But it's only Côtes du Roussillon/Mâcon Blanc/Crozes Hermitage – I can pay half what you're asking at the co-op.' (This is not an abstract possibility: one British high-street chain has had a policy that, irrespective of quality, Languedoc-Roussillon wines should be taken on only if they're in a medium-low to rock-bottom price band.)

For Etienne Pochon, who some years ago left the Tain l'Hermitage co-operative, his former colleagues 'endlessly play the Crozes-Hermitage card'; he now regards it as less significant than the name he can make for himself. Eighty miles to the north of Tain, Olivier Merlin thinks his local co-operatives are selling Mâcon short, making wines that conform to the *appellation*'s mediocre reputation at prices only a little above those of generic Chardonnay wines.

Reassuringly Expensive – Top Wines from Neglected Regions

A wine can be overlooked because it's from somewhere no one's heard of. The classic example is the 100 per cent Syrah from an *appellation* called **Brézème**, where **Jean-Marie Lombard** is virtually the only producer. His 1994 is light but juicy with a core of pepperiness. £8.25 from Yapp Brothers of Mere, Wiltshire (01747 860929). Odd: 0/5 Niceness: 3/5

Apart from Germany, Italy is a prime example of a region where some names have fallen into disrepute, obscuring the good work of a minority of growers.

Lambrusco di Sorbara 1994, Vigna del Christo, Cavicchioli & Figli (£6.55 Adnams 01502 727222). Foaming and invigorating, with the jewelled appearance and astringency of redcurrants. Three years haven't dented its freshness. The perfect wine to cut through rich food. Odd: 5/5 Niceness: 5/5. Red Vinho Verde from Northern Portugal scores similarly – it's the best drink with fresh sardines. At the time of writing the Selfridges wine department were considering bringing over a case or two from a reputable producer. Ring: 0171 629 1234.

Frascati can occasionally be wonderful. The producer to buy is Antonio Pulcini. His **Colle Gaio** from Alivini in Tottenham (0181 442 8215) is a textbook of how to make a great dry white wine

---

without looking over your shoulder at Burgundy: at once waxy, oily, floral and rich with aromas of sugared almonds.

Alivini also have a wine that manages to be both low-status and obscure – a still **Prosecco di Conegliano** from the hinterland of Venice from the **Gregoletto** family. Quite neutral in the way Italians like white wines to be, but with lovely flavours of pears and green apples. It's called **Ombretta** and costs £5.82.

Back to France: good Muscadet and good Beaujolais are almost always underpriced. Lay and Wheeler of Colchester (01206 764446) and Roger Harris in Norfolk (01603 880171) both have good Beaujolais lists.

You wouldn't expect people who are convinced of their superiority to be popular. And they aren't. What is even worse is their tendency to voice their views of their neighbours' shortcomings to foreign journalists. One such instance is the row described earlier between Telmo Rodriguez of Bodegas Remelluri and the *consejo regulador* of Rioja arising out of Telmo's unkind suggestion that a substantial share of that region's production might usefully be distilled into industrial alcohol.

On a different order of magnitude is the force ten storm tearing much of the German wine industry up from its foundations. But the fault-line is the same, splitting the 'élitist' single estates off from the mass of the ordinary growers. As in Rioja, the ostensible cause of the trouble is a British journalist.

In 1996 Hugh Johnson, the best-selling author of the *Wine Atlas of the World*, became the target for regular attacks in the German press. Growers met in heated sessions and vied with each other to denounce him as a meddling and ill-informed foreigner. 'It's like the Nazi era,' I was told by Ernie Loosen, an enterprising Mosel proprietor, using a comparison from which most non-Germans would shy away.

The problem facing his compatriots is that their country has lost its status as a top wine-producing country. This is measured by a general collapse in demand that has had dire effects both on once popular brands, like Blue Nun, and on estates accustomed to getting prices comparable with the top châteaux of Bordeaux. Johnson's offence was to have gone into print drawing attention to this fact and arguing that the root cause was the wine law of 1971.

This law was enacted after two decades that had seen German wines grow ever more popular. Its effect was to extend the use of the names of the best-known wine villages, allowing producers to put these prestigious names on their labels even if their vineyards were ten or even twenty miles distant from them. The result has been to devalue the currency. Believe it or not, Liebfraumilch was once a grand wine, taking its name from the vineyard surrounding a medieval church, the Liebfrauenkirche in the city of Worms in the state of Rhineland-Palatinate.

'Unfortunately,' wrote Johnson in a short foreword to a booklet put out by the VDP, the association of top estates, 'the philosophy pursued by the government authorities has been precisely to deny the basic facts of wine geography.' He continued, 'The result of these laws based on half truths, untruths and downright lies has been the depressing sight of an industry sinking lower and lower in international esteem.'

The thrust of Johnson's argument is that the authorities should redraw the maps, making it obvious to consumers which wines really come from top vineyard sites. But to expect widespread support for this plan is to ask turkeys to vote for Christmas. The growers of bad Mosel from overcropped, ignoble grape varieties are barely making a living as it is. Without the little scrap of grandeur in which they've wrapped themselves they fear that they'll freeze to death.

Good Germans

Even people who don't have much to say on the subject tend to be sure of one thing: the disgustingness of German wine. Everyone at some time has drunk Niersteiner or Liebfraumilch, but few can remember why they ever put up with these cloying, breath-tainting confections.

Unlike this meretricious stuff, the point of good German wine, especially from the Mosel, is that it's rather aloof and austere, even when it isn't dry. It doesn't make you very drunk (Kabinett, the least alcoholic grade, can have as little as 8 per cent alcohol), but it can give a feeling of almost spiritual uplift.

Ernie Loosen's philosophy results in excellent wines which these days are widely distributed. You can find the cheaper ones in the Bottoms Up/ Thresher/Wine Rack group and Majestic warehouses (with Victoria Wines the best high street outfit for Germany) and the single vineyard wines in Adnams of Southwold in Suffolk (01502 727 222), Amps of Oundle, Northamptonshire (01832 273502) and Zachys of Haverstock Hill, North London (0171 431 4412).

Oddbins import one or two growers' wines together with the dispensable **St Ursula** brand – look especially for the Rheinpfalz wines of **Kurt Darting**. The great thing about Victoria Wines is this group's tradition of selling mature Riesling, with sufficient bottle age to do justice to the latent smoky, oily, flinty notes. In the past Victoria have had a dozen single estate; the number's coming down but it's still impressive.

Of the supermarkets, Waitrose does the best job on Germany; the **Mönchof** estate in the Mosel is always a good bet. The names to look for in Tesco are the **Friedrich Wilhelm Gymnasium** and the **Grans Fassian** estate.

Any independent wine merchant worth its salt will do some justice to Germany, but Justerini and Brooks, London SW1 (0171 493 8721) are especially good.

The seeds of the confrontation were sown in 1987 in the library of Ernie Loosen's grand family home at St Johannishof near Bernkastel on the Mosel. Loosen had recently taken over the property which had been in his family ever since they bought it at the start of the nineteenth century, as part of the church estates sold by Napoleon to fund his campaigns.

Ernie had a visitor, Stuart Piggott, the English wine writer who was working on his *Wine Atlas of Germany*, partly funded by the German Wine Institute and he had something to show him: a Land Tax document drawn up by the Kaiser's authorities in 1901. From the different rateable values of the different vineyard sites it was easy to reconstruct a hierarchy corresponding to the French division of the vineyards of Burgundy's Côte d'Or into *grand crus, premiers crus* and *villages*.

Excited by this find, Piggott set to work turning it into graphic form. What made it controversial was that it told a wholly different story from the 1971 law which reclassified swathes of flat lands, until then used for growing sugar beet, deeming them worthy of bearing names no less revered than Montrachet or Chambertin.

The Wine Institute withdrew their funding. 'Stuart just couldn't understand it,' Loosen told me. 'Why didn't the Germans want to use a source that is older than the other classifications and that is so proper – done by a Prussian tax officer. So that was the start of all these discussions – which haven't been easy.'

Even if Piggott's new classification didn't appeal to the authorities it made sense to Ernie Loosen. Any wine from vineyards without historical status he now sells simply as 'Dr L. Riesling', leaving off the sonorous but irrelevant *Grosslage* name he is entitled to under the 1971 law. Other estates have done the same, and so too has at least one quality-conscious co-operative, at Ruppertsberg in the Rheinpfalz.

There is quite a solid consensus of British writers behind Johnson and the VDP. Certainly, the single estates make thrilling wines whereas the merchants and many of the co-operatives are responsible for a lot of dreary sugar-water that isn't worth even the tiny amount charged for it.

But, shamefully, I find it almost as difficult to follow the argument as I do to remember the names of the great German single vineyards. The thrust of the case is that, whereas in Bordeaux the good wine enhances the reputation of the mediocre stuff, in Germany the volume producers have dragged down the top estates in their wake.

But do the names make that much difference? To accept that it matters means believing that the following scenario is likely: you buy a wine called Piesporter Michelsberg assuming it to be from a top vineyard, but are so disappointed by the contents that you vow never to drink German wine again.

But since the Piesporter is likely to cost all of £2.99 you must be a bit of an idiot to make such an assumption. I think the reason Bordeaux has kept its reputation is nothing to do with *appellation* names and everything to do with the fact that even the cheapest Claret is a lot better than industrial German wine. It is not overcropped, it is not subjected to excessive chemical treatments and it is made from the noble varieties on which the region's reputation was created.

Before he took up the reins at the Loosen estate, Ernie worked at Geisenheim, the wine school and research institute on the Rhine.

It is hard to exaggerate Geisenheim's importance in the history of wine, whether in developing single yeast strains or creating new grape varieties that have been the basis of much of the modern German, and most of the modern English wine industries. Yet according to Ernie Loosen it has also helped wipe out the industry it was intended to serve. The direction taken by Germany has now been rejected by consumers, in consequence of which more than half the growers in the Mosel have gone out of business since the early 1980s ' . . . and a lot of these guys are in their fifties and sixties: they're just hanging on till they retire.'

It all seemed so different forty years ago. People couldn't get enough and to meet the demand new vineyards were planted, spreading outwards from the low-yielding riverside slopes into the hinterland. Farmers found that investing in a vineyard could yield startling rewards. The co-operatives led the expansion, but the bottling companies weren't far behind. These are the equivalent of the French *négociants* but, unlike their counterparts, they invariably buy made wine rather than juice or grapes.

The only problem was to make enough product. Yields per hectare doubled and trebled. As well as benefiting from richer soils, the new wave of growers turned to the high-yielding grape varieties developed at Geisenheim, abandoning Riesling in favour of Müller-Thurgau and other new crosses developed by the researchers.

'The area under vine had been about 6,000 hectares,' recalls Loosen. 'It went up to 13,000. These days the distribution is one-third steep slopes, two-thirds in the flat areas where they can mechanically harvest. They don't invest one penny in the wine-making. They don't chaptalize [add sugar to increase alcohol], not out of principle, but because they don't want to invest even in the sugar. The wine has all the technical faults you can find. They let the bottling lines use their high technology to clean it up.'

This stinginess is a reaction to current retail prices: 1.99 to 2.99 Deutschmarks, or about 80p to £1.40 a bottle. The growers are paid 1.50 Deutschmarks a litre. As it costs nearly that much to make, it's hardly surprising that they're going out of business in large numbers.

'It took the export market about fifteen years to wake up to the fact that the new German wines were crap,' says Loosen. Now, however, he and his fellow members of the VDP, who did not complain during the boom years, are also feeling the pinch.

The essence of great Mosel wine is that it comes from steep slopes where harvesting cannot be mechanized and whose cultivation is highly labour intensive. In these conditions a grower cannot cope with more than 2 hectares, a tiny holding, even by Burgundy standards. For wine made in these conditions the bottling companies pay two marks per litre. Wine made on the plain from Müller-Thurgau gets a lower price but gives high yields, at up to 140 hectolitres a hectare, and with mechanical harvesting, which anyway costs less, it's feasible to cultivate more land.

The economics still don't favour the hill slopes. Good vineyard sites identified by the Prussian tax officer are still uncultivated. When vineyards are taken out of production they will be on the slopes not the plain. 'Those younger growers who do still decide to continue doing grape production, most of them sell in bulk keep leaving the slopes for the flat land.'

The culprits? Loosen recalls that Geisenheim used to try to consign the link between low yields and high quality to history. The cult of old Riesling vines grown on unproductive slopes was said to be outdated dogma. 'Geisenheim always refused to accept that there's a quality-quantity relationship,' he recalls. 'And of course they were wrong.' Plus the majority of the growers.

'I hate these idiots. My father was president of this wine growers' association for twenty-five years. He always tried to make the case for quality. In France they make decisions in Paris. Everything is very centralized. Germany has the kind of democracy where any idiot can say something and it isn't based on logic or quality, it's based on majorities.'

He says the winegrowers' association downplays the importance of vineyard sites. 'They claim, "It's rubbish, just invented by the old estates because they don't want anyone else to use the traditional names and because they own all the *grand crus*." But it's a little bit funny. If it isn't true that these vineyards are better why are those guys paying so much over the odds if they want to buy one of those sites? Just look at the market prices.'

Isn't the skill of the wine-maker more important than the location of the vineyard? 'If you're a great wine-maker you'll always make better wine from a great site.'

Playing by the rules – different countries' AC systems

Europe's wine-producing countries all have wine laws specifying grape varieties, yields and vineyard regions. The European Union has harmonized them into the general category of 'Quality Wine Produced in a Specified Region', but as the table below shows the laws differ greatly in their antiquity and in the extent to which producers submit to them. The low proportion in England is caused by the use of the so-called 'hybrid' grape varieties: crosses with American species which are deemed incapable of producing high quality wine. But the amount of 'quality wine' a country produces hardly correlates with the quality of that country's wine.

Austria (since 1940) 78 per cent
France (1905) 50 per cent
Germany (1892) 95 per cent
Greece (1971) 8 per cent
Italy (1963) global percentage not collated
Luxembourg (1935) 100 per cent
Portugal (1756) 40 per cent
Spain (1932) approx. 45 per cent
United Kingdom (1991) 3 per cent

By using a simple phrase like Dr L. Riesling and ignoring a 'meaningless' geographical designation that he could legally use on his labels, Ernie Loosen is in line with a well-established European practice. There are any number of producers, especially in France and Italy, who sell on the strength of their own name rather than that of the region.

The trend began in Tuscany in the 1960s, only a few years after Italy acquired wine laws on the model of the French *appellations d'origine*. To this day there is little agreement on the value of Italy's *denominazione d'origine*. One criticism is that these laws incorporate bad existing practices such as high yields: 100 hectolitres per hectare, for example, for Soave. In France the creation of a new *appellation* can, and often does, mean measures to improve the wine. For example, when the new Côtes-du-Rhône *cru* of Vacqueras was created, 20 per cent of the vineyards around this village were excluded as too productive and yields in those that remained were cut by almost a quarter.

The Italians may have shown the greatest deference to the

requirements of the big producers, but local politics have helped determine the *appellation* rules of most countries. In Germany such considerations conferred an undeserved status on makers of industrial 'Mosel'; in France they dignified Carignan, a variety originally planted to make high-volume plonk, with a place in many southern *appellations*. In consequence many producers think that a legal guarantee of origin is a badge of mediocrity rather than of excellence.

The Marchese Mario Incisa della Rochetta was the first producer to release a wine with a humble designation – *vino da tavola*, or 'table wine' – but considerably greater ambitions. His Sassicaia was more like a red Bordeaux than a Chianti; influenced by the ubiquitous Professor Emile Peynaud of Bordeaux University, the Marchese used only Cabernet Sauvignon, the dominant variety of the top estates of the Haut Médoc, and like those estates, aged the wine in small wooden barrels, or *barriques*. The second of the 'super-Tuscan' *vini da tavola*, Antinori's Tignanello, dispensed with a *denominazione d'origine*, in this case not to explore a foreign tradition but to try to be truer to the local one. The motive this time was to evade the legal requirement for Chianti to contain a minimum amount of white grapes; the effect, according to Nicholas Belfrage MW, the expert on Italian wine, is to create 'what amounts to a modern Chianti'.

A few years later France got its first top-of-the-range wine not to bother with an *appellation d'origine*. Aimé Guibert, a former glove manufacturer, had been advised by Professeur Henri Enjalbert of Bordeaux University that the property he had recently bought in the Languedoc hills, Mas de Daumas Gassac, was on soil that had the potential to make great wine. 'Great wine' in the 1970s implied a 'classic' grape variety and on the advice of his Bordeaux experts Guibert planted the bulk of his new vineyards with Cabernet Sauvignon for red grapes rather than local varieties. As a result he was only entitled to call his wine a *vin de pays* or 'country wine'.

The Mas de Daumas Gassac story has parallels with Sassicaia. Other French growers opt for *vin de pays* status for the same reasons as Antinori with Tignanello – they want to work within the traditions of their region but think the rules fail to do justice to them. Gérard and Ghislaine Gauby are stars of the Roussillon *appellation* in the eastern Pyrenees. Their white wines blend

Maccabeu, the basic local grape for dry white, with Carignan Blanc and Grenache Blanc.

Gérard is especially fond of white Grenache, planted all over the region as a component of its local speciality, the sweet *vins doux naturels*, and likes to use a high proportion: 'It's something of a return to tradition.' They plant the vines much closer than legally required and this helps to get good natural acidity even when the grapes are fully ripe and bursting with natural sugars. Unfortunately for the Gaubys, the combination of Grenache and full ripeness makes for white wines that are stronger in alcohol than the *appellation* rules allow.

When these rules were drawn up at the beginning of the 1990s the authorities envisaged a different style of white Côtes du Roussillon. The easy way to get balanced whites is through picking the grapes early. They will then have plenty of acidity and low potential alcohol and make something satisfactory if less intensely flavoured.

But the couple won't do it. 'We're going to make the wines *we* want to make,' insists Ghislaine. In 1993 all the white wines were consequently downgraded to *vins de pays*. The following year they didn't even bother submitting them to the local committee. 'It was an experiment,' says Ghislaine. 'We put them on the market as *vins de table* [a grading lower than *vins de pays*]. We wanted to see if it would make any difference to our customers. It didn't make the slightest. They're obviously selling as Gauby wines, not because of the *appellation*.'

Another leading grower in the same region, Fernand Vaquer, designates his whole production *vin de pays*. He refuses to label his wine Côtes du Roussillon because of his anger at being excluded, for reasons of geography, from the supposedly more prestigious *appellation* Côtes du Roussillon Villages. This is not a cost-free gesture. If you leave the *appellation* you cannot benefit from the generic promotions mounted by the *Comités Interprofessionelles*, the regional bodies bringing together growers and merchants[1] (although it's also possible to be excluded from the journalists' circuit while remaining a member simply by falling out with the local head honcho).

Non Denominational

The Roussillon, the Languedoc and Provence each have out-standing growers who've stayed outside the *appellation d'origine*. They are:

Fernand Vaquer, whose red and white Vins de Pays regularly appear at La Vigneronne, London SW7, 0171 589 6113.

Aimé Guibert's red and white **Mas de Daumas Gassac**. Gassac used to be widely distributed, but is increasingly confined to independent merchants. Contact the importers, Haughton Agencies on 01502 727222.

Domaine de Trévallon from Eloi Dürrbach in Provence; as at Gassac there's a preponderance of Cab Sauvignon in the red. Lovely wine for long keeping. Imported by Yapp Brothers, Mere, Wiltshire 01747 860423.

Such writers as Tim Atkin and Robert Joseph have argued in the name of Aimé Guibert and other free spirits against legally controlled regional identities in general and the French *appellations d'origine* in particular. They take their cue from the Australians, who in the past have argued against any infringement of their freedom to grow what grapes they like where they like, saying that Australia's freedom from such regimes is one of its greatest strengths. Even so they sometimes worry that they may be missing out. 'The French *appellation* system is really nothing more than the most brilliant marketing tool,' one Antipodean producer told me.

The truth is that the New World countries are moving towards their regional classification systems. And when you look more closely, it turns out that the lone wolves in Europe are not against regulatory systems – they're just unhappy with the way they're interpreted.

Had he planted his vineyard a decade later, and with advice other than from experts from Bordeaux, Aimé Guibert told me, he might well have used the local varieties and so qualified for the *appellation*. Fernand Vaquer is not against *appellations* – he just feels he deserves a grander one. And the Domergues' disagreement with their local producers' syndicate does not mean they are opposed to the system. 'The INAO (*Institut National des Appellations d'Origine*) has actually kept quite a few things going which would otherwise have been lost,' says Patricia. 'And in a region like this one where people are looking for a local identity it's important to have some kind of overall view.'

In fact the history of the *appellation* system in France is closely linked with a drive for greater consumer protection. It belongs to the same movement which ultimately created the fashion for growers' wines: the campaign during the 1920s and 1930s by Raymond Baudoin and his new publication, the *Revue du vin de France*, against the unfettered right of the merchant houses to sell wine under any regional name they chose to use. Estate bottling and a system of law to banish fraudulent 'Châteauneuf du Pape' and 'Nuits St Georges' were two means to a single end.

Both of these reforms have helped shake growers free from the grasp of the merchants. But many have found that independence is not an easy or comfortable option.

1 The first of these, in Champagne, was created in 1941 during the Vichy regime. The one in Bordeaux was formed after the war following discussions and consultations during the war years. One model, according to Fiona Morrison MW of the Bordeaux Comité Interprofessionelle was the German system of craft and professional guilds. There are other agricultural reforms that outlived this appalling period, such as France's marketing organization for wheat and a reform of the laws of land inheritance.

8

Going Solo

━━━━━

'They're people who are taking their business in their own hands and want to push forward their own little ship. They don't have the benefit of a big name but because of that they have to make all the more of an effort on quality . . . It's never the wine itself you're really discussing but the person behind the wine.'

Alan Sichel, Bordeaux *négociant*

In the old days the growers occupied the lowest rung on the ladder. Tony Laithwaite of Bordeaux Direct helped overturn this hierarchy when he started bypassing the *négociants*. He recalls that, 'In the old-fashioned wine trade the merchant sat on a pile of cash and waited while the grower got increasingly desperate to sell.' Foreign wine merchants wouldn't meet the growers; it was even beneath the dignity of the local *négociants* or *commercianti* to go up country to meet their suppliers – instead they pronounced on samples brought for their attention.

The Englishman Alan Johnson-Hill of Château Méaume in Bordeaux summarizes the exchange that would then take place, as enshrined in the folk-memory of his neighbours: 'The *négociant* would say, "This is really terrible stuff – it's got every fault under the sun. Because of my connections I may just be able to find someone to look at it, so as a favour I'll take it off your hands." And of course then he'll go and sell this as the most wonderful discovery and make his huge profit.'

The alleged 'discovery' would not necessarily sell under its true name. Marcel Richaud of the southern Rhône village of Cairanne strongly suspects that the wine he used to sell in bulk to the *négociants* used to reach the customer re-christened as Châteauneuf du Pape. He would have been the last to be told: the point of the exercise was to enrich the middle-man, not the grower.

It was only the wealthiest and best-connected growers who could hope to right the balance of power. The Bordeaux estates had enjoyed some sort of brand recognition ever since the seventeenth century, when Arnaud de Pontac, the owner of Château Haut-Brion, created a name for his wine in London and so managed to charge a premium price. In 1924 Château Mouton Rothschild became the first estate to bottle all its wine on the property and so guarantee it as authentic.

In Burgundy the need was even greater. Beaune was the centre where the great wines of the Côte d'Or were matured and traded, but it was also the world capital of wine fraud: the place where wine from the Midi and Algeria came to be blended and sold under some more flattering name. Here too it was the nobs who cut free, inspired by Raymond Baudoin's campaign for authenticity, in which he was joined in the 1930s by the American writer and merchant Frank Schoonmaker. The Marquis d'Angerville in Volnay was the first grower to bottle his own wine. There was the financial motive of hanging on to a profit that would have gone to the middle-man, but the growers insist this wasn't their chief incentive.

'In those days Burgundy had a bit of everything in it,' according to Pierre Gouges, grandson of Henri, the first grower in Nuits St George to bypass the *négoces*. 'They used to make this *soupe* with wine from Algeria, the Midi, anywhere. My grandfather obviously wanted to get the best price, but it was also a question of being able to guarantee a pure product.'

Money has been the most pressing reason for selling directly, but it has generally been a question of survival rather than profit-taking. The inter-war economic depression triggered the first big move by the Burgundy growers to estate bottle: the *négociants* simply couldn't afford to buy. History repeated itself with the oil price crises of the 1970s. One of the best sources of inexpensive growers' wines in recent years has been the Languedoc, the western half of the French Mediterranean coastline. Here too the spur has been crisis, with the collapse in the market for bulk wines from the Midi. A similar price collapse affected Germany in the 1980s and Ernie Loosen noticed growers who formerly sold in bulk trying their hand at direct sales: 'But unfortunately if it's rubbish it doesn't make any difference who bottles the wine,' he observes.

Solidarity has been the other means of bucking the market and defying the merchants. For nearly a century the co-operative movement has offered humbler growers the prospect of better returns and of placing an unadulterated product before the consumer. Its origins were in Germany and its inspiration came ultimately from Friedrich Raifeissen (1818–88), who as mayor of Weyerbusch in the northern Rhine lands founded the first agricultural co-operative loan bank following the slump of 1846–47. The first wine co-op on what is now French soil was created in 1895 at Rapolsweil (now Ribeauvillé) in Alsace, annexed to the German Reich following the Franco-Prussian War.

In 1901 the first wine co-operative was set up on French national territory, at Maraussan, a little outside Beziers in the Languedoc. These were the years immediately following the crisis caused by the arrival of phylloxera in French vineyards. The Languedoc had been newly replanted with vines on resistant American rootstocks that were shortly to bring great prosperity to the region. But for the moment the market was depressed, both because the productive young vines were creating a glut and because of the difficulty of competing with the sugar-and-water pseudo-wines that had been created to fill the gap in the market and that could be sold without any legal restraints.

Henri Catala, the son of the co-op's first director, recalled that, 'There was hardly any market for real wine. The growers of Maraussan saw that they were going nowhere. Things were at this pass when a typesetter called Elie Catala, not a relative of mine, went up to Paris and came into contact with some people running a co-operative wholesaler, set up to supply farmers and craftsmen and enable them to sell directly to the public.'

Elie Catala returned to Maraussan with the co-operative message and soon afterwards the village was home to 'La Cave Coopérative de Production – Les Vignerons Libres'. (The first 'Cave' was actually a small shop belonging to one of the co-op members.) At that date the growers made the wine themselves, but blended it to create a uniform product.

The railway system was the key to their success. The next move was to buy cellars at Charenton, a riverside Parisian suburb on the southbound line out of the Gare de Lyon. From this base the co-op drummed up middle-class customers with the aid of flysheets. As was normal, sales were not by the bottle but by the 220-litre barrel, the *barrique bordelaise*. The Charenton outlet was a success and the next step was to build up a nationwide network of sales points at Limoges, Le Mans and smaller towns.

The movement swept through France leaving, especially in the Languedoc, a legacy of monumental Caves Co-operatives dating from between the wars. Although the Maraussan venture was a retail operation before it built communal vinification cellars, later the emphasis was the other way round. The co-ops made the wine and then sold it to merchants, but their members at any rate enjoyed a stronger bargaining position than they had had as individual growers.

In inter-war Europe the co-operative movement received strong support from authoritarian and fascist states. In Portugal, for example, Dr Antonio de Oliveira Salazar's government created regional growers' federations (the '*Federações dos Vinicultores*') charged with regulating the market and creating co-operatives, setting up the first Portuguese co-op in 1935.[1] With the Corporate State viewed as an alternative to socialism, co-operatives could redress the plight of peasant growers while maintaining the broad status quo.

These days there are stronger incentives for growers to go it alone, with new alternatives to the old-style merchants. Now that most people have cars there is plenty of business to be had from cellar door sales. An army of brokers and agents comb through the wine-growing areas looking for talent to buy from directly. Customers are proliferating: supermarkets, wine clubs and any number of new restaurants. Alan Sichel of the Bordeaux *négociants* Peter Sichel et Cie has become accustomed to seeing his long-established suppliers stray.

'The guy thinks Sichel is making a big profit out of him – that's the true peasant attitude – he thinks he's being done all the time and he tries elsewhere. He'll literally load up a van, go to Paris and knock on restaurant doors. If, say, Sichel had been selling his wine at twenty-five francs a bottle he'll offer it for twenty. The restaurateurs like that direct relationship. Well, he'll probably get rid of a couple of lorry loads before realizing that the overheads and time are making it far too expensive for him – then he'll come back to us.'

But Sichel has to concede that many prodigal sons are leaving for good. 'There is a definite movement to bypass the *négociant*. If the buyer likes the product, he likes the direct contact and from the producer's point of view he's getting more money. But we do provide a real service: promoting the wine, doing all the paper-work, all the problems with tax, the customers who don't pay . . .'

To be responsible for making and selling your wine is satisfying but stressful. With a husband away doing a nine-to-five teaching job Patricia Domergue complains of the combined responsibilities of a vineyard and child-rearing: 'Out here you're a prisoner.'

Recognition doesn't necessarily make up for the insecurity of going it alone. Maurice Gay is rated one of the top producers of the Beaujolais *cru* Moulin-à-Vent in the *Guide Hachette*, even though he still gives three-quarters of his grapes to the co-op and makes fewer than 450 cases himself. Still in his twenties, he is piling up certificates from the gold medals he's won at local blind tastings.

I congratulate him on his success. He shrugs: 'What success?' In his village the growers used to be able to count on cellar door sales to shift unsold stock. Now the motorway has killed the passing trade and he depends on good reviews. 'This year I'm in the guide, but what if I'm not next year?'

Unfortunately making good wine often goes with low levels of natural contentment. In the short time I'm with Maurice Gay he spots a vine he thinks is badly pruned, picks up barely detectable scraps of litter and decides to send back his business cards because of a minor error in keying in a block of colour. 'I can't help it,' he sighs. 'It's like a disease, it's genetic.' (This being Beaujolais and deep in rural France, he is not convinced by my idea that he should cash in on his name and go all out for the Pink Pound.)

Pierre Clavel is a grey-haired young man who suffers a similar form of angst. In the course of ten years he's gone from the life of a socially active student in the Mediterranean town of Montpellier, to what he calls 'being a peasant', either at home with his family or on his own out in the vineyard. In trying to establish himself he is desperate for feedback.

'I have to move so fast. I can't afford to spend any time groping towards a style, making experiments or changing my mind. I have to sell. That doesn't mean I'll make anything to satisfy my cus-tomers. But I want to have Blagden [Charles Blagden, his broker] on the phone to me saying "your wine is good". He does do it, but I wish he'd do it more often.'

Clavel has no desire to sell to the local association of co-operatives: 'They make very average wines.' But like many growers he misses the social setting provided by the traditional alliances of *appellation* or co-op.

1 See Richard Mayson, *Portugal's Wines and Winemakers* (Ebury Press).

9
Helping Hands

═══════

Not all good wines are made by small growers. No growers, in any case, are totally fenced into what Marx called 'the idiocy of rural life' (in the Greek sense of unsocial self-sufficiency). There are committed wine-makers who for one reason or another require a social framework, however informal.

For some, the old relationship of *négociant* and grower meets their needs; and as we'll see in the next section, in California and Australia the real guardians of tradition are the New World equivalents of small *négociants*.

Others get the guidance they require from a consultant oenologist. Members of this profession can be become over-committed to a single trademark style; but some are prepared to respect their clients' individuality.

It's possible too for co-operatives to hang on to the loyalty of a region's best growers, though to hold the ranks steady requires a director with a sense of vocation and the political skills to unite a community of turbulent individuals.

Successful Négociants

Négociants could use at least a book to themselves; in fact until recently they *were* the wine business. To generalize, finding the name of a good *négociant* on a bottle is almost, but not quite, as exciting as finding that of a top grower. In addition, some growers also run *négociant* businesses.

Olivier Leflaive and **J-P Moueix**, though with dissimilar pedigrees, are blue-chip names in Burgundy and Bordeaux (or rather the merlot-growing areas around Libourne) respectively. The basic O. Leflaive white Burgundy is found in lots of restaurants – the

---

bottom of the range equivalents from Moueix are the small but perfectly formed wines from properties like **Richotey**, whose soft but quite complex 1990 was available at the time of writing for £6.37 from Corney and Barrow (0171 251 4051) who import both these houses. Moueix also make the Marks and Spencer '**Merlot**' and **St Emilion** (£5.99 and £7.99 respectively).

Other trustworthy names include: **Bourée Faiveley** in Burgundy (look in Waitrose for **Mercurey AC La Framboisiäre**; the current vintage of this essential Pinot Noir is 1993 at £9.45) **Hugel** and **Trimbach** in Alsace, **Jaboulet** and **Guigal** in the Rhône.

The Champagne houses, the Sherry and Port houses, **Penfolds**, **Hardy** and **Orlando** in Australia and **Montana** in New Zealand are all also *négociants*.

Some merchants have acquired such a reputation that even in the era of independent growers they are still courted, rather than having to take what they can find. Etablissements Jean-Pierre Moueix of the small town of Libourne, who are possibly the Bordeaux region's most respected *négociants*, keep on their books a substantial number of named properties from whom they buy year in year out. This is in addition to one-off purchases from the scores of wines they taste every day, brought in by *courtiers*, the final link between merchant and grower in the traditional buying chain.

Claudine Pontallier of Château Richotey, a little 10-hectare estate in Fronsac, bottles half her yearly production on the property, much of which goes directly to clients in France. But since the time of her husband's great-grandfather the family have sold to Moueix; at present everything they export, half their production, goes in cask to Libourne.

One reason they do it is for the feedback. The casks that go to Libourne in the May following the vintage will be the responsibility of Jean-Claude Berrouet, Moueix's unassuming but celebrated in-house oenologist, the man in charge of the coveted Château Pétrus.

'Moueix come and work closely selecting vats,' says Mme Pont-allier. 'We value their input. They are very very conscientious.' One logical reason to prefer growers' to *négociants'* wines is that growers often keep back the best stuff to sell under their own name; but in this case you don't suspect any such thing. 'We're partners. They bought from us even in the two very difficult years, 1991 and 1992.'

Laurent Navarre, the Moueix export manager, insists: 'Everything is subjected to the most rigorous tasting.' So if Moueix bought Richotey's 92 it was not for old time's sake, but because it outperformed the phalanx of wines they taste daily.

The prospect of keeping J-C Berrouet as your consultant must be a strong incentive to stay with Moueix. The alternative, which has become very popular since the reign of Emile Peynaud, is to pay a retainer to a big-name oenologist. Oenologists can do everything from some rudimentary chemical analyses to all but make the wine for you. A link with a well-known one may well help you commercially; if as the owner of a Bordeaux property you can say that you retain the services of Denis Dubordieu or Michel Rolland, potential buyers will notice you and will have an idea of what to expect: modern aromatic whites from Dubordieu, dark oaky Merlot-based reds from Rolland.

The Rhône oenologist, *négociant* and consultant, Jean-Luc Colombo, will not only make your wine, if you want, but help market it. Once a year he stages a presentation at the 'Pic', the best restaurant in Valence, at the southern end of the northern Rhône, and invites the star tasters and journalists of the *Revue du Vin de France* as well as wine writers from further afield. It is a glittering occasion, but the two-Michelin-starred lunch is no free meal: as a guest it's odds-on that you'll be asked to speak on the merits or failings of the wines, irrespective of your competence in French and without regard to your native British reserve. Given that the growers are present and that it is extremely difficult for those who are anything short of bilingual to find words which combine politeness and reasoned criticism, it isn't surprising that the British contingent draws heavily on a critical vocabulary which runs the gamut from '*remarquable*' to '*excellent*' and '*très, très bon*'. On such an occasion you feel that Jean-Luc Colombo is earning every centime of his fees.

The accusation often made against name oenologists is that they impose the same style wherever they go. To go by his Valence tastings, it's not one which can be levelled at Colombo. In any case he's anxious not to upstage the distinguished clients of his wine lab. 'I work for Chave [the top Hermitage grower] – do you imagine that someone like Chave would let anyone dictate to him how to make his wine?'

Despite the advantages of hitching your train to the star of a Colombo or a Rolland, the best and most committed growers often choose someone with a lower profile – if, that is, they make much use of an oenologist at all. Those who dislike sprays in the vineyard and additives in wine view some consultants as unhealthily close to the agrochemical industry.

Francois Serres, who is based in Narbonne, is widely praised for not imposing a style. Daniel Domergue says, 'If you asked him to help you make a *rouge de zincs* [a rough red of the sort served by the glass in a bistro] he'd sit down with you and decide how to do it.' He works for big names like Château Rayas and La Prieure de St-Jean de Bebian and frequently gets called in by small growers in the Midi at the critical moment when they are deciding to try to make a name for themselves. He says however that he does not want to be seen as guaranteeing the quality of his clients' wine: 'There's only so much you can do with vinification. How can you be responsible for what they've done the rest of the year in the vineyard?'

For many growers, the transition to selling directly and making an independent reputation need not be too uncomfortably abrupt. At first only a little wine is kept back, then more each year, until finally the merchant is relegated to being a purchaser of last resort in years when the wine doesn't deserve the estate label.

But for growers who pull out of their co-operative the process is sometimes more painful. They will be lucky to get away with only a legacy of ill-feeling; there have been cases of mutual denunciations, in which both parties tell the authorities about unpaid taxes or undeclared yields, or other skeletons which tend to lie about in rural closets.

So it's hard to expect growers, especially recently established ones, to offer the most balanced view of their local co-op. Even so there is a case that the co-operatives have to answer: that by their nature they tend to sink to the lowest common denominator. They are plagued by the same problem as the school orchestras that never succeeded in persuading me to practise the clarinet: when you know your individual efforts are going to be swallowed up in a general pool you tend not to give of your best.

Telmo Rodriguez of Bodegas Remelluri has made wines on the premises of various Spanish co-ops. He says in one remote region he found his way there by following his nose to the source of an overwhelming smell of vinegar. 'It was crazy. It was like a machine to destroy any potential quality in the wine. The co-ops are a big problem in Spain. A lot of them date from the Franco era. It's obviously not a socialist mentality, but it comes from an attempt by the regime to help agriculture. I'd say though that the effect was destructive. In the old days the small producers knew what happened to their grapes. But with the co-ops they lost contact with the wine – they lost that sense that the wine should be the image of the grapes.'

In fairness, fewer Western European co-ops these days wreck their raw materials. In France many have invested heavily. When there's a problem it's more likely to come from the growers. 'I know the technicians at the local co-op and they're excellent,' I was told by an industry official. 'But they're simply at a loss. How are you supposed to make wine when they bring in grapes with a potential alcohol of only 8 or 9 degrees?' One reason for such low alcohol levels is high yields, sometimes allegedly in excess of those permitted by the *appellation*. In one French region growers are said to have built secret cellars in which to vinify the grapes they cannot legally sell to the co-op.

The French co-ops are losing members, and those who go tend to be those with the most to offer. Some of the French *appellations* came into being because of the lobbying of a co-operative. But where the new independents get to work they can achieve prices and a reputation for the *appellation* that the co-op couldn't achieve. One classic example is Crozes Hermitage, made, like the grander Hermitage, in the northern stretch of the Rhône where the river is still quite tightly hemmed in by the foothills of the Alps to the east and of the Massif Central to the west.

Agreeably Co-operative

Co-operatives make almost all supermarkets' basic lines, with or without 'flying wine-makers'. In some cases they inch up the price scale, either because they make top-of-the-range lines or because they work in a top-rated area. Here are some favourites.

The **Buxy** co-operative at the southern end of Burgundy

produces two core wines: the basic red Burgundy, which delivers a good reliable oaked **Pinot Noir** at a fair price and the more quirky white from the **Montagny** *appellation* (just under £7); this wine's combination of leanness and barrel ageing comes into focus especially well after some years in bottle. Suppliers include Marks and Spencer and Safeway for the white Montagny only, Tesco for both the red and white.

Amost all the Chablis in the high street comes from the **La Chablisienne** co-op and it's a good flagship-bearer with wines that are both reliable and have the characteristic apple and mineral flavours. Marks and Spencer have developed their relations with La C further than most, going both above and below the usual price range. Up market, they offer the single vineyard 'premiers' and 'grand crus'; at the other end they have the lesser **Petit Chablis** *appellation* and wines declassified because the vines are too young for Chablis.

The **Saumur** co-op on the Loire make a big proportion of the sparkling wines that benefit from coming from a variety – Chenin Blanc – which forces them to be themselves rather than imitation Champagne. They also make a red **Saumur** (similar to a light Bourgueil, see above page 5) usually stocked by Tesco, which is a bargain in hot vintages like 1995 and 1996.

Safeway have the best **Ruppertsberg** wine in the form of the **Nussbein Riesling Kabinett** (£4.49): a proper traditional German wine – not dry – which can take ageing and should probably be given some.

I quite like the prestige wines made by two southern French co-ops: the colossally large **Val d'Orbieu** from Narbonne and the more modest **Producteurs de Mont Tauch** who concentrate on the Fitou *appellation*. They're both dense and dark and given a sheen of likeability with the use of aromatic grape varieties: Cabernet Sauvignon in the case of Val d'O's **Cuvée Mythique** (£5.99 in Victoria Wines, Majestic and Safeway), Syrah for **Terroir de Tuchan** (£7.99 Wine Rack).

At the beginning of the 1980s there was only one Crozes that got talked about, Domaine de Thalabert from the *négociant* Paul Jaboulet. The heavyweight wines from the area came from the vineyards on the Hermitage hill overlooking the riverside town of Tain l'Hermitage. Crozes was made from the grapes grown down among the peach orchards on soil too productive for fine wine. The slopes classified as Crozes, with the best potential for quality rather than quantity, had mostly been abandoned in favour of new planting in the plain during the 1950s and 1960s.

Etienne Pochon was a co-op member who had inherited family holdings on the unproductive but potentially superior slopes. He says he left to go solo because he had no financial incentive to persevere: 'There was no distinction made; the good stuff just got mixed in with the rest. I had to leave to get an economic price.' Now he believes his top wine, Château Curson, is up to the standards of Hermitage: 'Though I don't know if it's up to the level of an exceptional one.'

(On the other hand, to do justice to Tain l'Hermitage co-op, it should be given credit for making impressive wines to a price: for instance the Crozes it supplies to Sainsbury's.)

However, good co-op wines confirm rather than invalidate the rule that the best wine requires the influence of a driving personality. A good outfit will be one led by a director endowed with Napoleonic powers of leadership.

Many of the German co-operatives are responsible for dull technically manipulated sugar-water. However the Ruppertsberg Winzerverein in the Rheinpfalz is a lot better than the rest, making, for those who like the style, classic Rhine wines at moderate-to-giveaway prices.

The secret of their success, as described by the young managing director Gerhardt Brauer, has a somewhat chilling ring: 'One hundred per cent social control.' What he means is that there is no question of co-operative members cheating in the fashion of their counterparts in some French regions.

What is at stake is yields. Gerhardt pays according to a notional yield of grapes per hectare of land. The growers are paid nothing for grapes over and above this yield, but are compensated if they grow less, on the principle that less production means more flavour and concentration. I mention the stories of the French growers and their secret cellars. This couldn't happen in Ruppertsberg, I'm assured: 'This is a small village of only 1,400 inhabitants. Everyone would know about such a thing and they would be in disgrace.'

Nor does Ruppertsberg have to worry about the talented growers stomping off in fury at seeing their ripe and concentrated grapes blended into mediocrity. Here, claims Gerhardt, it is a case of a talented majority with a small minority who deliver grapes with inadequate sugar levels (and for this they are made to suffer financially). Although there are 200 co-op members, a manageable number, just eleven in all, are responsible for three-quarters of the grape production. 'I don't want to tell you that every one of the eleven is the best in the Pfalz – there is one who isn't as good as the others – but it isn't a situation with just a few producing good grapes; there are a few who don't do the job as well as the others, but they don't bring down the quality level overall.'

Herr Brauer has a tiny vineyard holding himself and he believes it's important to think like a grower. 'Our niche is being like an estate, but producing in interesting quantities. We sell to the English supermarkets but we wouldn't sell to any in Germany.'

The village of Villeveyrac on the Mediterranean coast has witnessed the dramatic arrival of a man of destiny, serenely confident in his mission. It has a small co-op, and is three miles inland from the Mediterranean and less than twenty miles east of Maraussan where it all began in 1901. Despite the plight of the growers at the turn of the century it was not a region accustomed to hardship. One grower's daughter told me: 'We were richer here by far than the growers in the Côte d'Or [the most valuable chunk of Burgundy].'

This prosperity was founded on the high-yielding Carignan and Aramon grapes. The underpowered wine they made at just 7 to 8 degrees of alcohol was blended with the more concentrated produce of French Algeria and sent off on the railway network to fortify the industrial workers of Northern France. Despite the guff spoken about the civilizing effect of wine, one legacy was to put France at the head of international league tables for alcohol consumption, a distinction retained to this day. Britanny suffered an epidemic of alcoholism when cider, the traditional drink, was replaced by wine.

Algeria's independence from France in 1962 and a steady trend to drink less but better wine undid it all. 'The region was destitute. Everyone was bankrupt.' There was the traditional response: 'A series of little uprisings – people blocked the roads.' Finally the central government responded with a programme of subsidies to encourage the uprooting of vineyards.

The eighty-mile-long Carignan/Aramon coastal belt still produces more than a third of all French wine, or more than five times the total output of Australia. Many of the remaining vineyards have been replanted: the simplest method is often to take a chainsaw to an old Aramon vine and 'field-graft' a Chardonnay or Cabernet cutting on to the stump. Much of the output of the Languedoc is now in modern single varietals, as pioneered in California.

It's also a region of new single estates, the first and most celebrated of which is Aimé Guibert's Mas de Daumas Gassac. Now Guibert has become a guru to the co-operative members at Villeveyrac, encouraging them not to replant but to make better wines with what they have.

There isn't as yet a wine-producers' Hall of Fame, but if there were Guibert would be elected the first life member. One reason would be the mythic quality of his story, with chance leading him to the old mill on the river Gassac and chance revealing the potential of the virgin scrubland or *garrigue* to make great wine.

And today the Mas de Daumas Gassac recalls one of America's Homes of the Stars. There is a team of young women ready to take you on a tour of the cellars and, if necessary, translate the wall plaques telling the story of the estate. As in Hollywood or Nashville, there's a healthy emphasis on selling; your souvenir can be either the estate's first wine or the different *cuvées* produced under Guibert's helmsmanship by the Villeveyrac co-op. 'The whole thing grew out of M. Guibert's concern for the growers in this region,' I was told by Mme Chantalle Borreda, the great man's secretary.

It looked for a time as if Mme Borreda would be the nearest I would get to Guibert. He'd faxed a handwritten reply to London in response to my request for an interview. But after I reached France I rang to change the date. When I arrived at Daumas Gassac one of the hostesses told me that: 'M Guibert is very ill.' She mimed resting her cheek on her hands, assuming a sorrowful expression. 'He is up at the house resting in bed.'

Mme Borreda was charming; however I tried to demonstrate that I was not a man to be snubbed by firing off volleys of technical questions. It worked. After a while she slipped away, then returned, smiling, to announce that I would be received. She led me up a flight of steps and into the boss's office, where he had been all morning enthroned behind his massive desk. Beside him was a window overlooking the mill-pond which teemed with fishes and tadpoles.

Aimé Guibert, now in his seventies, believes in his own importance and invites, or commands, you to share this belief; and the effect is flattering. You are being offered something more than an interview: a chance to set down a first draft of history.

'I've never spoken at length before about my work with Ville-veyrac,' he growled. 'It wasn't easy; in fact it was a complex business, getting the confidence of a co-operative. The first thing was to find one with the right attitude. This is the Languedoc, and no one around here wants to do what someone else tells them to do. The principle was to find a co-op that would say: "Monsieur, I'm willing to take orders." Finally I found a co-op director at Villeveyrac who said "yes". Before I did a thing I talked to abso-lutely everyone. We had two general meetings of the entire village, and took a vote. I told them that there would be no written contract, which amazed them. The basis was just going to be loyalty.'

Guibert's first priority was to make a complete inventory of the co-op's vineyards, categorizing the holdings into fifty 'parcels' or separate sites. They were listed as young or old vines – meaning more than twenty-five years – and by location: at the top or foot of hills. He found the classic Rhône varieties, Syrah and Grenache; the less-regarded Aramon and Cinsault; and also Morrastel, a low-yielding, high-quality grape corresponding to the Graciano of Rioja.

Bien Aimé: Guibert's Villeveyrac Wines

Les Vieux Cépages Carignan NV £2.99 Tesco; **Terraces de Landoc Carignan 1995** £3.99 Booths Supermarkets. Whether at £3.99 or £2.99 this food wine is a steal, with the dried leaf tang of Carignan and lots of red fruit. Odd: 1/5 Niceness: 4/5.

Les Vieux Cépages Grenache NV £2.99 Tesco; **Terraces de Landoc Grenache** £4.25 Adnams (01502 727222). Spicy and juicy; quite light. Odd: 0/5 Niceness: 3/5

Figaro, Vin de Pays de L'Herault 1995 £3.59 Threshers/Wine Rack/Bottoms Up; £4.20 Adnams. A clever commercial wine to drink in the current vintage. Odd: 0/5 Niceness: 4/5

Aramon, Terrasses de Landoc £4.25 Adnams, £4.58 Avery's (01272 214141). A curiosity, considering that it comes from the most reviled grape variety of all, and pleasant in its pale, peppery way. Odd: 2/5 Niceness: 2/5.

Terraces de Guilhem 1995 £4.50 Adnams. Not exuberant, but I find this dark and characterful Carignan-based blend the best of the Villeveyrac wines. Odd: 1/5 Niceness: 4/5.

The big brother is the red **Mas de Daumas Gassac**. After six years the 1990 had become a smooth powerful wine with a mix of spiciness and classic Cabernet Sauvignon flavours (blackcurrants and cigar-box). I bought it for under £10 at Threshers, but these days it's more expensive and more narrowly distributed. Importers: Haughton Agencies, 01502 727220.

Ninety years earlier the pioneer co-op members had pooled their wines to create a standard blend. What Guibert now did was to unpick the separate elements. He made a blend of old-vine Carignan and Grenache under the name of 'Terrasses de Guilhem', which, he says, has been 'a world-wide success'. He describes it as: 'A wine to enjoy, not for spitting down the sink. I'm not really interested in the current mania for creating *une hiérarchie de crachoirs* [a pecking order of spittoons].'

Later Simon Loftus of Adnams, who sells Gassac (and who may have played a more significant part in the Villeveyrac project than Aimé volunteered), asked if it was possible to create a slightly cheaper *cuvée*. Under the brand name of 'Figaro' this was given the accolade of Wine of the Year in the London Wine Challenge awards.

'This was an incredible thing for the small-holders of Ville-veyrac,' says Guibert, 'that from this region they had made something judged to be one of the best wines in the world.'

Reading the Small Print – Who Made the Wine?

France
Mise en bouteille au domaine – 'estate bottled'.
Mise en bouteille par le vigneron/le proprietaire récoltant – 'bottled by the grower'.
There's a body for independent growers called the *'Confédération Nationale des Caves Particulières'* with a logo showing a peasant in a smock bowed under the weight of a barrel. Only a minority of growers belong.

'*Vin élévé et mis en bouteille par . . .*' – wine matured and bottled by . . . almost certainly a *négociant*.

Mise en bouteille à la propriété – 'bottled on the property': this phrase is sometimes used by co-operatives, to the indignation of the *Confédération Nationale des Caves Particulières*, who think it's intended to mislead.

Co-operatives feel they labour under a stigma and so dislike announcing themselves. Look for phrases like *caves* or *celliers* de ('cellars of . . .) '*groupement des producteurs*', '*des vignerons de*' or '*les producteurs réunis de . . .*' (united growers of . . .). Or they just take refuge behind a cluster of initials and a French postcode. My favourite is the melodiously named UCCOAR from the Midi.

Other clusters of initials, coming before a French producer's name indicate a small-scale concern: EARL (*Enterprise à Responsabilité Limité*) denotes a sole trader, GAEC (*Groupement Agricole d'Exploitation en Commun*) a family business and SCEA (*Société Civile d'Exploitation Agricole*) is a small firm created to make the wine and split, for tax and inheritance reasons, from ownership of the vineyards.

Champagne has its own conventions. The type of producer is shown by two tiny capital letters followed by a number at the bottom of the label. A grower is an RM (*récoltant manipulant*), a *négociant* an NM (*négociant manipulant*) a small *négociant* acquiring grapes only from family members is an SM (*société manipulant*) and a co-op is a CM (*coopérative manipulant*). The most ambiguous status is that of the RC or *récoltant co-operateur* who buys wine back from the co-op and sells it under his label, although only a homeopathic amount may have come from his grapes. *Manipulant* refers to the work done after fermentation to turn the still wine into Champagne.

Germany/Austria

A single estate is a *Weingut*, a co-op is a *Winzergenossenschaft* and regional co-op grouping is a *Gebebietsgenossenschaft*. *Gut-abfüllung* means estate bottled, *erzeugerabfüllung* bottled by the grower (*erzeuger* = grower or producer).

Most of the best German estates have taken refuge in a rather more select equivalent of the French growers' organization. It's called the VDP – the *Verband Deutscher Prädikats-und-Qualitätsweingüter* (Association of Certified Quality German Wine Estates) – and has a stylized eagle-and-grape-bunch logo which some, though not all, members print on the capsule (the metal or plastic covering the cork).

Italy
Azienda agricola, tenuta, azienza agraria all mean that the grapes are grown at the property on the label.
Azienza vitivinicola – a producer who buys in some grapes.
Azienza vinicola – the equivalent of a French *négociant*, buying both grapes from the growers and made wine.
Cantina sociale – co-operative.

Other countries
Portugal: *Produzido e Engarrafado* is 'produced and bottled' by, implying that the two are done by the same person. Spain: look for the words *Embotellado en la Propriedad* (self-translating). In Australia and the USA, as discussed later, many of the best wines come from the equivalent of what in France would be called small *négociants* – in any case there are no equivalent terms on the labels.

2

THE SENSE OF PLACE

You can develop a fondness for the sight of vineyards but the majority aren't places of great beauty. Stendhal said of the vineyards of Burgundy that 'Were it not for their excellent wines, I would find this the ugliest place on earth.' They are not as dull, it's true, as a field of sugar beet but they are considerably less attractive than an orchard or even a traditionally grown hop garden.

Photographers on assignment for glossy magazines and coffee-table books find ways round the problem. If it's Australia the picture will really be about the landscape: sunlight and Eucalyptus trees, with a vineyard reduced to a patch of green in the foreground. If it's Europe the focus will be on dry-stone walling, a wrought-iron Château gate, a strategically placed rose bush – anything to get away from rows of vines.

Recently I have come to think that this boringness conveys a certain truth about wine. There has to be something more than just vines and grapes. Imagine a wine produced by keeping vines under growlamps, in the same way that people grow marijuana in lofts and garages. You might be interested to taste it to see what it was like, but even if it was pleasant to drink it would be missing something. The point of wine is what it brings with it.

A habit has grown up of talking not about *where* a wine comes from but the *style* it is made in. In this section I want to show that most of the variations that give interest to wine are rooted in particular places and climates. Small growers have a vested interest in exploiting the power of the elements; unlike effects that can be created with high-tech winery equipment, they're free.

10

Ground Rules

―――

You may believe that growers are wrong about the influence of their vineyard sites on the taste of their wines, but you can't accuse them of faking their obsession. They insist on showing you round mainly so that they can unburden themselves of their passion, although of course they welcome the opportunity to tut-tut enjoyably about their neighbours: 'Look at all the dead foliage between the rows – he's just put weedkiller on the lot instead of ploughing.' – 'He's put his vines into a cordon to copy me but look, he's got the branches way too high off the ground.'

Emmanuel Reynaud, who at the time of writing (mid 1997) is the heir-apparent to the great Châteauneuf property of Château Rayas, doesn't have the air of someone who spends his day toiling under the Midi sun, but at certain times of year he can hardly bear to be indoors. 'It smells so good at this time of year – you know the smell when the vines are flowering?' I confessed I didn't, and in minutes we were outside bending down to sniff the thin, lemony smell of the little off-white flowers. 'I love everything about the vineyard – all the different jobs, pruning, tying back the shoots. You can start to tell what kind of crop you'll get from very early on. *Il faut être passionné de la vigne.*'

Dedicated growers can't leave the vineyard alone. Pierre Clavel is supposed to take days off to be with his young family, but has a habit of slipping off with the secateurs to 'tidy up'. One attraction of his vineyard, outside Montpellier and three kilometres from the Mediterranean, is the sea breeze.

'Do you do any sailing? Any sailor could tell you about thermal winds. They're to do with the different rate that the land and the sea absorb heat. What they mean is that at night the air pours off the land towards the sea and in the day it blows back from the sea to the land. There's always a breeze – there's always the cooling effect of the sea.'

I sense that I'm missing a punchline. 'So what effect exactly does this have on the wine or the grapes?' Pierre Clavel's expression tells me he's never heard a more stupid question, so he spells it out as if to a child: 'A good effect. It's good for the vines.'

This sort of attitude has two consequences. One is that all good growers believe they are uniquely fortunate in having *un terroir exceptionnel*. The other is that the best vineyards are pleasant places – they have to be, for their owners to want to spend so long in them. Dry-stone walls will be meticulously repaired; the vines, which in Europe are close-spaced, keep off the midday heat; even when the soil is stony it will have been turned over so regularly that it is as comfortable to walk on as a carpet.

Above all there are the views. When vineyards were planted everywhere as part of a mixed farming economy, they were given the poorest land. The fertile valleys were kept for the staple food crops; the vines did the best they could with the barren slopes, where nothing else would grow but wild scrub. There are great wines made on low-lying sites, but generally to see the vineyard means to go uphill, ideally in a car with four-wheel drive.

Although I made a social *faux-pas* by calling on Marcel Richaud on a Sunday, he couldn't pass up the opportunity to take me on a vineyard tour when I started questioning him about the meaning of the names of his different holdings.

Every patch of even the most monotonous-looking vineyard has to be separately named, otherwise it would be impossible to find anyone. A husband who goes off just telling his wife '*Je serai dans la vigne*' is as good as lost. Australia has sensible names like 'Old Paddock' or 'Church Block', unlike Burgundy, whose vineyards are sometimes odd or bizarre: *l'Homme Mort* (the dead man) in Chablis, *les Pucelles* (the virgins) or *la Boulotte* (the tubby little woman) in the Côte d'Or. In ancient vineyards the names are equally likely to be left over from a time when Provençal or Catalan was the local language.

'*Quartier des Combes* – combes means a fold in the ground between two ridges,' Richaud had told me. 'It's on the road going to Vaison-la-Romaine. White clay over blue marl.' I think at this point he saw the light go out in my eyes, as it does however much I try to pretend to be excited about the geology of a vineyard, and insisted that I see for myself.

It was a wet drive up a twisting dirt road. Richaud owns much more land than he's using as vineyards: 'I like to keep the forest to compete with the vines.' The English 'forest' suggests something taller and darker than the low-growing oaks, some of which have been deliberately planted in the hope of encouraging truffles. It's only when the ground opens up at the top of the hill that I realize how far we've climbed. 'On a clearer day you can easily see the Alps.'

On a hillside in Southern France in June it is hard to believe that someone hasn't been at work with a carload of plants from a garden centre. There are roses, deeply coloured honeysuckles, snap-dragons, pink cistus or rock-rose, as well as all the most familiar herbs.

And in fact Marcel Richaud does quite a bit of *ad hoc* gardening. When he makes a new vineyard in the ground, which has more pebbles than soil, he transplants the honeysuckles or rosemary he has disturbed. This is partly to create a nice place to work and partly a consequence of the belief that the grapes will reflect the scents and flavours of the place where they are grown.

In Britain we are used to a vocabulary that is reminiscent of a corner shop full of boiled sweets and bubble gum, especially appropriate for industrial wines. French growers don't always enjoy trying to pin down the taste of their wine in words, but when they do, the legacy of Jules Chauvet[1] is a vocabulary which recalls a country walk. There's an assortment of hedgerow fruits and flowers – may blossom, honeysuckle, blackberries, bitter cher-ries. There are hay, smoke and mineral smells as well as farmyard odours – rabbit guts is a tasting note as descriptive as it's off-putting.

This is one reason for the feeling against herbicides, pesticides and commercial yeast strains. The belief is that it is living micro-organisms, both in the soil and on the surface of the grape, that communicate the sense of place. If you kill them you break the link with the *terroir.*

Terroir of the Southern Rhône

The countryside that produces standard Côtes du Rhône, the archetype of good-value, bog-standard French red, has started to teem with ambitious growers. Apart from **Richaud** in Cairanne, names to look for include:

1. The various wines from the **Archimbaud-Vache** clan, the top growers of the village of Vacqueras, under the name of their estate **Domaine le Clos des Cazeaux**. Their Vacqueras wines come out quite unlike those they make from vineyards in the neighbouring village of Gigondas – unsurprisingly, due to the different composition of the vines (Vacqueras has half Syrah, Gigondas mainly Grenache). At the time of writing their available wines included **Gigondas Cuvée de la Tour Sarrazine Domaine le Clos des Cazeaux 1994**, £8.40. Tanners of Shrewsbury (01743 232400). Odd: 0/5 Nice 4/5. **Vacqueras Cuvée des Templiers 1993, Domaine le Clos des Cazaux 1993** £8.90, Justerini and Brooks, London, SW1 (0171 499 4653); **1994** £7.30 Tanners.

2. **Château du Grand Moulas at Mornas** Tanners and Adnams (01502 727222). One of the more northerly of the Southern Rhône growers, and lacking some of the richness and oomph of the others, but nevertheless delicious of its kind in 1995.

3. Various **Meffres**. (One is a big *négociant*, making a range called 'Les Galets' for various supermarkets.) There are **Roger** and his son **Jean-Pierre** at the village of Rasteau, imported by Yapp Brothers (01747 860423) and another, I think unrelated, Meffre called **Gerard** at Séguret. Bibendum Wine Ltd, London, NW1 0171 722 5577, has the 1991 at £6.50. The last two go for a Syrah-dominated style, creating a dark colour and brambly fruit. But the best, and most expensive, **Côtes du Rhône** of all leans on the lighter coloured, less aromatic Grenache.

4. Emmanuel Reynaud makes such a wine at **Château des Tours**. When you first pull the cork you don't get it; the only way you may become conscious of this **Côte du Rhône's** excellence is through the number of times you refill your glass. Adjectives: supple, resinous, intense. I don't find it expensive at £8, from Bibendum Wine Ltd. His **Vacqueras** is a tenner.

5. In Lirac, on the other side of the Rhône from the others: **André Méjan** and **Armand** and **Roger Maby** are the most widely distributed producers of a village whose wines supply the sort of comfort

associated with Châteauneuf-du-Pape, but much more cheaply (not much over £6). Sources include Yapp Bros, Mere, Wiltshire (01747 860423), the Wine Society, Stevenage (01438 740222). Davisons Direct (0181 681 3222) list a good Lirac from **Domaine Duseigneur** (as well as a fine Vacqueras producer in **Château des Roques**). Lirac rosé is good and cheaper than the original version from the neighbouring Tavel.

Richaud has learnt the sorts of wine he can expect from his different vineyards, and he uses them as the building blocks in putting together his different blends, starting with the cheapest, sold as a *vin de pays* and going up to a wine with the village *appellation* of Cairannes.

The alternative for those in the grip of this obsession is to carry out separate bottlings for as many sites as possible. In Alsace, the French Rhineland region where most growers are bilingual in the local German dialect, this process is especially far advanced.

Single Vineyard Wines You Can Afford

It's fun (well, very mild fun) to see if different vineyards really produce different wines when the grape variety and the producer are the same.

Take Nino Pieropan, who has to contend with Soave's uninteresting reputation while making some of the world's best white wines. You can find two examples of his **Soave Classico Superiore** in Britain from the **La Rocca** and the **Calvarino** vineyards. They're both concentrated wines, rich and crisp at once with the Soave flavour of freshly shelled almonds. The Calvarino makes most impression as the more floral and scented of the two. But La Rocca, more peachy and rounded, is the wine for the long haul; you can actually tell this by the respective speeds at which they deteriorate after pulling the cork – the *La Rocca* was still perfect after five days. Contact Enotria Winecellars in North West London 0181 961 5161 for mail order by the case or stockists.

If you want to go in for this exercise on a big scale but a small budget you have to look to the German single estate wines. Gelston Castle Fine Wines of Galloway in Scotland (01556 503012; London office: 0171 821 6841) allows you to brood over the nuances of difference between **Max Ferdinand Richter's**

Graacher Himmelriech and his **Wehlener Sonnenuhr**, both
under £9 and a host of other examples which, because of their
interminable Teutonic names, I can't possibly list.

Producers like to use vineyard names even when they're meaningless. **Jacobs Creek** is an actual place even if the grapes come
from all over South Eastern Australia; **Mouton Cadet** sounds as
if it ought to come from the vineyard of Ch Mouton, even if hardly
any of it does. The tendency goes even further with all those 'hill'
wines: **Echo Hill, Badger Hill, Winter Hill** . . .

But sometimes place names are genuine even when the wine
is apparently too cheap for a *lieu-dit*: one of the most reliable red
Burgundies is '**Les Bons Bâtons**' from Patrice Rion, which comes
from vineyard near Nuits St George in the Côtes de Nuits. Under
£10 a bottle from Morris and Verdin of London, SE1 (0171 357
8866).

Stockists of the **Rolly Gassmann** wines (see below) include
Bibendum, London NW1 (0171 906 7706) and Justerini and Brooks,
London SW1 (0171 493 8721). For stockists of **Guillot-Broux**, (see
below) contact Richards Walford, the importers, on 01780 410451.

Till recently the region was dominated by such famous *négociants*
as Hugel and Trimbach, and the label gave only the grape variety
and the generic Alsace *appellation*. But since 1985 fifty-one *grand
cru* vineyards have been recognized by the authorities, together
with rules on which variety should be grown where. The result is
that a whole new series of names are appearing on the tall Ger-
manic-looking bottles, requiring alert consumers to distinguish
between Moenchberg and Muenchberg, Altenberg de Bergbieten
and Altenberg de Bergheim.

Alsace is following in the footsteps of Burgundy, where decades
earlier growers had to agitate for the legal right to use single
vineyard names as part of the *appellation*. The process there is
still incomplete. Jean-Gerard Guillot in Mâcon used to work for
Michelot, one of the Burgundy producers who led the campaign
for the system of *premiers crus*. It may be this precedent which
drives him to sail close to the wind of the AOC rules and puts his
vineyard names on his labels, even though, as there is no *cru* system
in the Mâconnais, he isn't strictly entitled to.

'Here,' he says, pulling out the land register. 'Am I making these
place names up?' The names that appear as little outcrops of

defiance on Guillot's gothic labels are indeed listed: La Combette, Les Perrières, Les Renardières. 'These are the old vineyards of the monks of the abbey of Cluny. They used to receive 1,000 pilgrims a day and they had to give them all food and drink. It was quite an undertaking.'

I asked him to compare his vineyards with those of the Côte d'Or, where he learnt to make white Burgundy. In particular I wondered why the whites of the Mâconnais have higher acidity; being further south you might expect them to be softer.

'It's a question of altitude. The harvest here is always eight days after Meursault in the Côte d'Or. Here it's all short hill valleys, as opposed to the deep valley of the Saone. The Côte d'Or does have a better *terroir*. But the vineyards here have something to say too. We can make wines which go beyond the run-of-the-mill.'

French growers are always reaching for the land register. 'In our one village of Rorschwihr we have twenty-one different soil types,' says Pierre Rolly-Gassmann, the youngest son of an Alsace family with holdings dating back to 1666. 'The Geological Institute did a survey in 1975, but it was very inaccurate and the boundaries between the different soils didn't correspond with those on the old land register. When we did our own in 1989 we found that the old place names tied in exactly with the points where the underlying geology changes.'

Unlike some of their neighbours, the Rolly-Gassmanns have always made separate batches of wine from each vineyard site, even when they weren't legally allowed to name them on the label. 'The INAO [*Institut National des Appellations d'Origine*] said we couldn't and told us if we went ahead they would declassify our entire production.' So in those days they were single vineyard wines, but labelled as Riesling, Vintage Riesling and the top one, Riesling Rolly-Gassmann. This last *cuvée* would come from either the Kappelweg or the Pflaenzerreben vineyard, depending which was on better form that year.

Each of the wines from the three vineyards planted with Riesling is quite distinct in character. If the point of wine is to mirror its place of origin – the credo of the independent grower – the noble Riesling performs with exceptional fidelity, responding sensitively to every variation in soil and exposure.

But even a variety famously anathematized as 'a very bad and faithless plant'[2] can perform the same trick. When grown on light soil over granite in the Beaujolais hills, the Gamay grape makes the stuff we know and love (perhaps) – lively, fresh-tasting, red fruits and, if you're unlucky, synthetic bananas. On heavy clay in the Mâconnais it results in something less charming but more substantial with a peppery, earthy, rooty character. Then again, on the hill of the Beaujolais *cru* village of Moulin-à-Vent, the poor, manganese-rich soil with lumps of white clay turns Gamay into something which, with a few years ageing, can be confused for a Pinot Noir based Burgundy that would sell for double the price.

Henri Lafarge makes wines from Pinot, Gamay and Chardonnay. Of the three, he singles out Gamay as the most *'plastique'* (pliable and adaptable). His Gamays, grown on clay soils a few miles north of the ruined abbey of Cluny, turn out, his clients tell him, like Burgundies made from Pinot rather than like his near neighbours in Beaujolais.

Anyone can distinguish between Gamay from Mâcon and Gamay from Beaujolais. But even as you compare and contrast, glass in hand, you stray unintentionally into one of the great theological arguments of the business.

Gamay leagues

I really do like the less usual Gamay wines: i.e. those which aren't like conventional Beaujolais. It isn't just perversity – honestly.

At the cheap end, an ordinary **Mâcon Rouge** is often the best thing to come out of the co-operatives of Southern Burgundy. At any one time the co-ops of Buxy, Lugny and Igé usually between them send over at least one example of these acidic reds with their flavours of pepper and root vegetables. They're plonky and unpretentious, in the lightish style that's found all over wine-growing countries simply because it's so good with food. Writing in early 1997 there are such wines in the Fullers and Wine Cellars chains and in Waitrose – but they come and go.

Growers who send Mâcon Rouge to Britain Include **Jean-Philippe Baptista** (in Lea and Sandeman, London SW3, 0171 376 4767), the **Guillot-Broux** domaine (contact Richards Walford, 01780 410451), **Olivier** and **Corinne Merlin** (Bibendum Wine Ltd London NW1, 0171 722 5577), **Domaine de Rochebin** (Bibendum and Avery's of Bristol, 0117 9214141) and **Henri Lafarge** (Balls Bros,

---

London E2, 0171 739 6466). All are recommended, though they all rate 3/5 at most for upfront niceness. My favourites would be the oak-matured version from **Guillot-Broux** and the unoaked one from **Lafarge**, both of which are real Burgundies with quite a bit of ageing potential with much more concentration and character with many of their Pinot Noir rivals. They are all in the £5–10 range.

Jean-Paul Brun's 'untypical' Burgundian Gamay is his **Cuvée à l'Ancienne**; contact Adnams of Southwold, Suffolk (01502 727222). And for the top versions of Beaujolais, designed for bottle age, contact Lay and Wheeler of Colchester (01206 764446) and Roger Harris in Norfolk (01603 880171). I also particularly like the **Moulin-à-Vent** from **Maurice Gay** (see page 75) from Lea and Sandeman and the **Chénas** and **Moulin-à-Vent** from the **Duc** family, from Bibendum.

The question is whether their obvious lack of resemblance is down to the difference in geography or the difference in the ways that they're made. The best examples of Mâcon Rouge are made like classic Burgundies: the grapes are destemmed, thrown in open vats and prodded around with *pigeage*, using either poles or bare legs.

Beaujolais has its own technique: you fill a tank with whole grape bunches; the fermentation starts inside the uncrushed grapes and extracts the colour from the skins but not the tannins which make red wines tough and long-lasting.

Moulin-à-Vent is a deeper-coloured, longer-lasting Beaujolais; it comes as little surprise to learn that many growers there have a local refinement to the Beaujolais method (involving a wooden grid that keeps the grapes below the surface of the fermenting wine) that extracts extra tannin.

So is the real difference between the grapes or the way they're made into wine? The growers would be horrified to think that it's simply a matter of technique. The implication would be that their beloved vineyards are not as unique as they believe, that by going about things in a different way you could turn out a 'Beaujolais' in the Mâconnais or a 'Mâcon' in the Beaujolais. Jean-Paul Brun might appear to be doing precisely that and I think this contributed to the horror expressed by Anne Mathon from the *Comité Inter-professionelle* over his collection of 'untypical' *cuvées*.

But most growers will assure you that their wine making procedures are dictated to them by their vineyard sites, and the kinds of grapes they get from them. 'I'd have problems making the lively wines that come out of Beaujolais', says Henri Lafarge. 'So I go after something different.' Jean-Paul Brun would agree. He says that he uses a Burgundian vinification, as does Lafarge, precisely because it suits the character of his soils which, just like those in the Mâconnais to the north, are composed of limestone and clay. The only reason he makes a more conventional 'Beaujolais' is that he has large plantings of young vines; he finds they are well suited to making a less serious wine while they wait to acquire sufficient maturity to reflect their *terroir*.

It's the same story in Alsace though in a more extreme form. Grapes from different vineyards will undergo fermentations lasting different lengths of time, leaving different amounts of residual sugar. Growers like the Rolly-Gassmanns will tell you that these crucial factors aren't in their power, but are determined by the grapes themselves and the yeasts that make up the microflora coating them. 'Each *cuvée* gets precisely the same treatment. We just find though that year after year Silberberg, which comes from an acidic soil, goes through the most complete fermentation, whereas with Pflaenzerreben it naturally stops, leaving some richness and residual sugar.'

It is startling when a grower can demonstrate, glass in hand, the difference that a few hundred yards can make to wines that are otherwise identical. And if you're a grower, not a consumer, it is in these differences that the concept of *terroir* proves itself: the changes caused by a little outcrop of chalk soil or a south-facing sun-trap.

This is familiar territory. We all know that this is what expertise in wine is supposed to be about, the ability to deduce whether the grapes came from the eastern or western slopes of a given vineyard, or, as was said of the proprietor of Château Cissac in the Haut-Medoc, to be able to tell whether the tide was coming in or going out at the time that the grapes were picked.

This all adds to wine's mystique – too much so, in fact, even for my taste. I want to show why I think the best wines are those that strongly reflect their geographical origin. And the most important

ways in which soil and climate leave their mark are not mysterious
at all.

1 See page 34.
2 The reference is to the famous edict of Duke Philip the Bold of Burgundy, in
   1395, ordering the general uprooting of the *très mauvaiz et très-desloyaul
   plant, nommez Gaamez, du quel mauvaiz plant vient très-grant habondance de
   vins*, as giving excessive yields of dilute wine (quoted in Anthony Hanson's
   Burgundy).

11

What Makes a Good Vineyard?

Professor Gerard Seguin has made it his life's mission to discover what kind of soil makes the best wine. His conclusions are largely arrived at by poking about in the great vineyards conveniently close to Bordeaux University, his workplace; they explain why the best sites owe everything to their geology even if they seem to lack anything in common.

A good vineyard, the way Europeans picture it, has a hillside position and poor soil. The raised ground creates the necessary drainage, while the poor soil stops the plants giving a huge crop of underflavoured berries; despite counter-arguments that we will encounter in the next section there's a consensus that it's only with low yields that the complex, sometimes mineral-like flavours that are specific to the site can express themselves. Prof. Seguin told *Gault-Millau* magazine in 1996 what happened. 'Minerals and water will be available in such short supply as to bring the growth of the vine to a premature halt. Instead there will be an accumulation of certain compounds in the grapes, especially the chemical precursors of aromas, plus anthocyanins that produce colour and the tannins that give the wine structure.'

The original reason for parking the vines above the fields may have been economic: it would have been too wasteful to use deep soils other than for the annual food crops that can't do without them. But vines, even the selected varieties used for wine-making, are still quite close to their wild ancestors and they cope happily with adverse conditions.

Burgundy conforms to the pattern. The Côte d'Or is a thirty-five-mile east-facing ridge; as you climb it you go from vineyards classed as generic Burgundy to named *crus* whose wine will sell for at least double or treble the price.

But Bordeaux doesn't. The great names of the Médoc, to the north of Bordeaux, are on low-lying gravel. The best wines come from the sites nearest the Gironde, the wide stretch of water in which the Garonne and Dordogne come together as they flow out to the Atlantic. However, the hills and the estuary have something in common: infertile stony soil in which the vines have to send down long roots to search for water and nourishment.

Château Pétrus, the most highly priced Bordeaux of all, appears to break all the rules. This small vineyard in the commune of Pomerol has never lost the cachet it gained by making the preferred wine of the Kennedy White House. Yet its clay soil is on the rich side, and the roots hardly penetrate it at all.

You might conclude wrongly that any site can make great wine, but there is a common factor. Prof. Seguin has found that the best vineyards are those that supply just enough water and no more. Vines must have good drainage, but if they are completely deprived of water in a summer drought the plants stop functioning and the grapes don't ripen. To this extent the French proverb that 'the vine must be made to suffer' is wrong. It is right though to the extent that a good living for the vines makes for mediocre wine. Too much fertility makes for high yields of underflavoured grapes.

At Pétrus, where the soil is rich, the owners reduce the yields by cutting off some of the bunches while still unripe while avoiding all manuring of the soil. Pétrus makes the best wine of Pomerol because it is on top of a low hill; the lie of the land and the clay soil structure work against each other to give the vines just enough water and no more. It may not look like a classic vineyard, but it's less untypical than it first appears.

Not every village in pre-industrial Mediterranean Europe made good wine, or even made wine at all. But there was a certain fit between the village economy and the requirements of wine-making. People understood that vines required poor soil. In *Burgundy*, Anthony Hanson quotes a decree of the *Parlement* of Bourgogne (the regional supreme court under the monarchy) noting that people were 'corrupting the precious vineyards by making them too fertile', setting a fine for those who failed to remove any manure from their vineyards.

The belief in the link between good wines and poor soils remained entrenched until the last three hundred years. Two things changed: the discovery of new territories in America, Africa and

Australia enabled Northern Europeans without grape growing traditions to migrate to regions warm enough to plant vineyards. And in the last century wine growing in Europe itself was transformed by industrialization and the creation of new markets for cheap wine, which could easily be supplied by rail.

The first vines to reach the New World were brought across in the sixteenth century by Jesuits who planted vineyards in what are now Chile and Argentina. Just as Roman legionaries[1] planted vines wherever they went, the Catholic church took steps to ensure it had supplies of wine for the liturgy of the mass.

A hundred years later the first Protestant wine-makers began work in South Africa. The governor Jan van Riebeeck wrote in his diary on 2 February 1659 'today praise be to the Lord wine was made for the first time from Cape grapes'.[2]

Just after the turn of the next century the second governor Simon van der Stel planted the Constantia vineyard. The way he chose the site showed his limitations as a wine expert. He sent out riders to fill baskets with soil taken from different places across the whole region . . . and chose the most fertile. The same sites are still productive today: too productive in fact. At the Klein Constantia estate they have to practise crop thinning to make high-quality wine. The original Constantia wine, for which the Cape was world famous by the end of the eighteenth century, was its Muscat-based *vin de Constance* made from shrivelled grapes – a style of wine in which the African sun drives away any wateriness caused by overcropping.

The first wave of Europeans to settle in Australia were English and Scots who energetically set about putting vines in unsuitable sites. (They were not entirely without guidance – the first issue of the *Sydney Gazette*, in 1803, carried an article on the mechanics of planting a vineyard, translated from the French. The translator forgot he was in the Southern Hemisphere and advised pruning in January and February.)

The Hunter Valley a hundred miles north of Sydney was planted with grapes as early as 1828 at Dalwood, beside the Hunter River itself. The fertile soils gave masses of vegetation, prolific crops and, unfortunately, rampant mildew. With no chemical industry to bail them out with fungicides the pioneers had to try again. In the late 1850s a new vineyard area was opened up in barren land on higher ground at Pokolbin, ten miles to the south-west. Dave Broom interviewed Hunter Valley growers for *Wine Magazine* in 1995. Phil Ryan at McWilliams told him: 'The soil's so poor here that even the rabbits carry a lunch box.' And according to Peter Hall, chief wine-maker at Rothbury: 'There's just rock here. There never was any topsoil, so most vineyards are on clay – but that makes for concentrated reds.' Len Evans, Peter Hall's boss at the time, concurred: 'The old buggers knew where to go a hundred years ago.'

The other classic Australian vineyard area was also created in the 1850s: the Barossa in South Australia. It was planted by immigrants from Silesia, Posen and Brandenburg, regions with a mixed German and Polish speaking population then ruled by Prussia. According to legend they left their homeland during the 1840s because of the discriminatory religious policies of Friedrich Wilhelm IV. Giles MacDonagh, who is both a wine writer and historian of Germany, picks holes in this Teutonic version of the Pilgrim Fathers story. The Calvinist Prussian king might have taken a dim view of Roman Catholics, but these Lutherans were, after all, his fellow Protestants. MacDonagh thinks it more likely that the Germans and Poles had been involved in the Weavers' Riots of the period, and were the counterparts of England's machine-breaking Luddites. For whatever reason Germany became too hot for them and their pastor found them a new home in the Barossa thirty miles north-east of Adelaide following a deal with the local landowner, George Fife Angas.

The Barossa is now the base of all the biggest Australian wine companies. Charlie Melton, a small-scale independent producer, points the connection with the region's history. 'What the Germans brought with them was a culture which put together wine and the most delicious food. In a lot of the great wine areas you find that it's tied up with the local food – take Provence or Burgundy – but the Barossa is the only old-established wine area like that in Australia. There are all the traditional German wood-fired bakeries, the *wurst*, the pickled cabbage . . .'

Where they settled the Germans set up mixed farms. The land did not grow cereal crops but was good for orchards, cattle-grazing and vines. These were unirrigated and very low yielding by later Australian standards. In the 1970s they still included vines from that first settlement, a living museum unaffected by the phylloxera that had devastated European vineyards towards the end of the nineteenth century. Unfortunately it was a legacy for which few in the Australian wine business at that time felt any enthusiasm.

Australia was to go through a wine revolution like that of Europe in the late nineteenth century. Whereas in Britain the masses of poor people crowded into the new cities were anaesthetized with gin, the staple drink of the French working class was *gros rouge*. By the turn of the century consumption had risen to half a bottle a day per head of population. Wine's centre of gravity moved south. Just as the Germans were to do in the 1950s, Southern French growers abandoned the old, low-yielding hillside sites and planted vines in land previously thought more suitable for wheat and vegetables. High-yielding varieties came in, showering wealth on owners of vineyards full of Aramon and Carignan. The wine was thin and low in alcohol (though this could be remedied by mixing it with more robust imports from Algeria) but above all it was cheap.

With their Anglo-Saxon roots, the Australians' tipples were beer and spirits. The old Shiraz and Grenache vines cultivated by the Barossa farmers made a certain amount of red wine, known almost interchangeably as 'Claret' and 'Burgundy', a red sparkling curiosity called 'sparkling Burgundy' which mirrored a late nineteenth-century European fad for putting bubbles into everything, and quite a bit of fortified 'Port'.

The Barossa – dry country classics

How classic is classic? The **ne plus ultra** of Barossa wines is **Penfold's Grange**, which never costs less than £50 these days. The top wines from Charles Melton and Robert O'Callaghan are, respectively, **Nine Popes** and **Rockford Basket Press**, and they are good value even at around £15 each. All three wines could easily sell out in Australia, but an allocation is kept back for Britain. To track down Melton, try Enotria Wine Cellars, London NW10 (0181 961 5161). La Vigneronne, London SW7 (0171 589 6113) has regular Barossa offers. Noel Young, Trumpington, Cambridge (01223 844744) is a Barossa as well as an Austrian specialist and Adnams of Southwold, Suffolk (01502 727220) have a strong Barossa list. The London-based Fullers Wine Shops have a good

---

range; they stock the **Rockford Dry Country Grenache** which at £8.60 is a good introduction to the Barossa.

Then after World War II Australia experienced another wave of European immigration. There were two and a half million new arrivals, this time from the wine-drinking Mediterranean: Croatians, Italians, Greeks, even Christian Lebanese. In 1965 the demand for red table wine lifted off and in 1968 it rose by a third in a single year. There were new plantings, but emphasis was also on getting more fruit out of the existing vineyards.

The dry-country vineyards were irrelevant – even though it was the old, low-yielding wines that had begun to give Australia an international reputation, with names like Grange Hermitage and Hill of Grace. There were new plantings to capitalize on a new market for top-quality wine, but they weren't in the Barossa. All eyes were instead on Coonawarra, further south and therefore cooler, and plantings of the more fashionable Cabernet Sauvignon, which arrived wreathed in glory from Bordeaux and California. What was more, a combination of younger vines and irrigation gave Coonawarra substantially higher yields than the Barossa.

Robert 'Rocky' O'Callaghan was working at the time for one of the old family-owned Barossa wine companies. 'People thought this region was finished,' he recalls. 'We were supposed to be old-fashioned and inefficient.' The wine industry stayed put in the region but changed out of all recognition. The wineries turned into huge factories processing fruit from more productive irrigated vineyard areas. New owners came in, attracted by its sudden profitability: foreign firms from the UK and America like Reckitt and Colman, Philip Morris and Allied Vintners.

'I couldn't work for them,' says O'Callaghan. 'A lot of people couldn't work for the bloody multi-nationals. It was a different world. They couldn't be bothered with a load of dinky little farmers.'

With their usual customers looking elsewhere, the Barossa farmers saw prices for their grapes sink through the floor. And to complete the rupture with the past, in 1986 the Australian government instituted a 'vine-pull': a programme to grub up low-yielding vines. For the next few years production from the irrigated regions rose sharply, but in the Barossa it went into an equally steep nose-dive.

Several of the wine-makers from the old companies were out of sympathy with their new corporate masters, and they saw an opportunity as Barossa grape prices went into freefall. O'Callaghan left Seppelts to go independent; so did Peter Lehmann, his counter-part at Saltrams. Working in some cases with the cheapest and most rudimentary equipment, they plugged away making wine the way they knew how, in some cases reviving styles big firms such as Lindemans had abandoned, like Australian Sparkling Burgundy (now Sparkling Shiraz).

Sparkling Reds from Australia and elsewhere

Almost irrespective of their taste, I'd have a soft spot for these wines on the grounds of their ability to disarm wine-anxiety. As they have almost no status you just have to decide whether you like them for yourself. In general, they tend, when young, to be like a fizzy version of the free-run juice from a summer pudding; they have the rare quality of being drinkable with chocolate puddings. They all score 5/5 for oddness.

Lambrusco Grasparasso di Castelvetro Amabile, Cavicchioli & Figli £4.75 Adnams (01502 727222). Foaming rich sweet wine that smells of bramble jelly. Recommended, though the fizziness doesn't last long. Niceness: 5/5

Gratien & Meyer, **The Society's Saumur, Red**, £7.95 The Wine Society (01438 741177). Sweetish and fresh with simple red fruit. It would go with cherry-studded Madeira cake. Niceness: 3/5

Seppelts Sparkling Shiraz, £7.99 Tesco, Oddbins. Seppelts made the classic Australian 'sparkling Burgundies' but seem to have lost the script a bit with this fruity but thin wine. Niceness: 3/5

Chanson Sparkling Bourgogne Rouge £10.13 Averys (01275 811100) £8.70 Tanners (01743 232007). This is the wine that started the craze and it's . . . just like Burgundy that sparkles: very Pinot Noir, with some age-derived gaminess. If it really is in demand for ruby weddings, as Tanners say, there must be some strange families out there. Try one bottle in a mixed case, perhaps with game pie. Niceness: 2/5

Recioto Spumante 1987, Bertani £11.90 Adnams. A lovely combi-

---

> nation of sweetness and a touch of bitterness – deep-coloured
> with intense raspberry flavours. Niceness: 4/5
>
> **Sparkling Red 1991**, Charles Melton £13.75 Adnams. Again a
> proper wine and in this case a very good one with a spectrum of
> fruit, leather and tobacco Shiraz flavours. You could drink it now
> with a pudding but would do better to keep it a decade till the
> sweetness and fizziness subside, and use it as an exotic red.

'When the price went down and down it gave people like me
access to some fantastic fruit,' says O'Callaghan. 'If I was starting
now, if I was trying to do what I did in 1984, I wouldn't be able
to get a single berry out of these farmers.'

The wheel has now gone full circle; Australians are now in a
mood to appreciate their home-grown traditions and dry-country
Shiraz is back in fashion as a sort of national treasure. O'Callaghan
now has to bid against Penfolds, the biggest of the big companies,
who these days are prepared to pay almost any price when looking
for raw material for Grange, the classic wine invented by Max
Schubert in the days before Coonawarra came on stream.

Australians take some national pride in the prices Grange can
fetch, more than £60 a bottle for the most recent vintage. Robert
O'Callaghan's Basket Press Shiraz is made with the same sort of
grapes in the same long-lived style – it shouldn't be touched for its
first six or seven years – but it goes for only a fraction of the price.
'Grange is a great wine and maybe it's a better wine than mine,
though I'm not such a fan of all that new oak. But it's not five
times better. My accountant is always telling me that I've got my
pricing wrong, but I think the right way is to charge what it costs
me to make it, plus something on top.' This sounds almost like a
sales pitch, but from 'Rocky' it's a *cri-de-coeur*. 'I suppose I'm still
a bit of a socialist at heart.'

Charlie Melton or Robert O'Callaghan have never embraced capi-
talism to the extent of acquiring shareholders and a listing on the
stock-market. Had they followed the example of some more heavily
capitalized rivals they would almost certainly have lost control of
their businesses. They have what the big firms now want. The
corporations, which ten years earlier barely noticed what they were

up to in the Barossa, would now gobble them up given half a chance.

What has happened is that the Australian wine industry has discovered 'regionality'. It no longer makes sense in marketing terms to offer 'Chardonnay' or 'Cabernet' in a world up to the gunwales in varietal wine (much of it competently made by Australian expatriates). Even with their mechanized vineyards they find it hard to compete with Chilean and Eastern European labour costs. So we are being asked to respond to such nuances of difference as exist between McLaren Vale and Langhorne Creek, the Adelaide Hills and the Clare Valley.[3]

It would be a shame if this trend eclipsed the blended wines in the same way that the fashion for Cabernet devalued Shiraz or that the table wines boom relegated Australia's unique legacy of dessert wines. If you accept that port and champagne can be put together from fairly widely scattered vineyards, it makes no sense to jib at Penfolds number-coded blends (unless you have a bad head for figures): Bin 95 (more famous as Grange) and such other post-war classics as Bins 28, 407, 707, 389, etc. (Bins 707 and the no-longer-current 747 were, as you might suspect, named by an ex-Qantas employee.)

Having come round to the idea that one region's wines can be intrinsically better than another, Australians are now apt to display the zeal of a late convert. Len Evans, whom I met in the immediate aftermath of the loss of his Rothbury Estate to a hostile takeover, was sceptical when I told him I was writing a book on inexpensive hand-made wines. If they were cheap it had to be because they came from a second-rank wine-making area, meaning that they couldn't be much good.

This argument fails to take account of a centuries-long process of promotion and relegation between regions. Evans thought Cahors in South West France was the pits: 'I went there to taste the wines and I thought "Christ, how do people drink this stuff?" ' In past centuries, though, the 'black wines' of this medieval town had a reputation that put Bordeaux in the shade. In Bordeaux itself the tiny enclave of Pomerol has been recognized only in the last few decades, getting prices in excess of those realized by such famous names as Latour or Mouton-Rothschild. The Rhône had a reputation in the nineteenth century, lost ground in the twentieth, and is now back again at the top.

Cahors Lumme!

There are various wines you never forget; one of those, for me, was a Cahors drunk in a B&B in South West France, black-coloured, unlabelled, and with a bitterness that was exactly right with the fat-heavy local food. But traditional Cahors, like the equally dense dark Madiran, depends on this kind of setting, and you can see why Len Evans wouldn't have been impressed. The versions that come to Britain are usually tamed into fruitiness and drinkability, but if the process goes too far they lose their point.

Here are some examples.

Château Lacapelle Cabanac, 1994, £6.25 Yapp Brothers, Mere, Wiltshire (01747 860423). This has the savouriness of good Cahors: a smoky, tarry quality, bitter, wild fruit and a metallic tang. Odd: 3/5 Niceness 3/5.

Château de Gaudou, imported by Enotria (0181 961 5161) wholesale price £4.18 a bottle.

Clos de la Coutale 1994, £5.75, The Wine Society (01438 741177)

Domaine de Paillas 1988, £7.75, Bibendum Wines (0171 916 7706); £6.50 Raeburn Fine Wines, Edinburgh, (0131 332 5166).

One wine that shows how an uncompromisingly black, traditional wine can get away with it is from Madiran, deeper into the South West. **Madiran, Domaine Pichard 1985**, Vigneau et Tachouères, £11.50, The Wine Society, Stevenage (01438 741177). Dark, leathery, dry, blackcurrant and liquorice. Odd: 3/5 Niceness 3/5.

On the other hand there are names which defy the swings of fashion and always attract moneyed buyers, for example the Clos Vougeot in Burgundy. A guaranteed income ought to be ploughed back into the vineyard to keep up the quality of the wine; but it isn't always. Burgundy in particular has suffered from over-cropping and poor wine-making. It's also possible for a vineyard with a great history to be degraded by abusive treatment. What price *grand cru* status if a vineyard has had such an excess of chemical treatments as to render it 'more devoid of life than the Sahara desert', in the words of Claude Bourguignon, the soil microbiologist.

The judgement that one area can make wine and another can't has the same drastic finality as the business of 'red-lining', when finance houses and insurance companies give an all-encompassing thumbs-down to certain blighted areas of the inner city. Tony Laithwaite of Bordeaux Direct and the *Sunday Times* Wine Club, says that he began the 'flying wine-maker' movement of the late 1980s in a conscious attempt to prove that it was people, not places, who made the difference. He admits that he is biased by being the owner of a Bordeaux château which, because of the few kilometres that put it in the Côtes de Castillon rather than St Emilion, will never quite have the ring of greatness to it.

This isn't to play down the importance of site. But if good vineyards are isolated and lack enough growers to achieve the necessary political mass, they are unlikely to get official recognition.

The growers of Montpeyroux, a small hill village on the slopes to the north of the *département* of Herault, have felt hard done by for the past century and more. But when I went to visit their local champion, Sylvain Fadat, they were hopeful of better things. Sylvain, a young grower with a golden touch, was rather on edge. He was just a day away from a crucial visit by a delegation from the *Institut National des Appellations d'Origine* headed by no less than Marcel Guigal from the Rhône ('the world's greatest wine-maker' according to Robert Parker). At issue was whether Montpeyroux should become a recognized *cru*, with the right to use the village name on the bottle.

This doesn't matter to Sylvain Fadat, who after only seven vintages had made his name, but it means a great deal to his neighbours. In the years when there was money to be made in *vin ordinaire* their rocky and infertile vineyards were never able to produce even a third of the prodigal yields of the adjacent plain. As the *négociants* paid by volume rather than by quality this condemned them to poverty. These days they have a right to be called 'Coteaux du Languedoc', but it's not a name to conjure up much interest from the merchants, and the local co-operative sees most of its product taken away to be blended away into the anonymity of an *appellation* that sprawls across seventy-five miles of southern France.

One way to back up a claim to a *cru* is to show that your vineyard sites have always been considered special. When I called in, the tasting room at Sylvain's Domaine d'Aupilhac seemed halfway to being a village museum. His great-great-grandfather Marius Canaguier, like many in the village, had decided against trying to making a full-time living from the vineyards, but used his job as an insurance salesman as an opportunity also to drum up orders for his wine. He had a standard letter he sent to prospects, exquisitely printed, headed 'Extra Fine Table Wines, guaranteed absolutely natural, pure fresh grape juice' (a claim few modern producers could honestly make.) It began: 'I take the liberty, Sir, of approaching you with a view to obtaining the favour of your business regarding the supply of the wines necessary for your consumption.' I very much liked this last phrase, and also M. Canaguier's claim that this year's vintage had been 'exceedingly successful' – in view of the fact that this was a standard letter dateable any year in the 1910s.

When I mentioned this to Sylvain Fadat a slight cloud passed over his cheerful face. 'Mustn't write that down,' he directed. (Sorry Sylvain, I'm sure it's not a patch on the roguery of the pre-World War I Burgundians.)

More to the point, the letter showed that the ancestor's Montpeyroux wines were unlike most of the region's offerings in that he competed on quality not price. Canaguier appealed to potential clients 'not to allow themselves to be tempted by more attractive prices than mine, as this is always to the detriment of quality'.

I'm not sure whether the letter was produced for the benefit of the INAO or whether the delegation just tasted and looked at the vineyards. But the visit didn't do the trick, at least not in the short run. Three months later, Sylvain was down in the mouth. 'I expected some movement after all the work we put in but we've had no comeback at all. I must admit I'm disappointed.'

Perhaps the INAO delegation didn't detect sufficiently clearcut differences between wines from the Montpeyroux *cru* area and from the wider Coteaux du Languedoc wines. But I do find it easier to believe in a difference between hill and plain-grown wine from the same region than in the idea that Australian wines grown at the same yields, from the same varieties using the same technologies and the same yeast strains will really be very unlike each other, even if the vineyards are widely separated . . .

If you make everything else equal, geography cannot be relied on to leave its mark. But I feel the sense of place should be interpreted in a broader sense than simply a fix on a map. Theorists as diverse as Jules Chauvet and Peter Vinding-Diers have argued that the local yeasts are an important part of a *terroir*. I'd go further and say that the notion also should embrace the grape varieties traditional to the area and ways of turning them into wine. The local culture is the human element in the local landscape.

The rest of this section will show how particular places are expressed in wines, not in so subtle a way that only an expert taster can identify them, but unmistakably. A sense of place is the source and origin of each of the classic wine styles.

1 Commanded by centurions whose badge of office was a stump of vine wood.
2 Quoted in Hugh Johnson's *The World Atlas of Wine*.
3 A blind tasting conducted by *Wine* magazine in 1996 failed to pick out any regional patterns in a general tasting of Australian Chardonnays. The tasters did not even manage to identify the Western Australian examples although this different region is widely believed to have a distinct and more elegant style.

12

It's Alive! The Life that Lives on Grapes

'The final picking was in progress on the day of our visit, and judged by our standards it was only fit for pig fodder. Almost without exception the small, shrivelled bunches were covered with mould, and when they were tipped from the pickers baskets into the transportation containers, clouds of mould rose into the air. I could not find one bunch fit to eat, and to my suggestion that they would undoubtedly be used for distillation I received only looks of pained amazement. I was politely informed that some of the finest Sauternes in the world was made from grapes such as these.'

Huon Hooke, *Max Schubert, Portrait of a Winemaker*

As Max Schubert discovered on his fact-finding visit to Bordeaux in 1950, vineyards don't only teem with grapes. They are also a rich source of microbial and fungal life, which sometimes, as during harvest time at Château Yquem, can become distressingly visible. The modern international approach wants to clean everything up with the declared aim of letting the grapes' character emerge uncontaminated. But throughout history, wine-making, like cheese-making, has been about exploiting a partnership between the raw material and a particular microflora. Squeaky-clean wine-making claims to enhance the nuances of difference between vineyard sites; I think this is wrong and that we need local micro-organisms to transmit and accentuate the differences in the grape juice in order to bring them above the threshold of detection.

Take the Rolly-Gassmanns in Alsace, with the contrasting styles of Riesling wines from their *Silberberg* and *Pflaenzerreben* vineyards. One is drier and more steely; the other sweeter and more unctuous. As we've seen, much of the difference is caused by the fact that the first goes through a complete alcoholic fermentation, whereas in the second the yeasts give up, leaving some unconverted grape-sugar.

The modern approach would be to choose the style of wine, the options being either to leave a little residual sugar or to ferment it right out. In any case a strain of commercial dried yeast could easily be found which would finish the fermentation within a given time. The two vineyard sites would still come over as different, but not that different.

Fermentation yeasts aren't the only micro-organisms supplied with the territory. Wild moulds and infestations are inextricably linked with the creation of celebrated wines such as Sauternes, Tokay, Sherry and the top wines of Alsace and Germany. Fortunately these wines are protected by their reputations and the long purses of their clientele from being cleaned up out of recognition.

The mould Schubert saw at Château Yquem is *Botrytis cinerea*. In the wrong place it is no better than he imagined it to be. A fungal parasite that preys on a great range of crops as well as grapes, it was one of the organisms responsible for the failures of the potato harvests in Ireland in the 1840s. Growers fight back either with fungicidal sprays or by picking early, both of which have their drawbacks. The grey mould caused by *Botrytis* is an annual headache in vineyards as widely separated as Champagne and New Zealand.

But in a small number of regions a seasonal combination of humid mornings and sunny afternoons turns *Botrytis* from a blight to an eagerly awaited part of the grape harvest: *pourriture noble* or 'noble rot'.

The origins of many wines are lost in history, but a precise date and place have been assigned to the world's first noble-rotted one: the autumn of 1650 and the estate of Zsuzsanna Lorantsly on the Bodrog River, a tributary of the Tisza. This was under Habsburg rule, but near the frontier with the Ottoman Turks who had already conquered much of Hungary and who, three decades later, would sweep through to lay siege to Vienna. That autumn there were rumours of a Turkish attack; as a result the Abbot Mate Sepsi, who was responsible for the estate's vineyards, held off picking. When he felt it was safe to do so *Botrytis* swept in leaving the Furmint grapes shrivelled but intact.

Tokay, the wine made from the viscous juice of botrytized grapes, very soon became the most celebrated in Europe. Tsar Peter the Great bought an estate to which his grenadiers made an annual visit in order to oversee shipments of new wine to St Petersburg. Prince Ferenc Rakoczi II sent regular consignments to the court of Louis XIV. It was served at Versailles and was apparently the first wine to be dignified with what is now a much-used tag '*Rex vinorum, regum vinum*' ('the king of wines, the wine of kings').

The use of the stricken-looking berries spread through the German-speaking world, to the banks of the Rhine and Mosel; the essential factor is proximity to water. To get the best from an affected vineyard the pickers need to visit it again and again. This practice is celebrated in the superb name given to the top grade of German botrytised wine – *trockenbeerenauslese*: selection (*auslese*) of dry berries. From the pre-unification German state of Trier and its ancient vineyards the technique was taken to South Western France: in Bordeaux the necessary damp is provided by mists rising off the Garonne.

Some regions get different levels of *Botrytis* in different years. At its most extreme this variation means that producers on the Loire making white wines from the Chenin Blanc grape sometimes make no sweet wine at all. When there is a warm year it will still be a toss-up whether the sugar just comes from the grapes going raisin-like and dried out on the vines, or whether there is also noble rot both to accelerate the concentration of sugars and add its own haunting flavours.

Perhaps it's because of this lack of consistency, or if you prefer, this interesting vintage variation, that the sweet wines of the Loire are not understood or valued as they deserve. When he tries to communicate the qualities of his quince-like wines, Noel Pinguet of the Domaine Huet in Vouvray often makes the magnificent gesture of getting out a forty-year-old bottle. These wines, in the style called *moelleux* or 'unctuous' were not that sweet even when they were new; the intense acidity which you get with Chenin blanc grape stops them being cloying. After several decades the outright sweetness fades leaving layers of flavours which hover in the glass even after you've drained the last drop.

This style doesn't interest the mass market, so the growers don't have to worry about keeping supermarket buyers happy by coming up with a consistent product. The years 1989 and 1990 were both good for the sweetest style of Vouvray, but in 1989 the sweetness comes from vine-drying and only in the following year from *Botrytis*. The vintages are equal but different and there is no temptation to use the techniques developed in the New World for artificially culturing harvested grapes with *Botrytis*.

White Burgundy is the prototype of the full-but-dry whites, often also oaky, that these days are made absolutely everywhere. But according to Jean Thévenet of the Domaine de la Bongran the region also has a tradition of using shrivelled and botrytized grapes to make sweet and sweetish wines. He says it's well-documented, down to the technical terminology: 'Our ancestors used the word *levrouté* for what we'd call "bletted"[1] grapes.'

He tells me about a 1919 Montrachet – the most famous vineyard for dry white wine in the world – that had a bouquet like a Sauternes. This triggers a memory of the only detective story I know that turns on the sleuth's unerring palate – a Dorothy Sayers from the 1920s.[2] Two Englishmen have letters of introduction identifying them as Lord Peter Wimsey, authorized by the Foreign Office to collect a formula for poison gas from its inventor, who lives in a château with a superb cellar. The real Lord Peter also turns up under a pseudonym. The first impersonator is unmasked because he confuses Montrachet with Château Yquem.

The point is that today no one who knew enough to know that Yquem was a Sauternes could possibly muddle up a famously sweet and a famously dry wine. Seventy years ago it was a howler but not such a preposterous one. Thévenet asks for a photocopy; he'll add it to the dossier he brandishes in the face of those who accuse him of irresponsible innovation in making sweet white Burgundies.

Burgundy gets noble rot in dribs and drabs and growers who harvest early – too early according to Thévenet – can simply ignore it. But there are a small number of regions where great blankets of it arrive on cue every autumn. Tokaji is one of these: till recently it seemed as obscure as the Austro-Hungarian empire, but with the opening up of Eastern Europe this caramel-orange wine is becoming more familiar. Various Western consortia have invested in the region and are visibly nervous that Hungary's other main wine business, supplying budget deals to supermarkets, might endanger Tokay's aura of exclusivity.

In the Habsburg empire, Tokay eclipsed all other nobly-rotten sweet wines. But within the frontiers of modern Austria is one of the world's most perfect environments for *Botrytis cinerea*. It's created by the Neusiedler See, the country's largest lake, 135 square miles in area but little more than a metre deep. This great surface of water moistens the air but, with so little volume, does next to nothing to chill it.

Willi Opitz recently gave up his job with a factory making Mars Bars and M&Ms to devote himself full time to his small vineyard holdings around the village of Illmitz. As a producer of botrytized wines he finds the region 'a paradise'. 'On this east coast of the lake we have lots of little lakes; it's a national park shared with Hungary. It's very important to me because the vineyard gives directly on to a hundred little lakes. You get so much humidity – often the fog doesn't clear till noon.'

Opitz feels he's different from the other growers of Illmitz. He inherited nothing – 'we built up everything ourselves' – and goes his own way – 'we are not following the trend in our area which is people planting Chardonnay'. He acquired a British agent by chance rather than design: a colleague in Mars working for its petfood division in Melton Mowbray happened to be a friend of Trevor Hughes, a wine importer who till then had specialized in France. However, since acquiring an international presence, selling, for example, in Fortnum and Mason, Opitz has shown himself to be as imaginative at marketing as at wine-making. In 1996 he released CDs of his different tanks fermenting, evoking the sound of water dripping deep underground: at once haunting and boring. Whether or not the sales of *The Sound of Wine* were self-financing, it got him stories in wine publications around the world.

Opitz has an innovative sales approach. But when he turns to wine-making he looks not at marketing opportunities but at the potential created by the Neusiedler See. Apart from being a forcing-house for noble rot, the lake creates great expanses of reeds. He puts these to use to form a protective but airy surface on which to dry out those grapes which don't succumb to *Botrytis* and markets the result as *schilfwein* (straw-wine).

His other newly invented wine is even more unconventional. 'All the rule books tell you to protect your red grapes from *Botrytis*.' (The writers of these rule books can't get around very much; on the Rhine growers make incredibly long-lived and expensive *trockenbeerenauslese* wines from the Pinot Noir that makes red Burgundy.) However, he has defied local convention to come up with a sweet red wine, called Opitz One, using Blaufränkisch and Blauburger, the deep-coloured, velvety flavoured grapes you find only in Austria. He bubbles away even more animatedly than his CD: 'It has these flavours of cherries, berries, but the finish is dried plums – oh, and it goes with blue cheese.'

Finding that your grapes get noble rot is rather like discovering truffles on your land: an unsought windfall. Jean-Michel Vache of the Clos des Cazaux in Vacqueras in the Southern Rhône learned at college that botrytized red grapes are worthless. Like Willi Opitz his curiosity outweighed his receptiveness to received opinion and he pressed ahead and experimented with a tankful of nobly-rotted Grenache grapes.

The result is extra alcohol rather than sweetness, making the end product quite unlike Opitz One (or the German examples of sweet *trockenbeerenauslese* wines from Pinot Noir grapes). Grenache is anyway prone to make very heady wines and Vache would get his wrist slapped by assessors looking for 'balance'. No one would set out to put together this odd, dry, warming, rather medicinal style, but when you taste it you can see why the following year Vache would wait with impatience for the autumn mists and the *Botrytis* that settles with the autumn dews.

Aristocratic, Rotten to the Core, Available . . .

The least expensive one is Australian, from Lindemans, but the more place-specific botrytised wines are somehow sexier. The classics are Tokay, white Bordeaux and the sweet German and Austrian wines, but the best value sometimes comes from less well-known sources, for example:

Domaine des Forges, **Côteaux du Layon Chaume 1996**, Fullers shops, £8.99. As with other sweet Loire wines, this has lots of acidity from the Chenin Blanc grape to balance the sweetness and the exotic botrytis flavours. Odd: 3/5 Niceness 4/5

Gaillac Doux 'Grain de Folie', Lescarret, Morris and Verdin, London SE1 (0171 357 8866), £9.00 50cl bottle. The spectrum of botrytis flavours here runs through dried apricots, tropical honey and the penetrating edge given by the fungus itself; and, like the Côteaux du Layon, this pale golden wine has lots of citrussy acidity.

From Bordeaux the cheaper sweet *appellations* are, in a rough ascending order of grandeur, Premières Côtes de Bordeaux, Cadillac, Ste-Croix-du-Mont and Loupiac. If you get much botrytis character, as opposed to simple sweetness, for much below £10 a bottle you're lucky. Sometimes a climatic quirk will produce an extraordinary wine from an unpromising *appellation*, such as the ultra souped-up **Cadillac** Patrick Doche came up with in 1995. Ask Bill Blatch of Vintex (0033 5 56 50 85 72) for its progress if you want something extraordinary to drink for the millenium.

Otherwise there's Tokay from Hungary which is generally affordable, with the striking exception of a practically pre-communist wine: a 1947 **Tokay Pure Essence** which, at £495 for a 50cl bottle from Justerini and Brooks works out at £1 per millilitre.

Finally, Adnams (01502 727222) have Jean-Michel Vache's rule-breaking and brilliant botrytized red Vacqueras, **Grenat Noble 1995**, at £13.85.

A Microscopic *flor*

One of the standby topics of wine writing is the 'challenge' faced by those wanting to make crisp and fruity wines in a hot climate. There is a textbook modern approach, using refrigeration technology imported from the dairy industry (for example, New Zealand has been greatly influenced by its history of exporting dairy produce), plus high-tech means to banish oxygen, plus selected yeasts to stop fermentations spoiling.

In effect modern wine-makers are using grapes grown in hot places but creating an artificial climate in the cellar resembling that of the Loire, the Mosel or Chablis, the original homes of crisp dry white wines. In these regions it's enough to open a cellar door to create a chill that will slow down a fermentation or clarify a wine in cask.

One candidate for this treatment, you'd think, would be the baking plains of southern Spain. They grow great quantities of white grape varieties that make good raisins – one reason that the vineyards thrived even during the five centuries of Muslim rule –

but that mature in early September, when the days and nights are still hot.

But in Andalucía they don't need technology to make a crisp-tasting wine. For centuries they've been exploiting the local geology and microflora to make something that is as refreshing as dry white wine, but also startlingly unlike anything else. These are the dry, long-matured wines that in Cordoba are called *Montilla*, take the form of *Fino* sherry in Jerez de la Frontera; and in Sanlúcar de Barrameda on the estuary of the Guadalquivir river, down which Columbus sailed on his journey west out of Seville, they are known as *Manzanilla*.

According to local myth in Sanlúcar, the origins of Manzanilla are tied up with Columbus's voyage of 1492. I heard it reported with justifiable scepticism by Fernando Parais, the young, business-school trained export manager of Barbadillo, the town's largest producer. After travelling only the first eighty miles, the three ships found they were carrying too much ballast, and put into Sanlúcar, where they left some barrels of local wine. On their return they found the liquid had become covered with a thick coating of mould . . .

This sounds very similar to other tedious 'origins of a foodstuff' stories and almost exactly matches the 'origins of Worcester Sauce' tale which Lea and Perrin's export manager is no doubt sick of trotting out. In any case Roman sources talk about the same mould – *vini flos* to them, *flor* in modern Spanish – so we do not have to picture Columbus's ships riding at anchor on an unscheduled stop-over in Sanlúcar.

Back to Manzanilla and its cousins, created by these micro-organisms that only thrive in particular places under particular conditions. What *Botrytis cinerea* is to Sauternes and Tokay, a special group of *Saccharomyces* yeasts are to Sherry. In most wines, yeasts turn the sugar to alcohol until either all the sugar is used up or there is so much alcohol as to stun them into inactivity. At this point the spent yeast cells fall to the bottom of the barrel or tank to form what are called the 'lees'.

But in certain places and in certain conditions some of the yeast rises to the surface and lives on as *flor* (flower), nourishing itself not on sugar (which has all been used up) but a curious diet of vinegary acetic acid and unctuous glycerol. What is more, in its new guise the yeast uses air to digest its nutrients, whereas during alcoholic fermentation it doesn't need it.

Visitors to the Jerez *bodegas* get shown a glass-fronted barrel containing some scummy-looking *flor* on top of brownish liquid, back-lit with a light bulb. It's not clear, though, how far this really represents the contents of a typical barrel. The wine behind the glass is topped up, but never emptied, and keeping the *flor* alive for the tourists is one of the more fiddly jobs of the cellarman, or *capatz*.

A Hidden Flor

Why drink wines infected with a mould? Here are two occasions when there would be a strong case. Firstly if you're drinking socially but relentlessly you need something with enough personality to continue to register: after a few glasses of something light and fruity there's a danger that it will disappear like water. Secondly, *flor*-affected wines are perfect with not-too bland snacks: there is nothing better with poppadoms.

Some experts are doubtful about the idea that Manzanilla tastes different from Fino, but the distinction is borne out if you try the two leading brands side by side: **Hidalgo's La Gitana** (Majestic, Waitrose £5.99, Oddbins halves £3.49) and **Tio Pepe** from Gonzalez Byass (everywhere, around £7–8). The Hildago Manzanilla is lighter and more floral; the fino from Jerez has more nuttiness and weight.

Wine from Jerez can be quite good with only a little *flor* influence. Miguel Valdespino likes to show visitors his glorious '**Inocente**'[3] when it has only had about half the time it will spend in barrel: but he says he couldn't bottle it. Sandeman's have actually put something similar on the market under the name of **Soleo** at around £7 – call Seagrams on 0181 250 1801 for current distributors.

Ranked by weight and power, an ascending scale of *flor*-influenced wines would start with Soleo, go through the Manzanillas to the Finos and then to Australia, with the **Seppelt Show Palomino** at £5.99 a half bottle from Oddbins Fine Wines, ending with the peerless **Vin de Voile 1983** of Robert Plageoles from South West France (Odd: 5/5 Niceness: 1/5), retailing for at least £13. Contact Richards Walford (01780 410451) for distributors. This combines *flor* saltiness with acidity, a touch of vanilla, something floral on the nose and lots of concentration.[4] The oddest wine in

---

> the book?
> Final thought: the *flor*-affected pale dry Montillas, at around
> £3.50, are some of wine's best bargains.

Flor demands cool and humidity to thrive. In Sanlucar, Jerez and
Cordoba (the home of Montilla), they supply this by standing the
stacks of barrels on sand which is watered every day. But it is at
Sanlucar, near two great expanses of water, the Guadalquivir and
the Atlantic, that the mould grows most thickly and constantly.

Barbadillo claim to have bottled the first Manzanilla in 1827,
for export to the United States under the name of 'Divina Pastora'
('divine shepherdess'). The style of young, crisp wine then was
taken up in Jerez, twelve miles inland, where Manuel María Gon-
zález Angel, the founder of Gonzalez Byass, named his small
production of *fino* in honour of his uncle Jose, a native of Sanlúcar.
(The casual form of Jose is 'Pepe' – hence the brand name 'Tio
Pepe').

In Sanlucar they regard *flor* as their own local phenomenon. At
Barbadillo, Fernando Parais showed me a *bodega* not reached by
the moist wind coming off the Guadalquivir because of intervening
buildings. Here the *flor* thrives only in the spring and autumn
and the company accordingly sells the wine as a *fino* and not a
manzanilla.

The more *flor* there is, the fresher the wine tastes. This is because
the white coating lives by scavenging up substantial amounts of
both vinegariness and the oxygen that makes wine taste old. Instead
you have a unique range of tastes: salty, marmity, almond-like . . .
Fino Sherry is perhaps a taste you have to acquire, although drunk
chilled on a hot day with a plate of big Atlantic prawns it doesn't
take long.

Fino and its cousins may seem surprising candidates to be included
in a guide to unorthodox, left-of-field wines. It's hardly obscure:
there can be few supermarkets where you can fail to find a bottle.
It's mass-produced: the bigger *bodegas* are on such a scale that it
takes visitors up to an hour to walk round them, and even then
they miss out the less picturesque modern pressing plants and
cellars on the edge of the town. It's made by arms of huge multi-
national companies: Gonzalez Byass and Pedro Domecq are linked

with IDV and Allied Domecq respectively, and Sandeman are owned by Seagram.

Yet Sherry is the opposite of a modern wine. Anyone today who proposed launching a drink requiring five years' maturation would soon be clearing their desk. The ideal accountant's drinks are vodka, Beaujolais Nouveau, rosé wine, all of which can be sold rapidly without tying up capital.

Manzanilla and *Fino* would also get pretty short shrift from the marketing department. According to the boring standards of modern international wine-making, they are all wrong, lacking the sugar and/or glycerol that give a flattering 'fatness' and deficient in acidity and 'fruit'. So why are they still made and distributed on such a scale?

What they have in common with all the other wines in this book is that they are a labour of love rather than a commercial exercise. For historical reasons they are at the heart of the drinks trade: in the mid-nineteenth century Sherry accounted for nearly half the wine imported into Britain. This connection is embodied in the physical fabric of Jerez de la Frontera, an Andalusian town which, with its narrows streets and single-storey buildings, still keeps something of the Arab identity it lost on its reconquest more than seven centuries ago. Like Bordeaux and Oporto, the British links are everywhere. The Sherry *bodegas* have something of the air of Oxbridge colleges, with their courtyards and immaculate displays of flowering plants (not to mention the all-pervasive smell of Sherry).

Sherry is allowed to buck the trends partly because it's sustained by receipts from the more profitable 'Brandy de Jerez' (distilled three hundred miles away in La Mancha but matured in the city). But even hard-faced drinks magnates sometimes take time off from the demands of the bottom line. There is an element of prestige: the historic *bodegas* are useful in hosting corporate events, performing the same role as Wimbledon tickets or a box at Covent Garden. Also I think that it would be hard to own a Sherry company without feeling a sense of stewardship towards one of the strangest and most romantic of wine traditions.

But not all the Sherry houses are multi-nationals. Miguel Valdes-pino, the current head of an almost unimaginably old Sherry family, embodies the triumph of romance over reason. Without the support of any big institutional partners or shareholders, he has become the last producer to continue to ferment in barrel rather than in tank. 'Every January I make the decision to go into tank – and every vintage I make the decision to carry on in cask. I think I'm mad to continue with this.'

. In Jerez, as in Burgundy, barrel-fermentation gives terrific results. With the juice from the fat white Palomino grapes divided among hundreds of batches of only 500 litres, the fermentation stays at an even temperature without refrigeration. But it's hugely costly, because of the labour needed to fill, empty and clean the barrels.

Valdespino explains why he can't break the habit: 'I feel it's a bit like my old camera, which gives me two or three outstanding pictures, two or three good ones and maybe one goes blank. That's the vinegar: if you barrel-ferment you make good wine and some-times good vinegar.' (Fortunately this is a prized commodity in Jerez.) 'If you ferment all in one single vat you get what I get with my automatic camera. All the pictures are good but none is really outstanding.'

Until 1264 when Jerez was taken back from the Muslims, the Valdespinos lived in Castilla in Northern Spain. Don Alfonso Val-despino fought with King Alfonso X and was rewarded with a grant of land in the newly conquered territory: 'I don't know if he was some sort of mercenary or what,' shrugs Miguel. The family have been in the wine business since the fourteenth century and exporting since 1837.

As the sole proprietor, Miguel can indulge other foibles as well as barrel-fermentation. One is the right to mark a barrel with the word 'No'. This tells the cellar staff that he considers the contents too good to be included in the usual system of blending and topping up. His successors will have the pleasure of tasting from these casks, just as he can tap into the barrels that enthused his prede-cessors. Again, it makes no economic sense.

The Valdespinos are vineyard owners, with a holding in the celebrated Macharnudo district ('the Montrachet of Jerez' as Miguel immodestly calls it). But where a grower would go to potter among the vines, he is addicted to sloping around his various small Jerez *bodegas*, each numbered, and each unlocked with a key whose cross-section is the relevant number.

Next to his office is a *bodega* full of Oloroso: in Jerez this dark sherry isn't sweet, but is a wine chosen as likely to develop interestingly without *flor*, hence in the presence of oxygen. He has set aside a special barrel with a tap, but concealed it with a hinged false front: 'I don't want it to look too Chef and Brewer.' The wine is dark brown and as savoury as the concentrated juices around a pan of roast meat.

The other whitewashed *bodegas*, containing an endless number of separately fermented barrels, offer plenty more chances to compare and contrast. There are the different nuances of the different ages of his best Fino, which he likes to take out to drink with food before it's really become sherry. There is a decades-old butt of orangey-coloured wine that is somewhere between a Fino and an Amontillado. Again, the proper meaning of Amontillado is not something sweetened, as in the English sense, but rather a Fino in which the *flor* has died, permitting the start of oxidation. Then there is another teasingly intermediate category, Palo Cortado, which has the nose of an Amontillado and the body of an Oloroso or the nose of an Oloroso and the body of an Amontillado, depending on who you listen to.

'Here's an experiment,' says Miguel confidingly, rounding a whitewashed corner under a pointed arch. 'But don't tell my accountant. I'm trying to set up the largest *solera*[4] of Palo Cortado. When I find an Amontillado with a tendency to grow 'fatter' I bring it here; but it's horribly expensive.

Valdespino's most notorious product is Coliseo. An Amontillado, already the most pungent Jerez style, this is super-concentrated through great age. When Miguel's nephew, the London wine-merchant Patrick Sandeman, held a tasting, a single glass of Coliseo created such an overpowering presence that guests found it impossible to smell any other wine.

The barrel Miguel shows me which demonstrates the Coliseo effect most clearly isn't Sherry, but vinegar: a solitary butt in the middle of a courtyard, that long ago had to be accounted as a failed fermentation. He takes out of it a glass full of a substance as dense as treacle and pours it away, then refills it laboriously from a pump (you might guess there wouldn't be anything as straightforward as a tap). The second glass is hardly less coloured or pungent than the first.

1 bletted – intentionally over-ripened.
2 'The Bibulous Affair of the Matter of Taste', from *Lord Peter Views the Body*.

3 £7.50 from The Wine Society 01438 74177; £7.95 Lea & Sandeman 0171 376 4767.

4 Maturation cellar in which wines of different vintages are blended to create a consistent style.

13

Body-Heat

Without Sherry's appeal to Northern Europeans, it would never have been more than an obscure local curiosity, like other old-fashioned *flor*-affected wines, in Rueda, Gaillac, the Jura or Sicily. Sherry's success may owe something to *flor*, but probably much more to the fact that when it comes here it's sweet, usually after blending with the sweetest Sherry of all, named Pedro Ximinez (PX for short) after the grape from which it's made. PX is brown and opaque, the colour of prune juice, with a texture like a thin smooth fruit purée and a taste of raisins and dried figs. As with most wines there's a received opinion on it – that it's good poured over ice-cream, as they do in Southern Spain, but too sickly to be drinkable on its own.

I was sipping a glass of 'PX' in the Valdespino *bodega* and gearing up to voice this reaction when Miguel Valdespino launched into an anecdote. He had had a couple in the *bodega* recently and offered them both a glass of old PX. 'She said: "I love it. What a wonderful wine." He'd shaken his head and said: "Give me a glass of dry Oloroso." ' (This shows them to have been Spanish, probably at least into middle age. Dry Oloroso rather than Fino used to be the drink of the Jerez bourgeoisie.) 'And the wife said: "How can you say that to Miguel. Last time we had a bottle of PX in the house you finished it all on your own." '

The truth is that PX is no more undrinkable than Twix bars are uneatable. It may not be fashionable for wines to be sweet, but it's such a fundamental dimension to wine that you'd think there would be some clever technical way of achieving it. There is in fact – the combination of sterile filtering, sulphuring and refrigeration which creates Liebfraumilch. For a wine to be sweet and to taste good as well the high sugar levels have to be the gift of the local climate. In Bordeaux, Tokaji and the Neusiedler See this happens through the agency of *Botrytis cinerea*. In Jerez it's just done by the sun.

My Sherry Amour

If you tell most people that you like dry sherry you risk being thought odd. So is it possible to put in a word for sweet sherry, of all things, without appearing outright barking?

Yet in the wine business sherry is so 'in' it's almost a cliché – and in the International Wine Challenge, which is judged by the trade, the top trophy most years goes to a sweet version, the great but expensive Matusalem from Gonzalez Byass.

One difficulty is the lack of an obvious moment. It strikes us as a bit gross to choose a sweet wine, as the French do, as an aperitif, and by the end of a meal people are looking for a break from alcohol. But the point of eating socially should sometimes be an unconditional surrender to pleasure, and that's what is provided by port and by these following wines:

Lustau Old East India £9.99; Majestic, Booths supermarkets. At once sweet and savoury, like Chinese crispy duck and with the burnt tang of Madeira. Odd: 4/5 Niceness: 4/5. Lustau say that unlike most sherries it will improve in bottle. This is something it shares, believe it or not, with **Harveys Bristol Cream**. This rather bland sherry that loses some sweetness and gains nutty flavours after ten years in bottle. However the screw tops are not made for long storage, so you have to spend around £12.50 on a ready-aged bottle with a cork. 'Old bottled' **HBC** only comes from Harveys directly on 0117 927 5010.

The best PX is the **Valdespino PX** £7.95 from Roberson in West Kensington (0171 371 4010), imported by Lea and Sandeman (0171 351 0275) and Hall and Bromley (0151 525 8283): almost opaque with a dense texture and flavours of dried figs and prunes. Odd: 5/5 Niceness: 4/5.

Again, the final thought is a Montilla; this time it's the **Alvear Pedro Ximenez Cream of Cream Montilla**, £3.95 at Sainsbury's for a convenient half bottle. An economical way to find out if this strange drink is for you.

The heat of the autumn weather of Southern Spain is used to turn the ripe grapes into something not far off raisins. The technique is a little similar to the *schilfwein* of Willi Opitz: after harvesting the bunches are laid out on esparto mats to concentrate the sugars. The resulting juice is so dense and sweet that the yeasts can hardly get to work and the fermentation falls far short of creating a dry wine.

This is a very ancient practice which you find, with variations, all round the Mediterranean. It was also used long before the days of Max Schubert or Maurice O'Shea to create the first uniquely Australian wines: the 'Tokays' and Liqueur Muscats grown in the hot plain of Rutherglen in the state of Victoria.

Australian 'ports' and 'sherries' have been the subject of much research by the wine companies to bring them closer to the European originals. The so-called 'Rutherglen stickies' *are* originals, with perhaps some resemblance to PX Sherries.

'Tokay' in particular has not the slightest resemblance to the wine of Tokaji in Hungary but because no one has come up with another name it cannot legally be imported into the European Union. This gives it a forbidden lustre. I was tasting a range of Australian curiosities at the London office of Southcorp, the holding company for many of the country's biggest names, when the phone rang. It was the owner of the Parker Estate, the haughtiest property in Coonawarra, who had been scouring London for a bottle either of Lindeman's Rutherglen 'Tokay' or Liqueur Muscat to give to a friend as an example of the best of Australia. As the Oddbins Fine Wine shops had sold out of their limited allocations, we had the only bottle in London; but as it was a third empty he didn't feel it would do.

A decade after the revival of Barossa Shiraz, both still and sparkling, a new generation is starting to slurp its way through Australia's treasured reserves of dessert wine. This is lousy news for the rest of the world. When Australian wine first began to be known in the 1970s its country's producers met the demand by turning up the taps. But you can't mass produce the 'stickies': like Sherry, they come out of a *solera*, in which one row of barrels is topped up from one filled with younger wines, so ensuring that the end-product is well aged and impregnated, through blending, with the concentrated flavours of truly ancient wines. And there is only so much of the venerable stuff, which creates its character, to go round.

In 1996 Rutherglen Brown Muscat cost between £15 and £20 in Britain. Compare this with the price of a European rival. Until the end of 1995, the last year in which it was available, Scholtz Hermanos 1885 Solera Malaga Dulce was less than £4 *a half bottle* in Waitrose. Sweet Malaga is like Rutherglen Muscat in various ways: the grapes, a mixture of Muscat and Pedro Ximinez; the climate; the *solera* system; the nineteenth-century heritage (at the peak of its fame, Malaga or 'Mountain Wine' was quite a lot more popular in Britain than sherry).

In the end Scholtz was sunk by its low prices. At the beginning of the 1970s the owners sold up the old *bodegas* in the centre of Malaga and moved out to a bypass leading to the airport. A quarter of a century later the benefit given the company's balance sheet by this deal had long ago worn off. In the autumn of 1995, instead of making wine, Scholtz began selling off its equivalent of the family silver. The stocks of maturing wine were disposed of and a year later only the oldest, most concentrated barrels were left; these were said to be so outstanding that their rivals could not use them without unbalancing their own house style.

But it is far from being all up with the sun-dried sweet wine styles. The Vin de Constance from Constantia in South Africa, which is supposed to have consoled Napoleon in exile, is being revived at Klein Constantia, part of Simon van de Stel's original eighteenth-century estate.

And even Malaga has found a friend. Telmo Rodriguez of Bodegas Remelluri in Rioja has carried out projects in association with Adnams, the English wine merchants, to make inexpensive wines in Navarra and Rueda. But the scheme closest to his heart involves reviving the Mountain Wine of Malaga, although, because he does not plan to age it within the city limits, he may be disbarred by the *consejo regulador* of the *denominación* from using the Malaga name.

The Muscateers

Muscat grapes get their name from their peculiar attractiveness to winged insects (Latin: *muscae*). The same unusual aroma chemistry appealed to the creators of the **Piat d'Or** blends: the red as well as the white contain a percentage of dry Muscat wine from French Catalonia. Its role is not simply to add the grapeyness of Muscat but to bring out the other less expressive varieties, rather as salt or lemon juice in cooking help other flavours to emerge.

Muscat comes in sweet and dry forms, and, as a dessert wine, it can be pale like white wine or as brown as a PX sherry.

Hungary makes a lot of dry Muscat, though few good examples are currently reaching us. This leaves Alsace, which isn't cheap: the **Rolly Gassmanns** make this variety their speciality: the spicy, floral **Muscat 'Moenchreben'** 1993 is £14 from Bibendum, London NW1 (0171 916 7706).

There are sweet Muscats all round the Mediterranean, from Portugal to Greece, via France's *Vins Doux Naturels* (see below). From Sicily, for example, there's a **Moscato di Pantelleria** 1994 Sainsbury's £5.45 half bottle. Very pale colour, faint ethereal orange-flower scent, sweet but fresh and well balanced by acidity and a hint of citrus peel bitterness. Odd: 3/5 niceness 3/5.

Australia's dark brown Liqueur Muscats are intensely sweet with flavours of oranges and roses. Names that are imported include **Brown Brothers, Mick Morris**, **Seppelts** and **Stanton Killeen**, and they cost around £5–£6 a half bottle. Stockists include Oddbins Fine Wine shops, the Thresher/Bottoms Up/Wine Rack group and Majestic Wine Warehouses.

The world capital of Muscat is the island of Samos, where the growers, organized in a single co-op, make wines from off-dry to sweet to the top, '**Nectar**', from semi-dried grapes. For suppliers contact the Greek Embassy Commercial Office (0171 727 8860).

Wines from raisin-like or super-mature grapes can owe their sweetness simply to a sheer concentration of sugar which overwhelms the yeasts, but distilled spirits often play a part as well. They're used in PX and the Australian 'stickies' to fortify the treacly juices and make sure they don't go off. Port depends on brandy, not just to make it stronger but to make it sweet – once the spirit has been added, the yeasts give up for good leaving high levels of unconverted grape-sugar.

Distillation was brought to Europe by the Muslim Arabs. Was Muslim rule in Spain and, briefly, in south-western France, connected, as has been claimed, with the practice of fortifying either Sherry or the *vins doux naturels* of Maury, Rivesaltes, Banyuls, and so on? You wouldn't think so, even though it is only recently that Muslims have demanded total prohibition in territories under their political control. Wine went on being made in Muslim Spain by and for the Christian and Jewish communities, and was enjoyed by Muslims including al-Mu'tamid, the last Emir of Seville.[1]

But most sweet wines began to be fortified many hundreds of years after the reconquest and the stimulus came not from the Arabs but the Anglo-Saxons. Marc Parcé, a qualified child psychiatrist, left Paris to begin a second career as a wine-maker when he jointly inherited his family estates: part of the spectacular terraces of Grenache vines that hug the coastline as it twists around above the Mediterranean between the little ports of Banyuls and Collioure. Parcé dates the invention of the *vins doux naturels* as recently as the nineteenth century. He quotes a letter from a M. Retche to an importer in the United States saying that he has added a little spirit before shipping the wine to stabilize it.

This letter shows how Banyuls differs from port, in that the spirit is described as being an addition to the wine rather than as an essential element. It doesn't, though, prove that alcohol was never added before that date; M. Retche might just have wanted to brief his new client on an unfamiliar style.

Vin Doux Naturels

The best known and most widely distributed VDN, to use the trade abbreviation, is **Muscat de Beaumes de Venise**, which is sweet and lush. But if a VND is going to be Muscat-based I prefer it to be fresher and more definitely fruity, like the versions from the Rivesaltes *appellation* with their balance of citrus and exotic fruits. The very best comes from **Cazes Frères**, imported by Enotria Wine Cellars (0181 961 4411) at nearly £10 a bottle, but not far behind is the one from the **Rivesaltes** co-op, imported by Mistral Wines, London W2, (0171 262 5473). Ring Mistral for stockists.

The other VDNs are based on the less aromatic Red Grenache and White Grenache. They're either tawny and oxidized, with caramel flavours, or red and retaining their fruit. If you're drinking them with fruit or puddings, they come effectively colour-coded: light Muscat with white fruit salad (melon, bananas, peaches), tawny with crème brûlée or caramel/toffee puddings and the red VDNs with chocolate.

> For example: the orange/tawny **Rivesaltes Tuilé (Cazes)** from
> Enotria (wholesale price of £9.27). (Sweet red) **Banyuls Parcé
> Frères** from branches of Wine Rack (£5.79 per half bottle) or
> **Vintage Maury Mas Amiel** from one of Lea and Sandeman's three
> London branches (0171 376 4767) (£12.95 per bottle), both of
> which are a spicier, juicier alternative to Port.

Whatever its origins, the essential ingredient in the success of
Banyuls, according to Marc Parcé, was the support of the church
hierarchy. Parcé, who is a lay Catholic activist, belongs to a family
which, like many in the region, built its fortune in the nineteenth
century on supplying altar wine. 'It was a theological principle that
wine used in the Mass should be pure, without any addition of
sulphur dioxide, and because it was fortified, Banyuls didn't need
any. Nicolas was a local firm from here. These days its altar wine
is a white, from the Entre-deux-mers, but it grew to be what it is
today by supplying altar wine from Banyuls.'

One benefit of fortification is that it stops the unconverted sugar
setting off a second fermentation in the bottle. The alternative is
to use sulphur as, for example, in Sauternes and in many sweet
German wines. Was this especially unacceptable to the church
because it is a smell that has always been associated with the
underworld, the kingdom of Christ's arch-opponent? The church
has for long periods been concerned that altar wine should reflect
its symbolic meaning, according to the *négociant* Louis Latour,
quoted in Anthony Hanson's, *Burgundy*. Latour argues that the
Cistercian Order created the modern style of deep red Burgundy
at the Clos de Vougeot in the twelfth century in order to have altar
wine which more approximated to the colour of Christ's blood
than the previous pale wine made without maceration with the
grape skins.

The church also apparently feels that sweetness, in altar wine,
conveys the right sacramental meaning: the modern version is
sweet, and technically is not wine at all, being made from unfer-
mented grape juice stabilized with pure alcohol. In Italy the sweet
wines of Tuscany and Trentino in the North East, are called *vin
santo* (holy wine) and the most usual explanation for this term is
their sacramental use in the Mass. Vin Santo has something in
common with Sherry, being a blend of younger wine with the

contents of a barrel, called the *madre* (mother), which is ancient and oxidized from air content. But they aren't fortified – the sweetness comes from the *passito* technique.

All round the Mediterranean you find different ways of drying wine grapes to create more sweetness and concentration. The most basic approach is to spread them out in the sun. The Roman natural historian Pliny (AD23–79) says such grapes are called *passi* because they have 'suffered' in the sun[2] (from the same Latin word that gives us 'passion' and 'patience' – though Pliny's translator H. Rackham more prosaically derives *passi* from *pandere* to spread out). Alternatively the grapes can go raisin-like on the vine, with the stems twisted to block off their water supply. Or where autumns are mild, but there is still a threat of rain as the year comes to a close, they can be brought under cover to dry.

This last method is widely used in modern Italy for it is the *passito* wines that turn up through the length and breadth of the peninsula. In Tuscany *passito* grapes can be used to referment Chianti and to make *vin santo*. In Piemonte they make the sweet wine of Caluso, and in the hills to the east and west of Verona that produce the *recioto* wines, respectively, of Soave and Valpolicella.

The sight of a loft full of trays of *passito* grapes gives meaning to the phrase 'hand-made wines'. The grapes must all be perfect, otherwise these would soon be spoiled by the wasps which buzz in intermittently through open windows. These do not admit direct sunlight, but they let the air circulate as well as offering glimpses of hills soaked in a golden autumn haze.

There are places where wine intrudes on a landscape, with regimented rows of vines that are really little more attractive that a monoculture of cabbages. A big modern winery with its stainless-steel tanks, often out of doors, can look very like an oil refinery. But in the hills above Verona everything is of a piece. The vines are on pergolas, a bit like an old-fashioned Kent hop garden, with grass growing underfoot; the effect is of a landscape in three dimensions which looks as if it was created, long ago, for pleasure rather than to raise a crop. (Pergola training is a variant on the ancient technique, practised in Italy within living memory, of growing vines up trees and still found in the *vinho verde* (Minho) region of Portugal.) Inside the lofts the landscape has been recreated in grapes: one set of trays will go to make sweet *recioto* wine while beside it are the grapes that will become *amarone*. This latter is fermented right out to make a slightly bitter, cherry-like wine with a concentrated texture and great intensity of flavour. Grapes for *amarone* come from warmer, better-exposed sites than those for *recioto* which give the grapes a balance of nutrients to nurse the yeasts through to the end of the long and arduous fermentation.

The proprietor, Giuseppe Quintarelli, looks round the scene, taking pleasure in its uniqueness. 'We press these grapes well after Christmas. I think that is the latest anywhere in the world?' Before I left the Quintarellis, I saw another sight that was equally unique. As small producers now do throughout the world, they were bottling their own wine. But instead of using a bottling line, whether their own or hired, they were doing it by hand. Signora Quintarelli had postponed her outing to look for wild *funghi* in order to run a pipe into a barrel of Cabernet Franc (which, in this corner of Italy, can make a sweet red wine). Her daughter was pasting on labels and an assistant was whacking in the corks one at a time.

All this weight of the past seems appropriate for a maker of sweet and highly alcoholic wines – less so for the dry, light styles that have been more fashionable in recent years. But as we'll see, crisp and fruity wines have their origins, not in a consumer trend, but in the combination of soil and a more English sort of weather.

A Mixed Bag of Sweets

A few more sweet wines, all nice but obscure:

1 What Australians used to call 'Port':
Tesco Oak-Aged Tawny Liquer Wine £6.99 (in most large stores). Rosemount Estates make this lovely version with its leathery Christmas-cake aromas and balance of an almost salty tanginess with intense sweetness. There's another classic Tawny from **Seppelts** called **Old Trafford**. (£7.99 Threshers/Wine Rack/ Bottoms Up). Much gooier than the real thing from Portugal – the outstanding example of which is the 10-year-old-Tawny from **Niepoort** (see page 42): £15.50 from Gelston Castle Fine Wines, Castle Douglas, Scotland and London SW1 (01556 503012 or 0171 821 6841) or Bibendum Wine Ltd, London SW1 (0171 916 7700).

2 Australian 'Tokay':
In Britain this has to be called after the grape variety, Muscadelle.

The Australian sweet wines have a strong family resemblance, whatever grape variety they're made from, but if you want to try the most obscure and least imported, contact the importers, Walter S. Siegel Ltd or Odiham, Hants on 01256 701101 and ask about the **Stanton & Killeen Rutherglen Muscadelle**; it should be about £5.99 a half bottle.

3 Marsala.
There is one highly reputed producer: **Marco de Bartoli** whose wines are imported by Adams of Southwold, Suffolk (01502 727220), but who have such low stock they were unwilling to open a bottle when I tasted with them. I brought a bottle of his wine back from Sicily – not technically Marsala because of his disdain for the DOC rules – but dropped it at Kings Cross Thameslink station: the nearest I got to a tasting was getting saturated in the rich and complex aromas that rose from the booking office floor. 'It's all right,' said the station staff. It wasn't.

4 Non-botrytized, unfortified sweet table wines.
For example **Jurançon Moelleux, Clos Lapeyre 1993** from the French Pyrenees (£9.90 The Wine Society, Stevenage, Herts, 01483 740222). Exotic fruit, mainly guava, with the same balance of sweetness and acidity that you find in other examples of this category such as the *moelleux* ('marrow-like') wines of Huet in the years they're non botrytis-affected. Another of the zillion things the French suggest drinking with *foie gras*. Sorry, animal lovers. Odd: 4/5. Niceness: 4/5.

---

1 Drink is a major theme of the poetry of pre-islamic Arabia and of the Muslim world. Even Ayatollah Khomeini uses it as a metaphor in his devotional verse.
2 One of the favourite grapes for making *passito* wines, Pliny tells us, was Muscat – just as it is two millenia later in Malaga, Setubal or Rutherglen.

14

Well Chilled

Here is a hard nosed thesis. It maintains that many vineyards are in the wrong place, and would never have been developed except for the transport requirements of previous ages. Some places, on the other hand, are ideal for all sorts of wine growing. On France's Mediterranean coast, or central Chile, or much of South Eastern Australia, vines will ripen reliably every year, rather than being at the mercy of a climate that plagues more marginal places with 'off-vintages'. With this perfect raw material, producers can used modern technology to craft whatever styles the market demands.

For a great number of growers, this is more than a debating point. Sauvignon Blanc is today grown in the Languedoc in mechanized vineyards at costs that are a fraction of those in the Loire, three hundred miles to the north. People have heard of Sancerre and Pouilly Fumé, so producers of these Loire Sauvignon *appellations* can continue to sleep soundly. Those making less grand wines – Quincy, Menetou-Salon or just Sauvignon de Touraine – might want to keep an eye open for vacancies at the local nuclear power station.

I have been privileged to see producers responding *en masse* to the suggestion that they're fighting a losing battle with nature. It was at a dinner given by the Hunter Valley Growers; this region of New South Wales is, as mentioned earlier, conveniently close to Sydney, but has a sub-tropical climate that is apt to engender drought during the growing season and bucketing rain at harvest time.

Robert Joseph, the publisher of *Wine* magazine, was speaking. Many others had previously ascended the rostrum (one sign of Australia's debt to Bordeaux is that so many of its wine-makers feel at ease in formal evening wear). Far from being stuffy these had been very funny on the theme of their sufferings as pioneers of the Hunter; life there in the post-war years was one of unremitting harshness, while the interest in wine that brought you to this bleak place publicly certified your status as a poof.

The previous speakers' stock in trade had been irony. Perhaps this emboldened Robert J to be puckish. He was going, he said, to talk about a region which had its great producers, but also made a great deal of indifferent wine, where vintages could all too often be disappointing, which owed its importance not so much to its intrinsic suitability as a vineyard site as to historical accident and which could be stripped of a substantial proportion of its vineyards without any great loss to anyone.

The faces on my table had grown strained and incredulous as he moved towards his punchline: 'But that's enough about Bordeaux in the 1990s!'

A moment's silence, then some relieved laughter, but a certain continued coolness. From the rostrum, Robert sensed the frost in the air, and shifted tack to telling stories against the French in a Clouseau voice. ('He's got the accent just right, anyway,' said my neighbour.)

The Hunter Valley growers are an exception among a nation who believe that their continent is the perfect place to make wine, and has a climate to which more traditional regions aspire in vain. Richard Gibson, a senior manager with the Southcorp companies, was interested when I suggested that a big switch away from claret in British customers' pre-Christmas buying could be connected with the poor Bordeaux vintages of the 1990s. 'So you think people in Britain are finally getting the message?' he asked.

This is the modern business point of view of someone looking for a consistent product and continuity of supply. If your vineyards will guarantee this, with a dependable supply of ripe grapes, why should you envy regions that cannot be relied on to deliver?

Northern Europe has never been satisfactory seen from this light. Take England, where monks in the Middle Ages did indeed cultivate vineyards; however Prof. Roger Dion, in his general history of French wine making,[1] points out that in most years vineyard owners so far north did not count on making any wine at all. Except when the season had been untypically warm the grapes ended up being used for *verjus*, the acid juice used in cooking in place of vinegar. You could argue that in modern times it is only the availability of cheap sugar, used (legally) to bolster alcoholic strength that has kept the vineyards north of central France alive at all. As recently as the late nineteenth century output could lurch between extremes: Germany made 16 million gallons of wine in 1891; 111 million five years later.

The question is whether the good years make up for the ones that are a washout. Does a marginal climate make grapes taste better?

You would think that it might, looking at the analogy of other fruits grown near their geographical limit of cultivation. Redcurrants and raspberries seem more fresh-tasting from Scotland; English Coxes have a big edge on Golden Delicious from France or Red Delicious from California.

And, irrational as this may seem, it is the vineyards with the least perfect climates that seem to make the most indispensable wines. The most widely imitated wine styles come from marginal growing regions: Mosel, Hock, Chablis, Champagne, Burgundy, and, the newest addition, the New Zealand re-interpretation of Loire Sauvignon.

England is the country to test this theory to destruction. It's too cold for consistent success with the famous grape varieties; this leaves us with the option of planting Pinot Noir or Chardonnay and crossing our fingers or going for stuff the rest of the world regards as second rate.[2]

And yet after less than half a century of the revival of English vineyards there is evidence that our cool climate does transform very ordinary grape varieties into something much better. But it does so only if the vineyard owners submit to the same rules that apply in other countries – and this does not necessarily come easily to those who regard viticulture as anything less than their life's work.

Robert Hemphill makes his own wine at Shawsgate, five miles north of Ipswich, and also acts as a contract wine-maker for a dozen vineyard owners, including Carla Carlisle, the Mississippi-born proprietor at Wyken Hall, near Bury St Edmunds. For years he was irritated at being sent grapes from Wyken which he felt had been harvested too early. His ambition, he says, is to work without 'messing the wine about' by being compelled to use techniques such as chemical de-acidification.

'In her early days she never, never picked them properly. This happened over many, many years until one year she delivered a load of grapes that I refused to make wine out of. I just had them spread over a field.' Was this not rather brutal? 'They have to learn the hard way – it's going to be my name behind the wine even if it's very second rate.'

Hemphill's message: 'We want our growers to do the majority of their work in the vineyard. They must spend time removing leaves, not using machines that also damage the fruit, pruning the right way to restrict yields and getting ripe fruit through low yields.' He admits that it's difficult to persuade vineyard owners to go for quality not quantity: 'They think of the number of bottles they can produce and you see the pound signs in front of their eyes.'

Robert Hemphill believes that England's cool climate can coax the best out of lesser grape varieties and that with enough commitment and hard work in the vineyard it's possible to cut down on the amount of sugar used to boost alcohol levels, and do without chalk as a de-acidifying agent: 'Whatever you do to wine, whenever you intervene, you're going to change its character.'

Terribly English?

With grapes, unripe equals nasty and English grapes are often picked unripe. The formative influence on our infant wine industry was German and pioneers in this country all too willingly embraced techniques designed to rescue dud prime material; for example, chemical de-acidification and the use of stabilized grape juice or 'sussreserve' as a sweetening agent.

More recently the spotlight has turned on to the Australian John Worontschak who goes in more for New World techniques such as oak chips. Ho hum. His work, while OK, still feels like an exercise in making a silk purse out of a sow's ear, rather than in showing off great fruit to its best advantage.

Robert Hemphill at Shawsgate at Framlingham in Suffolk says all the right things about the importance of ripe fruit and concentrating on the vineyard, not wine-making techique. That it isn't just talk is shown by the wines he makes from the Shawsgate vineyard and for other growers such as Carla Carlisle at **Wyken**. The style is out-and-out dry, needing and getting bottle age. Even the reds are good. The **Wyken** wines are at Adnams, Southwold, Suffolk, (01502 727220); most of **Shawsgate's** sales, as is often the case here, are from the vineyard (01728 724060).

The best of the rest include **Barkham Manor** (01852 722103) in East Sussex and **Tenderten** in Kent (01580 763033) where two wine-makers, Stephen Skelton and David Cowderoy, exercise their divergent talents under a single roof, responsible respectively for the estate wines and for the **Chapel Down** contract wine-making operation. **Chapel Down** made a lovely delicate botrytized wine when noble rot unexpectedly visited one of their growers' Bacchus grapes two years ago.

Sugar additions are a long-established way of creating a warmer-climate character. The more recent drift of wine technology has been to make wine from a warm zone take on the character of something grown in a cool climate. The forms of intervention in this case will be refigeration to imitate the natural cellar temperature of northern Europe, night harvesting to reproduce daytime picking conditions and tartaric acid to counter any tendency to flabbiness. The results may be OK but are unlikely to be exciting.

As the guru of the American wine industry, the late Frank Schoonmaker, counselled as long ago as 1941, 'We may expect, but we shall not get, fine Chablis, Port, Hock, Claret, Riesling, Sherry, Moselle, Burgundy, Angelica,[3] St Julien, Sauterne, all from one vineyard, even in California, no matter now large.'[4]

These days, when a dry white is no longer automatically called 'Chablis' or a sparkling wine 'Champagne' it is easy to forget that bubbles and acidity came originally, not because people asked for that particular 'style', but because people's tastes coincided with, and perhaps were formed around, what could be coaxed from local grape varieties and climate.

Chablis can be thought of as one extreme in the spectrum of styles of white Burgundy: the liveliest, greenest-tasting of a range of chardonnay-based white wines which shade through to Meursault with its rich, buttery, nutty flavours. It's a measurable difference: a proportion of the acidity in Chablis is given by malic acid, as found in apples, with a sharp, crisp, unripe taste; in Meursault it's been replaced by lactic acid, the acid that gives sourness to milk cream and cheese.[5]

Bacteria create lactic acid from malic in a secondary fermentation that sends occasional small bubbles of carbon dioxide popping to the surface of the wine. Since this process became understood in the course of this century, wine-makers have had the choice of letting it happen, so making a softer, more buttery wine, or blocking it by knocking out the bacteria with sulphur and making a fresher-tasting wine.

But left to themselves, the malolactic bacteria naturally accentuate the differences between various wines. All living things find it a struggle to survive when pickled in acidity and these bacteria are no exception. Grape juice from Chablis, in the north of Burgundy, will tend to be more acidic than in Meursault, which is fifty miles further south and where the vineyards are arranged in a low-lying, south-east facing sun-trap.

Left to themselves, the vineyards of Chablis and Meursault will turn out two classic contrasting wines. If out of perversity you wanted to make Meursault into 'Chablis' you'd have to block the malolactic fermentation with sulphur; to turn Chablis into 'Meursault' you'd have to de-acidify the wine chemically and inoculate specially cultured malolactic bacteria (*Lactobacillus*, *Leuconostoc* and *Pediococcus*). It might be fun, but after one experiment you'd probably choose to let nature take its course (while scooping in the handsome income that comes to those with holdings in these *appellations*).[6]

Champagne, in an even more marginal zone than Chablis, gives growers the highest returns of all. Through much of its history this region eighty miles east of Paris made pale red wine from the Pinot Noir grape, as it still does, in tiny quantities, for drinking as well as for colouring rosé Champagne. The wine is good, in the style of the other northern French red vineyards in Alsace, Irancy (near Chablis) and Sancerre, but, like them, it only makes much of an impression in hot years; when rail transport brought Burgundy within easy reach of Paris we can assume that a Champagne making red wine would have been as eclipsed as Irancy has become.

Why bother?

Gustave Flaubert was fascinated by the idiotic and unvarying phrases used by the French bourgeoisie in response to everything from actresses to yawning, and immortalized them in his *Dictionary of Received Ideas*, (drawn on extensively in *Madame Bovary*.) Much wine writing could be similarly catalogued. When confronted with a Pinot Noir wine from anywhere north of Burgundy's Côte d'Or – like Alsace, Champagne or the Loire – the stock phrase is 'why bother?'

For an answer look no further than the pale, piercing fruity **Bourgogne des Côtes d'Auxerre, William Fève**, £5.30 Longford Wines, Lewes, E Sussex BN8 5TB 01273 480761. Odd: 4/5. Niceness: 2/5 on its own in front of TV; 4/5 with grilled tuna or swordfish.

Other far northern Pinot Noirs: from Yapp Brothers of Mere, Wiltshire (01747 860423), **Bruno Paillard's Bouzy Rouge** £15.75 (Bouzy is one of the Champagne villages) and **Schléret's Pinot Noir d'Alsace 1995**, £10.25. Bibendum, London NW1 (0171 916 7706) have the **Rolly Gassmann's Pinot Noir** 1990 for a dreadful £22. More reasonably priced is the **Sancerre Pinot Noir**, André Dezat et Fils 1994, at £9.40 from Tanners of Shrewsbury (01743 232400) . . . also a **Pinot Noir de St Bris** from **J–M Brocard**, £6.85 for the 1995 Vintage from Adnams of Southwold, Suffolk (01502 727222).

Except that by the nineteenth century the Champenois had discovered bubbles. These, like the paleness of the white wine made from red Pinot Noir grapes, are the gift of the region's northerly latitude. The bubbles got into the wine originally because winter brought fermentation to a premature stop; when the casks were shipped the next spring it restarted, saturating the container with carbon dioxide, and when English clients opened the barrels and put the contents into sealed bottles, they created the world's first sparkling wine.

The climate of Champagne had another effect. Although yields in the region are not especially low, grapes here produce juice with exceptional concentrations of protein. This is the secret of Champagne's bubbles, that are so fine and persistent in a high-protein medium that Coca Cola made them the subject of a programme of research. For one of the world's most northerly wine-growing areas, Champagne seems in little danger of being marginalized.

Growers' Champagnes

You save money by choosing a Champagne from a small grower rather than a *Grande Marque*, as the widely advertised *négociants* are known. The main difference is that a grower will make champagne from only a single village and hence, probably, a single grape variety, whereas the Champagne houses, who buy from throughout the region and beyond (in the Aube valley for example) are free to blend Pinot Noir, Pinot Meunier and Chardonnay.

In *Wine Snobbery* (Faber and Faber 1988), Andrew Barr questions the sense of buying *Grande Marque* Champagne and draws attention to what I'd agree is the scandalous practice of some *négociants* buying in Champagne in bottle when their own stocks run low and simply slapping their label on it.

But after tasting through some growers' Champagnes on sale in Britain I can't believe the *Grandes Marques* would succeed in passing them off as their own. (Perhaps the region's co-ops offer more opportunities for this practice.) Single varietal Champagne is really not very like **Mumm, Pommery, Lanson** et al.

The best widely available grower's Chardonnay has to be **Gimonnet**. Oddbins follow the vintage versions: at the time of writing the 1992. This exhilarating pale golden wine starts with the unripe almond flavour of far-northern Chardonnay, adding the sweet notes of patisserie and hedgerow flowers, £15.99.

Albert Beerens from the Aube, a long way south of the three classic Champagne vineyard areas, makes a coppery-tinged wine from Pinot Noir and Chardonnay. You can taste the redness of the Pinot fruit as raspberries or cherries. A slightly acquired taste but very good. Bibendum Wine Ltd, £15.

Champagne Château de Boursault from Fullers (£14.99) doesn't come across like a growers' Champagne: it's marked NM not RM on the label (see the note on decoding labels on page 88) and with its toastiness and its blended-champagne flavour you'd think it was a well-aged *Grande Marque*. What's unusual about it is that the owners have planted their single 16-hectare vineyard in the Vallée de la Marne not with Pinot Meunier alone, as would be customary, but with roughly equal proportions of the other two Champagne varieties as well.

Another lovely growers' champagne from the same corner of the region is carried by the larger Safeway stores: **Champagne**

> **Chartogne-Taillet** at £15.99 at the time of writing.
> Threshers have been experimenting with growers' Champagnes, working with a producer called **J. L. Malard** who has been marketing his own wine and those of colleagues in the top-named Champagne villages. Originally there were six – this year there are likely to be just two or three, from the red grape villages of **Bouzy** and **Ambonnay** and possibly the white grape *terroir* of Cramant. In their last incarnation the wines ranged from good to great.
>
> Other merchants offering growers' Champagnes include Roger Harris, Weston Longville, Norfolk (01603 880171), T & W Wines, Thetford, Norfolk (01842 765646), The Wine Society, Stevenage (01438 741177) and Yapp Brothers, Mere, Wiltshire (01747 860423).

There is one final reason not to move the world's wine production into the most apparently logical sites: red wine grown in a cool climate appears to be better for you.

In his '*Save Your Heart Wine Guide*', the Canadian journalist Frank Jones looks at research aimed at finding out whether some red wines are better than others at preventing blood-clotting disorders. A pattern emerges: hand-made wines and wines from cold climates have more of the desired anti-oxidant compounds such as resveratrol. Healthiest of all is red wine from Pinot Noir, almost irrespective of origin.

One interpretation is that grapes produce anti-oxidants as an auto-immune response to the threat of an invasion of mildew or grey rot, always more likely in cool vineyards. But why should Californian Pinot be good for you?

Length of maceration is also cited by Frank Jones. The healthy substances in grapes are found in or just under the skin. In hot countries it makes sense to limit the contact between the juice and the skin to prevent the wine becoming excessively dark and tannic. With Pinot Noir it is a struggle to get enough colour from the pale skins to make an acceptably rich-looking wine. The process of extracting the colour-bearing anthocyanins, conducted for example by the wine-maker physically treading the skins during *pigeage*, also sends resveratol, trans-resveratrol, quercetin, catechin and the other anti-oxidant flavonoids tumbling into the juice.

In asking whether it is the site or the variety that makes the difference, we are re-opening a question that Pliny the Elder thought he'd settled when he wrote 'It is the country and the soil that matter not the grape.'⁶ In fact the issue is still bitterly contentious.

1 *Histoire de la Vigne et du Vin en France des origines au XIXième siecle.*
2 For white wine, the hybrid grape Seyval Blanc and a clutch of varieties developed by the Geisenheim Institute on the Rhine such as Muller-Thurgau, Reichensteiner, Huxelrebe, Schônburger and Bacchus. As Seyval Blanc contains genes of the American wild grape *vitis labrusca*, not a 'true' grape vine, it cannot be used in the European Union for any quality wines claiming a specific geographical origin. The Geisenheim creations are regarded by Germany's top growers as second rate and designed for quantity rather than quality. For red: Rotberger, from Geisenheim and Triomphe d'Alsace which, despite its name, I suspect of having German origins (Pierre Galet certainly doesn't list it in *Cépages et Vignobles de France*).
3 Angelica was a cheap sweet wine, made in, and taking its name from, Los Angeles.
4 *American Wines* by Frank Schoonmaker and Tom Marvel, Deull Sloan and Pearce 1941.
5 Which makes muscles ache after exercise.
6 To try to turn Chablis into Meursault you'd also have to (a) ferment in small barrels and (b) after fermentation stir the dead yeast cells. No one can surely have ever attempted such a nutty exercise, but if they did it would answer some fundamental questions about what creates the taste of wine. Would a true wine-buff spot that the fake Meursault showed the influence of Chablis's Kimmeridgean clay soil or that the fake Chablis had really been grown on limestone?
7 He gives examples of how grapes change according to site concluding: *quibus exemplis, nisi fallor, manifestum est patriam terramque referre, non uvam, et supervacuam generum consectationem in numerum, cum eadem vitis aliud aliis in locis polleat.* (Unless I am mistaken these examples make plain the importance of a country and a *terroir* rather than grape varieties, and the pointlessness of an endless enumeration of these, given that different vines react in different ways to different places.) Pliny *Natural History* Book XIV, VIII, 70.

3

THROUGH THE GRAPE VINE

Half a century ago only the most dedicated wine-buff would know that red Burgundy was made from Pinot Noir grapes, or even recognize the name as a grape variety. Today, spotting the variety has become an essential part of learning about wine. There are fears that what began as a way of increasing people's understanding has begun to obscure it. Worse, there is the prospect that the emphasis on grape varieties will actually make wine less diverse; to keep more than a handful of names alive in people's imagination is a task to overwhelm even a marketing genius. Despite this there are producers who, rather than choosing to work with Chardonnay in Chile, have managed to make a success out of Charbono in California or Cinsault in the South of France. This section of the book is dedicated to them.

Such growers will be just as concerned about how a vine is being looked after as what variety it is. The classic approach, that suits most small-scale producers, means endless hard work by hand, with the aim of limiting yields of grapes in the interests of quality. But is this back-breaking toil necessary at a time when many large companies have turned much of the traditional work of vineyard management over to machines?

15

Grape Nuts

———

In 1934 Frank Schoonmaker, the American travel writer, emerging wine pundit and author of *Through Europe on $2 a Day*, came up with the most influential marketing idea in his new area of interest since the invention of corked glass bottles.

According to tradition in the family firm of Wente Brothers it happened at their house over the road from their vineyards at Livermore, a small town forty miles inland from San Francisco, set in a plain full of orchards and field crops. Through his travels in Europe Schoonmaker knew about wine. His education had been undertaken by no less a figure than Raymond Baudoin, the founder of the *Revue du Vin de France* and leading campaigner against fraudulent descriptions of wine. Now, with the ending of Prohibition, Schoonmaker was going into the business himself, writing about it for the *New Yorker*, and looking for products to put on the market.

Despite the 18th Amendment, the Wentes, like other wine firms, had kept afloat; during this period California's total acreage of vineyards had actually increased. Large numbers of boxes of grapes crossed the continent by train for the attentions of home wine-makers, largely Italian immigrants exempted from the general ban on manufacturing alcohol. Wente Brothers also benefited from a lucrative contract with the Catholic Diocese of San Francisco to supply 'altar wine'. Phil Wente, who currently runs the business with his sister, says it then went through a kind of trickle-down effect, accompanying the meals of the clergy, with enough left over for generous distributions among lay parishioners. You feel that the twenties were probably growth years for the Church.

'Schoonmaker had approached us to suggest he represent us,' says Wente. 'He was convinced there was an opportunity for a new start, a new presentation to the public. They wanted a new name to identify themselves with, to mark them off from the traditional European-type names everyone was using: Chablis, Burgundy, etc. So, according to my grandfather's version, they all sat round the table and, after brainstorming and brainstorming, they all agreed about naming the wines after the variety of grapes from which they were made.'

So the first varietally-named wine in the western hemisphere was Wente Brothers' 1932 Sauvignon Blanc, soon followed by their Sémillon and Chardonnay. In the same year Schoonmaker visited Louis Martini at his winery a hundred miles further north in the Napa Valley and made another convert to the new way of describing wine.

The New World's First Varietal Wine

Ah, Sauvignon! That tang of gooseberry and tomcat that's a give-away even to the novice taster.* An appropriate vehicle, you'd think, to launch the world's first wine to be sold by grape variety rather than region.

But actually Wente Brothers' Sauvignon Blanc is barely recognizable as the stuff made by modern flying wine-makers in Hungary, Southern France or Chile. This is oily and peachy with a smokiness that comes from some ageing in American oak barrels, rich smooth texture with a hint of residual sugar. I'm not sure I'd spot it as being Sauvignon at all.
Wente's Sauvignon Blanc, around £7 from Cheviot Wine Agencies, G43 1QQ (01844 291 080).

In hindsight this has been acclaimed as a milestone in democratizing wine. Oz Clarke describes varietal labelling as one of the most important ways of simplifying wine for the consumer and making it possible for growers in non-classic areas to find a market.

It wasn't how it seemed in the early 1930s. 'At that time their market was very, very limited,' says Philip Wente. 'This wasn't a nomenclature for the average public. It was designed for sophisticated and knowledgeable people.' Then, as now, only a minority

---

* Novice wine writers might want to memorize this. Remember Ah! rather than Oh! or Ooh!

of customers find it as self-evident as writers assume it is that Chardonnay means a kind of grape rather than a place or a brand name. (It is currently also a make of cheap shirt.)

Only in the 1940s did a varietal wine become a big seller: the Grenache Rosé made by Almáden, which, like its predecessors was the result of a brainwave by Schoonmaker. His inspiration was to find a new use for the huge Californian plantings of Grenache, the grape that makes Tavel, one of France's best-known rosés. Even today in California Chardonnay and Merlot occupy a separate niche in the market to such people's favourites as Gallo's 'Hearty Burgundy', which is made not from Pinot Noir but from the Mediterranean varieties that have always made California's staple wines.

Australia, as a result of signing a treaty with the European Union, is finally having to phase out its equally long-established use of names like Houghton's White Burgundy and St Henri Claret. The alternative of varietal naming really got under way in the 1970s when the first Chardonnay was planted, aimed at wine-literate people who had heard of its success in California. 'Riesling' had already been a long-established wine name in Australia indicating not that it actually comes from the Riesling grape (which would be called 'Rhine Riesling') but in a Germanic style. Till recently many 'Rieslings' were made from Sémillon (following the same logic by which the dish sold as 'seaweed' in Chinese restaurants is actually made with Chinese Cabbage).

Some of the first single varietal wines to be sold in Australia were made by the Purbrick family at their startling-looking property, Château Tahbilk, in Victoria, eighty miles north of Melbourne. With its odd pagoda-style farm buildings dating from 1870 and its vineyards planted ten years earlier, Tahbilk is the state's oldest winery.

The three long-established varieties were Cabernet Sauvignon, (derived, according to the former wine-maker John Purbrick, from cuttings taken from the vineyard of Château Lafite) and two varieties from the Rhône, Shiraz (pronounced Shirah – the French Syrah) and Marsanne. With all the logic you'd expect the Cabernet was sold as 'Burgundy', the Shiraz as 'Claret' and the Marsanne was the Tahbilk 'Chablis'.

But in the early 1950s John's father Eric followed the Californian example. The 'Chablis' became 'Chablis (Marsanne)', then 'Marsanne (Chablis)', finally daring to go out only under its varietal name. As in California it was less an exercise in demystifying wine than a step designed to confer more authenticity on what was already a classy product. Tahbilk's wines had been presented to Queen Victoria, the Marsanne was served at the banquet for Queen Elizabeth's coronation and the range was stocked by the P&O liners.

Marsanne as grown in the state of Victoria is an Australian classic. The way it's handled at Tahbilk recalls the treatment Maurice O'Shea prescribed for Sémillon in New South Wales. The grapes are harvested when barely ripe, given between eight and twenty-four hours skin contact and bottled without any time in wood. Until 1978 the winery was technologically rudimentary, using hundred-year-old open vat fermenters and no temperature control other than pipes carrying cool river water. 'If we got cool nights this automatically brought down the temperature,' says John Purbrick. 'It would give us long fermentations and we made some stunning wines. But we only used to get them in a cool vintage.'

When young the wine is simple, dry, citrussy; after some years in the bottle it blossoms, deepening in colour to what Purbrick describes as 'wedding band gold' and producing tropical scents that are customarily compared to honeysuckle. 'They start to round out and become like a butterball. One person will call it dry and another will call it sweet. But the beauty is that they'll both feel quite safe buying it.'

However it was a commercial mistake to do away with the familiar name of Château Tahbilk 'Chablis'. When the world in the 1950s began to be familiar with the names of the grape varieties that made top Bordeaux and with red and white Burgundy, it also began to assume that the reason for the obscurity of other varieties was that they weren't much good. Despite the wine's previously high reputation, says John Purbrick, it suffered a rapid eclipse. 'Marsanne was a variety that no one wanted to know in Australia, from the 1950s through the 1960s, 1970s and 1980s. They kept saying to my father: "Get rid of it. Pull it out." He said, "No no no." It's only in the last ten years that it's started to move again.'

Ironically it isn't even straight Marsanne; the vineyard is actually a hodge-podge. It is old-fashioned because it contains genetically diverse plants rather than the single clones promoted by vineyard researchers and consultants. Even more unconventionally, it contains more than one variety, with stray specimens of Chardonnay, Riesling and Sémillon.

This unique mixture has migrated beyond the Tahbilk vineyards. Eric Purbrick wasn't the only wine-maker of the 1960s to think it gave outstanding results; another enthusiast was Colin Preece, who at that time had just retired as wine-maker at the Best's Great Western estate near Ararat in Victoria. Preece, who died in 1978, was one of the handful of strong personalities responsible for the post-war reputation of Australian wine, alongside Max Schubert at Penfolds, Maurice O'Shea at McWilliam, Lindemans' Karl Stockhausen and Jack Mann at Houghton.

In 1967 he was commissioned to plan a new vineyard in Victoria for Ross Shelmerdine, who was the heir through marriage to a substantial retail fortune. In the event the site he selected on the Goulburn River was less than five miles from Tahbilk, and he planted it up with vines propagated from the Tahbilk vineyards, two-thirds Shiraz and one-third more-or-less Marsanne. It's a tribute to Preece's reputation and force of personality that no one questioned his choice of two such unfashionable varieties. It wasn't just the Marsanne. John Purbrick says of Shiraz: 'It used to be thought of as the workhorse of the industry. Then it became a dead horse.'

Don Lewis, who's now in charge at Mitchelton, spent two years working under Colin Preece. 'He was a very respected man and what he said went. If he said, "Plant Marsanne," that was what got planted. The industry was anyway in such a flux at that time, just on the edge of a boom, that they were willing to try anything.' The wine from Mitchelton was called White Hermitage. Those who took a pessimistic view of Marsanne's commercial prospects were right; Don Lewis admits that even now it's difficult to sell.

Is it Chablis? . . . Is it Hermitage? . . . No it's Marsanne!

Marsanne, together with the Chenin Blanc-based Houghtons White Burgundy (see page 209) and the various Sémillons has become an Australian original. You can choose the more traditional unoaked style, represented by the first three wines listed below, or the oaked version created by Mitchelton. To continue with my scoring system, the unoaked wines start life neither very strange nor with any exceptional appeal and, with bottle age, develop

THE WILD BUNCH

strong individual personality. This is usually compared to honeysuckle, though this underplays the exotic, tropical honeyed
character. You could score young unoaked Marsanne Odd: 1/5
Niceness: 2/5, changing with five years in bottle to Odd: 3/
5 Niceness 4/5.

Thomas Mitchell Marsanne 1995, £5.29, Oddbins

Château Tahbilk Marsanne 1994, £5.79, Oddbins and 50 per
cent of Tesco stores

Dalfarras Marsanne 1994, £6.20, The Wine Society (01438
741177).

Mitchelton Reserve Marsanne 1993, £7.99 Oddbins, £8.40
Tanners, Shrewsbury (01743 232400). Justerini and Brooks,
London SW1, have the 1992 for £8.50. This is barrel-fermented
and aged, and the result is to bring on the 'honeysuckle' character
much earlier. You might think that adding the rich toastiness of
white Burgundy to the grapefruit/honeysuckle quality of Marsanne
would make for a dog's breakfast – but it doesn't.

In California and Australia the boom in wine drinking and the
move to varietal names were unconnected events. But because in
Britain they happened at the same time they have been thought of
as two faces of the same Wine Revolution. This has created a
handicap, both for French growers of non-varietal wines and New
World producers of obscurities like Marsanne – a handicap that
should be unblushingly exploited by the bargain hunter.

In Europe some wines have always been named after grape
varieties. No hype attached to Riesling, Gewurztraminer or
Muscat in Alsace, even less to the scores of Italian varieties in
unmemorable combinations with place names: Vernaccia di San
Gimignano, Dolcetto d'Alba, Verdicchio dei Castelli di Jesi, Greco
di Tufo . . .

That was the old Old World. The 1980s in contrast introduced
the so-called Fighting Varietals: Cabernet Sauvignon, Merlot, Sauvignon, Chardonnay. The Svengali grooming them for stardom was
Robert Skalli, one of the many former Algerian *pieds noirs* retur-
nees to become big league successes in the wine business. His first
base was a wine estate in Corsica; next he bought St Supery, a
substantial estate in California's Napa Valley. While there he struck

158

up friendships with the local big shots, Robert Mondavi, Michaela Rodeno and Bernard Portet, and became convinced that the future lay with single-variety wines. He took this philosophy to Mediterranean France and in the late 1970s established a newly built winery at Sète, on the coast between Beziers and Montpellier.

The business was different from the other *négociants* of the region. It would receive, not made wine, but grapes, and these grapes would be the noble varieties, not Carignan, Alicante Bouschet or Bourboulenc. The wines looked different, too, with labels so chic you'd think they had to be Italian and, for the top of the range, embossed bottles with a little glass grape cluster above the label.

Skalli's corporate literature stresses that the company's approach doesn't aim to replace the *appellations d'origine*: 'AOC and varietal wines are complementary; far from competing with each other each plays its role in different parts of the vast world wine market and enables France to attack international markets with renewed vigour.' In fact even the more staid end of the wine trade approves of Skalli and hopes his approach will hold the line for wine against flavoured vodkas and alcopops.

Chardonnay and Cabernet Sauvignon are no longer names to create a buzz, but fashion does help sell wine. Viognier in 1997 still has the sheen of newness. In 1979 there were little more than a hundred acres left of this great white grape of the Northern Rhône. When Jancis Robinson published *Vines, Grapes and Wine* in 1986 it was still on the endangered list. Then, largely thanks to Robert Parker, there was a huge international revival of interest in the Rhône and in Condrieu, which is one hundred per cent Viognier becoming, as they say, a wine to die for. At a dinner party in *Brightness Falls* by Jay McInerny the characters fuss over a bottle just, as one of them observes, as they would have done a few years earlier when they were drug connoisseurs. In the early 1990s the plains of Southern France rang to the sound of chainsaws slicing off Chardonnay saplings (which had themselves only recently been field-grafted on to the roots of old Aramon or Carignan) for replacement with thousands of hurriedly propagated canes of Viognier.

In the course of a few weeks in the summer of 1996 I saw the same process starting with Sauvignon Gris, AKA Sauvignon Rosé, a close cousin to Sauvignon Blanc, the 'cat's pee on a gooseberry bush' grape.[1] This starts from a far lower base of recognition even than Viognier.

It doesn't figure in *Vines, Grapes and Wine* by Jancis Robinson (not a Sauvignon Blanc enthusiast) and gets three lines in Pierre Galet's monumental *Cépages et Vignobles de France*. He describes it as 'barely in cultivation, occasionally encountered as isolated examples in plantings of Sauvignon Blanc, from which it is distinguished only by its pink berries'.

I first heard the name at a tasting in London. Mme Florence Cathiard, a proprietor from the Pessac-Léognan region of Bordeaux had a proportion in her Château Smith-Haut-Lafitte Blanc. 'Our oenologist says it tastes of pears but I think it's peaches. People can't believe that the wine's Sauvignon.' I made polite noises of agreement and turned away; then after I'd already half forgotten the conversation found a strong lingering taste of peaches.

When I was in Bordeaux soon afterwards Sauvignon Gris suddenly went from being an obscure reference – something you might invent to tease wine snobs – to a genuine and ultra-fashionable grape variety. A young grower called Stefan Defraisne proudly showed me some rows of the distinctive pink grapes at Château de Fontenille, his property in the Entre Deux Mers. Peter Vinding-Diers, the Danish wine-maker currently making Tokay in partnership with Hugh Johnson, turned out to have a big planting at Nôtre Dame de Landiras. And later that day I met Mandy Jones, the Australian wine-maker at Château Carsin, not far away, and she not only had some hectares but was using it, unblended, to make the top wine of the property. She thawed a frozen bottle of Sauvignon Gris juice in a microwave so that I could contrast it with the finished wine. Back in England I saw that Tesco already had a Sauvignon Gris. And so it all starts.

I liked Mandy Jones's wine and I think I understood how Sauvignon Gris could help Bordeaux. No one is very interested in white wine from the Entre Deux Mers, and it hardly helps to put the name of the main variety Sauvignon Blanc on the label: customers are likely to be disappointed when they fail to encounter the intense, nettle-like flavours they would be familiar with from Sauvignon from the Loire or New Zealand – Bordeaux is too warm to produce them.

But no one knows what this grey/pink version is meant to taste like and its spicy, peachy flavours could create a different range of expectations for Sauvignon. It might even give white Bordeaux that Holy Grail of marketing: a Unique Selling Proposition. Putting the name of a variety on a label may or may not make wine simpler to buy; it can certainly make it easier to sell.

Going Grey

For a rare variety, there seems to be quite a lot of Sauvignon Gris wine coming into Britain. In ascending order of price:

Sauvignon Gris 1995, Yvon Mau, £5.49. In 15 per cent of Tesco stores.
Château Carsin Sauvignon Gris 1995, price unknown at the time of writing – details from the Château on 0033(0)5 56 76 43 06

The flavours I associate with this grape are peaches and a trace of white pepper. The Yvon Mau is lighter and bubblier, with floral notes and higher acidity – the Château Carsin is more unctuous and concentrated with a little wood influence.

If you want to see what Sauvignon Gris is like when used more traditionally, in a blend, and are much better off than I am, you might be interested in **Château Smith Haut Lafitte Blanc 1993 Pessac-Léognan**, £21.30, Corney and Barrow (0171 241 4051). Up to 10 per cent is Gris; what's unusual is to have such a silky wine with all Sauvignon and none of the oily Sémillon.

The hyping of varieties has made wine much more like a fashion product. It used to gain value both from being scarce, like a single vineyard Burgundy, and because of the need to pass on the high production costs created by doing things by hand. Fashion adds value without adding to production costs; fashionable grapes can come from countries with rock-bottom labour costs or from highly mechanized vineyards. And it creates extra demand.

The cult of fashionable grape varieties may be good marketing sense but it infuriates many wine-makers, even if they work with the so-called 'noble' varieties. For Peter Sichel, the Bordeaux *négociant* and owner of Château d'Angludet, its chief offence is that it makes blended wines as traditionally made in his region less attractive to customers than single varietal ones. He tried to hit back by taking a kind of 'varieties don't matter' floorshow to the 1994

London Wine Trade Fair. In 1989 he had made separate bottlings of the three varieties grown at his property in the Haut-Médoc. He challenged an audience to identify which was the Cabernet Sauvignon, which was the Merlot and which the Petit Verdot (the least well known of the Bordeaux varieties). If you took Jancis Robinson on trust when she says that one sniff of Cab Sauv is enough for experienced tasters, the challenge should have been easily met. In fact the overwhelming majority of the wine professionals got it wrong.

In Bordeaux the different kinds of red grapes are close cousins. Cabernet Sauvignon is valued because it makes powerful wines that keep well, not because it creates a particular spectrum of flavours. Merlot ripens more reliably each year and contributes softness when the wines are young – in fact some in the trade think so much is being planted that the character of Bordeaux will change for the worse. But again, it isn't a simple question of the taste of different varieties.

Olivier Sèze has carried out much the same exercise as Peter Sichel. These days he now makes an accessibly priced *cru bourgeois* claret at his Château le Charmail, some eighteen miles up the Gironde estuary from Angludet, but his family comes from St Emilion on the far right bank of Bordeaux's rivers. 'The vats I make from the Merlot I grow here have no resemblance to Merlot grown in St Emilion,' he declares. 'I've entertained myself by asking experts who are very well known to taste and try to name the grape variety. They got it wrong. Flavours aren't a function of grape varieties, they're a function of the character of the soil and of the way the wine is made.'

Peter Vinding-Diers specializes in the white Bordeaux grapes. Sauvignon and Sémillon really are quite unlike: Sauvignon Blanc is strongly aromatic, whereas the point of Sémillon is its rich unctuous texture, not to mention its suitability as a vehicle for *Botrytis cinerea*, or 'noble rot' because of its tough skin. Yet the whole subject of varieties makes Vinding-Diers tetchy. 'To talk about varieties is completely wrong. Wine has nothing to do with varietal percentages. What it is about is an enormous amount of work blending – that's when you make the wine, when you put it together – but it's about the taste of each barrel, not whether it's called Sauvignon or Sémillon. I think the consumer is misguided by the whole idea. When people come up at a tasting and say "what's the grape composition?" I find it the most irritating question. It's nothing to do with what's in the bottle.'

So are varietal names making things clearer or not? You could use apples as an analogy. Coxes Orange Pippins are a distinct variety and New Zealand and English Coxes can both be very good, but they're less like each other than they're like other varieties of apples in their own respective countries.

The same principle can apply to wine. Pinot Noir is now widely grown outside Burgundy and you might prefer the products of California, Oregon or Australia; they tend to be richer and much more consistent. But they are less like a 'real' Burgundy than a Beaujolais from a traditionalist grower. A Moulin à Vent or even the supposedly lightweight *cru* of St Amour, after a few years in the bottle, can fool tasters, even though it's made from the much less 'noble' Gamay. And a further complication is that the name on the label is not even a guarantee that you're getting what you think you've paid for; in California a declared variety need make up only a high percentage of the wine. One widely grown wine grape in Australia is Sultana, planted originally in the irrigated areas as a source of dried fruit. It does not make distinguished wine. If varietalism was all about public information you might sometimes hope to see its name on a label. I predict that you never will.

Frank Schoonmaker helped educate the world to recognize the names of grape varieties: Cabernet Sauvignon, the grape that makes the best red; Chardonnay, the variety behind white Burgundy. But the effect of making one or two 'noble' varieties internationally famous was not simply to drive out those he saw as inferior, like Carignan or Alicante Bouschet. The victims of this new form of brand recognition were equally distinguished varieties that lost out simply because of consumers' limited attention span.

One classic instance was in Australia, where the big companies' stampede to plant up Coonawarra with Cabernet Sauvignon left the Barossa growers high and dry, with few takers for the fruit of their old, low-yielding Shiraz vines. The growers' misfortune was an opportunity for Charlie Melton, Robert O'Callaghan and those lucky enough to be their customers. They swooped on sources of wonderful grapes that ordinarily they could never have afforded to buy.

Almost exactly the same thing happened in California. Here it was a young graduate of the Davis University wine-making course who made history by swimming against a tide of Chardonnay and Cabernet Sauvignon. He was Randall Grahm, the Rhône Ranger.

1 Peter Vinding-Diers disputes that it is related to Sauvignon Blanc – he believes it to be a Sémillon-Muscat hybrid.

16

Old Vines

Had his Pinot Noir turned out better, Randall Grahm would have become a member of the diaspora of Burgundians-in-spirit described in Chapter Five. He resembles Gary Farr in Australia in his sense of internal exile and of taking a different path from the rest of his country's wine-makers. But even if he had knuckled down and spent his first fifteen years turning out Cabernet and Chardonnay he would deserve at least a footnote in history for helping make wine less stuffy. If he hadn't existed, you feel, Oddbins would have to have invented him.

Grahm's company Bonny Doon makes Californian wines using the Southern French and Mediterranean varieties that once dominated the state's vineyards. If Bonny Doon was a record label, magazine publisher or Internet site its choice of text and graphics would be par-for-the-post 1960s Californian course: verbal and visual puns, an ironic obsession with beautiful downtown Gilroy, America's garlic capital, and a pantheon of heroes taking in Frank Zappa and Marcel Proust. He likes practical jokes: Remington Norman in his *Rhône Renaissance* describes him as compelling visitors to one of his vineyards to converse in whispers, on the grounds that a particular variety was sensitive to noise.

This is fun with a purpose. The well-known grape varieties are brands, easily recognized by wine buyers. As Norman points out, if you are going to sell wines without this convenient hook you have to find other ways of being recognized. Randall Grahm has come up with plenty of these. Starting from the useful inheritance of a surname from which one of the letter 'a's seems to have dropped out he has acquired other media tags like the Rhône Ranger and the ABC mnemonic, signifying, variously, Anything But Cabernet and Anything But Chardonnay.

The idea of selling wines as coming from a single variety is, he says, essentially dumb. 'It's a very American thing; you know, Château Latour is 85 per cent Cabernet Sauvignon. OK, we'll go one better and have 100 per cent. More must be better.'

What's more the grapes used to 'improve' the vineyards have been the wrong ones: if you take cool-climate varieties of grapes from central France and grow them in California, on the same latitude as Sicily, they lose their acidity by the time they're ripe. Wine-makers then have to choose either to harvest unripe or to put back the acidity in the form of white powder.

Randall Grahm's strategy is to play to what he sees as California's strengths. These don't include superlative vineyard sites: 'We don't have great *terroir* – we don't have really interesting sexy soils.* But as we grow grapes in a warmer climate than Europe we can ripen them more completely and we can get a healthier grape. The trade-off is that we don't have the acid balance so we tend to acidulate. It's a cultural thing: Americans seem to be less sensitive than Europeans to acid additions. My thinking has been that if you get the right grapes in the climate that's appropriate for them at the appropriate yield then you don't have to make that trade: you don't have to add acid.'

Getting the 'right grapes' has been a protracted business. To begin with Grahm had hoped to turn the 28-acre vineyard he bought with family money in 1975 into a little corner of Burgundy. He planted Pinot Noir and Chardonnay and even imported large quantities of limestone. The soil may have begun to resemble the Côte d'Or, but the wine didn't.

'The Pinot that we grew wasn't terribly interesting. I was buying grapes in from Oregon. I came to think that if I can buy better Pinot grapes than I can grow then it isn't worth it. I concluded that the area was too warm, that for whatever reason I can't make a great Pinot. Maybe I didn't give it enough time.'

---

* Paul Draper of Ridge Vineyards, who makes perhaps the very finest wine in California, is however convinced of the opposite. He told me: 'Randall is a great friend. He's done almost anything that's of interest and does it every year differently. Never doing the same thing twice. It's the opposite of me, trying to persevere. He says. "We don't have the soils." I'd say he's absolutely wrong. He doesn't have those soils because he hasn't been able to find or purchase those pieces of ground – and it's a problem for him. I've had the luxury of searching for and purchasing great pieces of ground – so I'd disagree with Randall on that.'

Grahm is a little vulnerable on this last point. 'How many times has he replanted that vineyard?' another wine-maker asked me, with a note of disapproval. The original site is in any case currently laid low; a bacterial infection has required that it be reconstituted from scratch.

Fortunately California has a reasonable number of proprietors who have been content to leave their vineyards alone despite changing fashions. The main side of Bonny Doon's business is that of a *négociant*. Grahm in fact bought his first Southern-French-style grapes even before his own planting of Pinot had matured.

'It was 1982; the vineyard wasn't yet in production, but I wanted to get things going. I didn't know how to make wine so I thought: "I don't have to trash my own grapes; I'll trash someone else's grapes." So I bought some Grenache and made a small quantity, just two or three thousand cases, and got a little money in.'

Today Bonny Doon and a couple of similar operations hunt out old vineyards planted with the Italian and Mediterranean French varieties that Grahm thinks are most suited to the region.

Steven Edmunds started up in 1985 in Emoryville, a suburb of Berkeley, with a winery but no vineyard. 'Randall didn't know I was doing it; I didn't know anybody else was doing it. I began because I was unsatisfied with the direction Californian wines had gone. There was a character that was lacking in style and imagination. There had to be some explanation why Californian wines seemed to be so boring.' He worked in the wine trade, and so was in a position to make comparisons with the stuff he liked to drink, which came largely from Southern France and Italy. Along with Randall Grahm, he was drawn to explore the varieties traditionally grown in California: Barbera, originally from Piemonte in North West Italy, Grenache and Mourvèdre.

It is odd that Grahm and Edmunds never met up on their respective Mourvèdre hunts. Randall Grahm says it took a while before he worked out that the widely planted Mataro was just the Spanish name for the variety that makes the powerful wine of Bandol in Provence.

The quest involved Steven Edmunds and his wife Cornelia in some anguish. 'At the time we started so many of these vineyards were being torn out. It's true we were able to find some nice old vine sources for a few varieties but the search for Mourvèdre was agonizing. We kept getting the same two responses from farmers. One: what do you want with that stuff? Two: you should have called me yesterday/last month/last year. We just tore it out. It's kind of amazing that we did find Mourvèdre. It was in the very best place I think it could possibly be, south facing on a slightly calcareous ridge, and it's the best Mourvèdre in the western hemisphere. Later the growers, who were sort of local legends, asked me if I'd liked the grapes. I said I did. They said "Did you really like it? We had another four and a half acres till we tore it out last year." '

Some Californian old-vine hunters

Randall Grahm. His main importers are Morris and Verdin, 10 The Leather Market, London SE1 (0171 357 6575).

Pacific Rim Riesling 1995 around £8.50. This was designed for California's fusion cuisine – the seafood-based ancestor of all the tide of lemon-grass flavoured risotto which descended on London in the mid-1990s. This smells a bit floral but isn't at all mimsy to drink: it's concentrated and acidic, £8.50.

Ca' del Solo Malvasia Bianca 1995. This is another white wine that is tougher than it appears: it smells of roses, lychees, clean linen but is pinned up with decent acidity – a bit like a lightly sugared red grapefruit. Other than in Portugal, wines from this ancient variety are quite rare in the Mediterranean, let alone California, £8.50. (For another sighting try the distinctive **Loire Malvoisie** from Yapp Brothers' Pierre Guindon at £6.25.)

Ca' del Solo Big House Red 1996. A bit of every Mediterranean grape variety has gone in, but the flavours (mainly red fruit and canned cherries) don't cancel out.

Il Fiasco 1995. This has 85 per cent Sangiovese, the chief grape of Chianti, but the jammy, raspberry quality reminds me of the Burgundy that Randall Grahm was trying to make when he started out, £13,00.

Le Cigare Volant 1992. This is a tribute to Châteauneuf-du-Pape, but despite its southern inspiration goes for balance rather than power. With four years' age it's no longer about primary fruit but clubland aromas like tobacco, leather and the spiciness that's a

Rhône trademark, £15.50.

Doug Danielak, also from Morris and Verdin.

Jade Mountain Le Provencale 1995. Like Grahm, Danielak is inspired by Burgundy, where he learned to make wine, but in California turns to Mediterranean varieties. This blend is 40 per cent Mourvèdre from a source of 105-year-old vines: deep-coloured liquoricy wine, not really ready for drinking but so sumptuous it might almost work with food, £15.50.

Steven Edmunds and Cornelia St John. Oddbins Fine Wine Shops.

Edmunds St John 'L'Enfant Terrible' Mourvèdre 1994. Powerful autumnal smelling wine – spice, smoke, leaf mould and leather. £9.49 from Oddbins Fine Wine Shops.

This approach also enabled Grahm and Edmunds to offer affordable wines made with a personal touch. Otherwise California divides into two markets. On one hand there's mass-produced stuff like 'hearty Burgundy', using grapes from the industrialized vineyards of the Central Valley between Sacramento and Bakersfield, with, sometimes, an ameliorating dash of old-vine Mourvèdre. On the other there are the products of the 'boutique wineries': hand-made but heart-stoppingly expensive.

'California's big failing has been in not providing entry-level wines,' says Grahm. 'The only way you can do it is by finding grapes that other people don't want.'

Today the Californians, like Robert O'Callaghan and the other South Australian champions of the 'dry vine' Shiraz of the Barossa, are suffering from their own success. 'The strategy has been to find grapes that are inexpensive because they're slightly out of fashion. But when they come back into fashion, like old dry-farmed Zinfandel, then the prices come right up.' Steven Edmunds paid $550 a ton for his first batch of Mourvèdre back in 1985; now it costs him $1,800, hardly less than the going rate per ton of $2,000 for Merlot, just now California's most fashionable variety.

Yet though the price gap has narrowed, it is not enough to put the old vines out of danger. Many acres of old Mediterranean grape varieties in California are still threatened by the chainsaw.

Grape growers are as keen on money as anyone else. When a shift in fashion determines that they would enjoy greater prosperity by yanking out a row of old vines they are likely sooner or later to bow to market forces.

However those who make the best wine rarely follow the crowd. When it comes to grape varieties this is because:

a they like to explore their personal theories about the best match between a site and a grape variety,

b they have an obsession with the history of their vineyard and a desire to maintain a link with the past,

c in Europe few growers will admit that the variety is more important than the vineyard and

d many growers are distinguished by counter-suggestibility and cussedness.

In the New World most do go with the tide. This explains the relative lack of interest within California in the rich and complex wines that can be made there and nowhere else in the world; the secret is the mysterious grape called Zinfandel, recently identified with the Primitivo grape grown in the heel of Italy. Because it makes no great wine in Europe, Zinfandel never appeared in Frank Schoonmaker's shortlists of high-quality varieties and was generally thought fit only for bulk wine production. It took a couple of pioneers, working, like Randall Grahm, chiefly as *négociants*, to demonstrate the capabilities of the long-established plantings of Zinfandel. Joseph Swan's winery in Russian River, Sonoma County, has since 1969 relied on long contracts with mainly Italian–American vineyard owners. The great Paul Draper of Ridge Vineyards pre-dated Grahm in hunting out pockets of old vines.

The Languedoc-Roussillon region of Southern France, which follows the Mediterranean shoreline from the Pyrenees to Nîmes, makes more wine than Australia and New Zealand combined and, rather than having a single current of opinion, is criss-crossed with different viewpoints. It had a reputation for its wine during the Roman Empire, which is too remote a period to count, but also in the eighteenth century, when the wine of the Minervois sold for the same price as that of Beaune in Burgundy. As we've seen, it more recently supplied factory workers with industrially made wine, until the price collapsed in the 1960s, causing some disturbances among the *vignerons*.

The estates are spreading and the distances between them can be interminable. Compared to Beaujolais or the Northern Rhône, where the vineyards are cheek-by-jowl and manageably small, the region can seem out of scale and confusing. Everyone agrees that the wines have to find a new, more financially lucrative identity, but what should they taste like? In fact many pioneers find this lack of certainty stimulating. As Patricia Domergue puts it: 'In the Minervois everything's up for grabs, unlike in Bordeaux, where they've nothing left to discover.'

The most pressing question concerns grape varieties. When the French try to puff this region they like to play up the idea that it's Europe's answer to the New World. And in several ways there are parallels with Australia or California. There is a Mediterranean climate; there is little continuous tradition of making fine wine; there is a legacy of gnarled vines originally planted to pump out high-volume wine but now achieving a certain venerable status with their great age. To give force to the New World analogy, Robert Skalli and similar-minded wine-makers have set off a replanting programme with Cabernet and Chardonnay.

The idea that the South should replant with international varieties gets support in some surprising quarters. Cazes Frères in Rivesaltes make some of the best examples of those most idiosyncratic products of Southern France, the *vins doux naturelles* – both delicate Muscats and the caramelly brown oxidized styles. But André Cazes, joint head of the family firm, believes in giving the public what they want and has been disappointed to find that what pleases wine writers and the *Revue du Vin de France* isn't necessarily what sells.

'When foreigners had the pick of our grape varieties, did they choose Carignan or Maccabeu?' he asked. 'I don't think so – they went for the best ones France had to offer.' As a result he perplexes visiting journalists, for whom local colour is all, by seeking their opinion on experimental Cabernets and barrel-fermented Chardonnays. But he has a fair question.

Aimé Guibert is a vociferous champion of underrated varieties;

one of the wines he makes at the Villeveyrac co-op is actually Aramon, the most despised grape of all. 'The idea that one is all good and another is all bad is a gangster mentality,' he rumbled. Yet for his own red wine at Mas de Daumas Gassac this elder statesman of the Languedoc chose to plant an obscure southern variety called, er, Cabernet Sauvignon.

I asked him about this but drew the question's sting. After all, I suggested, it was in the 1970s that he planted up Daumas Gassac's porous slopes. That was still the era in which fewer than a handful of 'noble' grapes were supposed to be capable of making decent wine. What's more, his friends and advisers were from Bordeaux where Cabernet Sauvignon is the top variety even though it often has difficulty ripening. This property at Aniane, a hundred miles further south, must have appeared Cabernet heaven.

Yes, he said, but there was another aspect as well. His vines were no ordinary Cabernet Sauvignon, but came from a vineyard planted experimentally in 1944 with cuttings from all the greatest Bordeaux estates: Lafite, Margaux, Latour. In 1956 the Ministry of Agriculture had urged Latour to replant with a clonal selection of Cabernet and the wine had suffered a great drop-off in quality as a consequence. In 1970 the same busybodying ministry had ordered the owners of the experimental vineyard to grub it up. So Mas de Daumas Gassac was more than a vineyard, it was a sort of Ark, conserving the genetic diversity of the ancient vineyards of Bordeaux.

The Domergues, fifty miles further west, have a more formally organized rare vines collection, started in 1991. This is largely stocked from the collection of 3,800 pre-phylloxera vines grown by the *Institut Nationale de la Recherche Agronomique* in the protective environment of the Mediterranean sands outside Sète. Daniel's collection numbers about fifteen different varieties. One point of doing this is to have a living link with the pre-phylloxera South and its all-but-extinct varieties – and to know what its wines actually tasted like.

This sort of experience of the subject is not always required in order to be considered an expert. Daniel enjoys telling the story of one of his academic colleagues, a professor who lectured at one of France's leading oenology departments. This man had spoken inspirationally on the delicious flavour of Piquepoul Noir, formerly one of the noblest varieties of the Languedoc, described by one authority as making wines 'rich in bouquet, full of scents of flowers and fruit, not tannic, elegant and very original'.[1] Daniel was inspired, tracked down a source offering a small quantity of Piquepoul grapes, and did a micro-vinification – the tricky procedure of making wine in a container little bigger than a piece of kitchen equipment. He presented the resulting wine at a conference. 'Ah,' said the delighted professor, taking a glass, 'the first time in my life that I've tasted Piquepoul Noir.'

As noted in Chapter Three, the Domergues have plunged into the debate over Carignan, the variety planted after phylloxera to meet the demand for bulk wine. There are those, like Sylvain Fadat in Montpeyroux, who claim these old vines as a neglected treasure. However, one thing the couple especially dislike is visitors who gush about *le vieux Carignan*. Patricia thinks the only reason people don't grub it all up is a pious reverence for the grapes that made their families so much money in the past.

You can be interested in obscure varieties while still believing, *pace* Aimé Guibert, that there is some sort of hierarchy of excellence in grapes. Randall Grahm, who has popularized many neglected varieties and makes quite a bit of Carignan, has reluctantly come to accept this. 'I hate to admit it as it doesn't tie in with my egalitarian principles,' he sighs.

In the Languedoc-Roussillon, Syrah, Grahm's all-time favourite variety, is the 'improving' variety of choice. Faugères is one of the smallest of the Languedoc *appellations*, its separate existence due to its pioneer status. The Alquier family, who have lived there for five generations, were the first in the Languedoc to plant the varieties of the Rhône and Provence: Syrah, Grenache and Mourvèdre. It was the idea of Gilbert Alquier, the father of the current proprietor, who had been a *négociant* in Paris selling rather ordinary wines, including a little from his, then, insignificant vineyards. This property has anticipated the trend of the more ambitious growers of the region: the change from selling wine in cask to selling in bottle and the move away from Carignan. 'We don't do much with it now,' says Jean-Michel, who's now in charge. His wines are big but elegant, admired even by those who normally shy away from the all-stops-out, oaked wine experience.

Syrah is carrying all before it just now. It has a big exponent in Gérard Gauby, a wine-maker down in the French Pyrenees. Like the earlier pioneer Gilbert Alquier, Gauby is a great fan of the wines of the Rhône. The character they display in the Rhône's northern sector – leathery, liquoricy, black-curranty – comes from using Syrah on its own. Gérard is big, slow-moving, relaxed; his wines follow the general rule and reflect his personality. He likes the extra oomph that comes from new barrels, provided that the stuff that goes into them is dense and extracted enough to shrug off oak flavours without being dominated. His wine runs no such risk. 'Here,' he says, with a twinkle, filling a glass from a barrel with a pipette-full of an impenetrable black liquid. 'Try something lightweight. Beaujolais-style.'

Marc Parcé likes Syrah too, but rather in the way that English conservationists have a soft spot for grey squirrels. He's worried that this brash intruder will crowd out the local Grenache from its traditional niche in Collioure, a small port on the Mediterranean coast some thirty miles south of the *Domaine Gauby*. In particular he's upset about a change in the *appellation* rules for Collioure, that in future will permit other producers, notably the local co-op, to make a wine that has little or nothing to do with its historic identity as a dry, Grenache-dominated wine.

Grenache is the world's most widely planted red grape, so it may seem unnecessary to be overprotective of it. As it also makes the greatest Châteauneuf-du-Pape, contributes to the most sought-after Spanish red wine, Vega Sicilia, and is the variety used for the irreplaceable sweet red and tawny wines made in the vicinity of Collioure, at Banyuls, Maury and Rivesaltes, you might think that its reputation was secure. But it suffers from a possibly fatal handicap: it's almost impossible to come up with a snappy description for it, along the lines of the famous equatings of 'cat's pee on a gooseberry bush' for Sauvignon Blanc, 'blackcurrants and cigar boxes' for Cabernet Sauvignon or 'sweaty saddles' for Syrah.

In desperation you find yourself hunting for points of resemblance between Marc Parcé and the grape he is championing. It would be pushing even the bounds of wine writing a little too far to say that Grenache was articulate, feline, smart-but-casual in the way of successful French middle-class professionals – just as it would be to say that the neatly bearded M. Parcé was high in natural alcohol, low in colour and tannin and prone to partial flowering or *coulure*.

When Marc Parcé gets talking on the subject of the change in the *appellation* he is so fluent that my notes hardly keep up. His gist is that his fellow growers are suffering from an unnecessary ebb of confidence. 'The real issue is whether Collioure is to be something that expresses a particular history and a particular culture, or whether it's going to reflect a market trend and become a varietal wine. Sure, Syrah happens to be in fashion. But if the wine loses its distinctive character the price will collapse with it. Look what's happened to the price of generic Chardonnay, it's down to four to eight francs a litre in bulk. This is the threat facing all the French *appellations*. We would be crazy to imitate the Anglo-Saxons. The *appellations* are where our real richness lies – in the fact that one *terroir* is different from another *terroir*.'

Super Carignan, Super Cinsault, Super Grenache, Super Mourvèdre, Super Syrah

Super Carignan: **Domaine d'Aupilhac, Vin de Pays de Montbaudile**, £6.50, Adnams. When a grower gives you a bottle to taste at home you're meant to make notes, not swig and forget. But I wasn't so doped with pleasure as to forget the point of this wine: its fruitiness makes you believe you love the sometimes dusty-tasting Carignan for itself, and not just as raw material for clever wine-making.

Super Cinsault: **Clos des Centeilles, Minervois 1990, P&D Domergue**, £9.70, Adnams (01502 727222). Ethereal and unique: a light but concentrated dry red wine with hints of sugared almonds, spice and violets. You have to pause in order to get it, hence this unflattering-looking rating: Oddness: 4/5 Niceness: 2/5.

Super Grenache: there's lots of virtually straight Grenache in Spain and the Southern Rhône, but in the Languedoc-Roussillon there are fewer champions. **Jean-Marc Jeannin** at **Mas Cremat** has stuck with Grenache for his basic **Côtes du Roussillon**, from Gelston Castle Fine Wines, London SW1 (0171 821 6841), and there's **Marc Parcé** with his **Collioure**, from Tremayne and Webb, Bacchus of Olney and Gauntley's of Nottingham (numbers below).

Super Mourvèdre: **Séléction du Vieux Relais, Costières de Nîmes 1993**, approx £7–8 from Bacchus of Olney, Bucks (01234 711140) Gauntley's, Nottingham (0115 9110557), Tremayne and Webb, Essex (01277 890525). This producer's Mouvèdre is a dark, meaty wine and reminded me of dried fruits: prunes and figs.

Super Syrah: this dark aromatic grape is the variety everyone reaches for. Pioneers include: in Faugères – **Gilbert Alquier et Fils**, in Booths supermarkets, Tanners, Victoria Wine; in Costières de Nîmes – **Château Mourgues du Gres**, Enotria Winecellars, London NW10 0181 961 4411, around £6.00; in the Roussillon – **Gérard Gauby** at Threshers and the Wine Society, among others.

After a while you can't escape the 'who cares if it's authentic provided it tastes good?' question put by Anglo-Saxon pragmatists. If Syrah makes the wine more attractive and saleable, why fight progress?

Robert Plageoles has been listening to this argument for twenty years, not least from his former clients, Mark Williamson and Tim Johnstone, the English proprietors of Willi's Wine Bar in Paris. They were thrilled with the Sauvignon Blanc he made on his 25 hectares of vineyards in Gaillac, thirty miles north-east of Toulouse. But the Sauvignon was never a labour of love; he planted it because, under the rules of the Gaillac *appellation*, it was a mandatory 'improving variety' (*cépage ameliorateur*). Now he's tearing it out again, quite happy to do without the orders from Willi's and, if it comes to it, to have his wine delisted and be required to sell as a *vin de pays*.

Like Marc Parcé, he thinks the rush to embrace internationally known varieties is self-defeating. 'We're competing against New Zealand, Australia, Chile. Making our wines closer to international tastes only makes sense if you go in for this globalist philosophy. It's the outlook that says you have to go for the lowest common denominator, to let consumer fashions dictate everything. What we're doing is to rediscover our own wines and then to find a clientele that's interested. We are about creating a fashion of our own, not following a global trend. And we're not forcing anyone to share our point of view.'

South-West Trends: Gaillac

Whether the wines of the South-West are called Bergerac, Côtes de Duras, Côtes de Buzet or Côtes de Marmandais they're still Bordeaux grape varieties. But Gaillac, a bit further on from Bordeaux, is an oddity, even if you discount the off-dry, lightly sparkling white wine (a modern invention of the local co-op).

Domaine des Tres Cantous and Domaine Roucou-Cantemerle, Robert Plageoles. Tel 0033 (0)63 33 90 40

Plageoles' **Vin de Voile** (see page 125) is imported by Richards Walford, Stamford, Lincs (01780 460451), who also have stocks of his dessert wine, **Vin d'Autun**.

Domaine des Causses Marines, Patrice Lescarret

Les Greilles: a blend of Muscadelle and Len L'El ('out of sight' in Languedocian French). Cooked apricots and something recalling the long lost flavour of Barretts Sweet Cigarettes.

Mauzac: pears, white cherries and angelica. Surprisingly robust. Lescarret actively combats the tendency of Mauzac to sparkle by exposing the wine to tiny quantities of oxygen, following the technique devised by Patrick Ducornau in Madiran (see page 226).
Plus, **Grain de Folie**: the botrytized dessert wine, described on page 112.
£8, £8 and £9 respectively from Morris and Verdin, London SE1, 0171 357 8877.

Without compulsion, though, he has acquired one local disciple (apart from his son Bernard). This is Patrice Lescarret, a young oenologist who was drawn to put down roots in Gaillac by his admiration for Plageoles' lack of compromise. 'The easiest thing would be for me to plant Sauvignon everywhere, ferment with selected yeasts and I'd have a perfect marketing project. But my conception is about making wine and not perfume; I'm not interested in making an aromatic wine.' And is this approach catching on? 'Well, locally they call me "the mad *vigneron*".'

The traditional-variety crowd certainly seem to want to make life hard on themselves. To get their Cinsault on song, the Domergues have settled for yields roughly a quarter of their neighbours.

As Cinsault is light in tannin and colour they have to macerate it in the fermentation tanks for no fewer than eight weeks, with constant *pigeage*. It would be so much simpler to pump the wine up with some Syrah and reap the rewards available to those who conform.

Robert Plageoles makes no fewer than twenty different wines on his property. Most of these are from Mauzac, his apple-scented variety that makes the sparkling Blanquette de Limoux of South Western France. In its other manifestations it's something less than a crowd-pleaser; in *Vines, Grapes and Wines* Jancis Robinson sides with her compatriots at Willi's Wine Bar and dismisses it as 'a bit tart'. Yet Plageoles manages to find in it potential for a huge gamut of styles. There's a dry white and an unctuous *moelleux*. There's a sherry-like *vin de voile*: certain strains of Mauzac are apparently especially favourable for the development of the same *flor* yeast that grows on Fino. There's a *gaillac nature*: this is like an early evolutionary cousin of Champagne and used to be the main speciality of the area. The wine is fermented, filtered several times through muslin and bottled before all the grape sugars are fermented out. Next spring the returning warmth creates a slight second fermentation in the bottle.

It seems unfair that growers like Plageoles, Parcé and the Domergues should live at odds with their local *appellation* committees when what drives them on, above all else, is local pride. The Domergue's pure Cinsault wine, called Capitelle de Centeilles, is conceived almost as a manifesto for the region. The variety is the most ancient one still in use in the Minervois *appellation*. The style is fine, lively and perfumed. Patricia wants to convey the idea that the old culture of the Languedoc was one of grace and refinement, not a message sent out by the huge, black, oaky Syrah wines that are fashionable just now.

Robert Plageoles takes the same historical long view. He believes the property at Sallettes that his family has occupied since 1430 to be the oldest vineyard in Gaillac, itself perhaps the oldest of all the French vineyards, with a history pre-dating the Roman occupation of Gaul. When, fumbling for words, I talk about him 'creating' a style of wine he immediately pulls me up short: 'I'm not inventing anything. I'm rediscovering what had been lost.'

The world has so many different grape varieties. For a grower it would take many lifetimes to find out how each one performs on a given site. For people like Plageoles the right solution is to begin where earlier generations left off and explore to the full the possibilities of the best local grapes. Just because such growers don't replant and replant with the restless New World energy of a Randall Grahm does not mean they can spend most of the year sitting back and waiting for their ancient vines to ripen. Far from it.

1 Pierre Galet, *Cépages et Vignobles de France.*

17

A Yielding Disposition

It's a struggle to translate the modern word wine-maker into French. Surprising as it may seem in a country that has had wine for at the least two thousand years, the best bet is to say *'un wine-maker'*. Small producers in France are, as they have always been, *vignerons*: growers whose first concern is the vine. Wine-making requires skill and it's vital not to throw away in the cellar what has been achieved in the vineyard. But the major task each year is to grow the best possible grapes.

This will rarely involve thinking about grape varieties. In most areas there is no choice: if you want to make fine wine in the Mosel you have to grow Riesling; in the hills around Verona, Corvina; for red wine in the Loire, Cabernet Franc; for Burgundy, Pinot Noir. If you want higher yields you may be tempted to replant with selected clones offered by your local research station, but ambitious growers are more likely to want to keep long-established vines, which give low yields but the best and most complex flavours.

Since most writers are chiefly interested in the-winemaker-as-hero and in discussing the relative merits of different varieties, the grower's work in the vineyard doesn't get much attention. Nor is it in the interest of the major players in the industry that it should. In rich countries where labour is expensive, the last fifty years have seen every possible effort to mechanize the vineyards and hence cut costs. In poor countries like Chile or South Africa, the pruning and training of the vines is done by estate labourers, who don't attract much notice from visiting foreigners.

A traditionally managed vineyard almost always has people in it. Where the soils are rich and the vines are closely spaced a conscientious owner will plough the soil. There are three separate operations, and in France each has its own associated term.

After the grape harvest there is *buttage*, with the plough creating a v-shaped groove between the rows of vines, banking up earth over the graft where the vine joins the rootstock and so protecting it from frost. Ploughing in the spring, or *debuttage*, is to uncover the vine so that the grower can remove all unwanted sideshoots. The final task, in the early summer, is called *griffage* (scratching). This time the plough lays the soil flat, digging in the weeds and opening up the surface so that rain can penetrate to the roots of the vines.

The alternative, for the last few decades, has been to treat the soil with herbicides. But for many independent growers, ploughing is a badge of honour and a sign that they're not to be numbered among their time-serving neighbours (who, typically, will sell to the local co-op rather than bottling their own wine). The ploughing faction claims that the main benefit lies in stopping the plants developing a shallow root system and forcing them instead to send their roots deep into the ground. Shallow-rooting vines in unbroken soils, it's alleged, become waterlogged when it rains and drought-stricken when it doesn't. Deep roots find the marginal but constant supply of water that gives great wine.

Henri Goyard of the village of Mâcon-Viré is passionate on this topic. 'Once you've started with chemicals you can't stop; the roots of the vines come up to the surface. If my neighbours restarted ploughing now they'd kill off half their vines.' French wine journalists are equally sold on the practice, to the extent that even growers who use herbicides find it politic to turn over the soil in the most accessible part of their vineyard.

In *Burgundy* Anthony Hanson reports on the firmly rooted belief in ploughing among growers of that region. He suggests, though, that it is quite recently acquired. Before the mass replanting of the late nineteenth century in the wake of the devastation caused by phylloxera he notes that vineyards weren't planted in orderly rows but in a huddle (*en foule*) and in these conditions, he contends, ploughing would have been impossible.

Ploughing by horse certainly would have been impossible. But the terrifying fact is that the ancient French vineyards *were* worked – by hand. Bollinger, the Champagne house, maintain a tiny walled vineyard behind their headquarters in the village of Aÿ planted *en foule* with ungrafted vines never affected by phylloxera.

I visited Bollinger with a group on the day in late September that this unique vineyard was picked. For a while there were more journalists, visitors and TV technicians than pickers; then they got going in full swing and in half an hour the crop was gone, to make a tiny number of bottles of ultra-expensive Champagne.

Looking at a living medieval vineyard is like experiencing the sight of the Elgin marbles still with their ancient Athenian colouring or a Gothic cathedral with all its stained glass intact. Whereas European vineyards are planted about twice as close as those in the New World, these are twice as dense again. The grapes are borne in pitifully low yields on four shoots, each of which represents that year's growth. After the harvest three canes will be removed and one cut back to four growth-points and then entirely buried in the ground. In the winter nothing shows but the huddle of stakes to which the four new shoots will be attached.

(One consequence of this technique is that the whole vineyard is creeping uphill. Each time the cane is buried the new growth emerges a foot or so distant from its previous position. So each year the vines at the far vineyard wall have to be dug up and replanted at the bottom.)

And the soil of the vineyard is worked by hand. I didn't see the special hoe ('binette'), but Corinne Bricout of Bollinger described it. It apparently looks much like the hand-tool used to scrape tartrate crystals off the inside of old barrels.

Even a conventional vineyard, planted to allow a special tractor to be driven straddling the vines, demands endless work if it's to be kept in order. Small growers do this using their own labour, while bigger scale producers with many acres to manage are generally eager to take up cost-cutting innovations.

In the Entre Deux Mers, one of the less highly-rated sub-divisions of Bordeaux, you can see the two philosophies in competition. Until after the war the area was dedicated to inexpensive sweet white wines, that only rarely had the benefit of the *Botrytis* infection that descends regularly on Sauternes on the other bank of the Garonne River. The Sémillon and Sauvignon vines were grown according to the same system used elsewhere in Bordeaux, trained on cordons one and a half metres high in rows one metre apart.

Benjamin Mazeau's father changed the face of the region. René Mazeau settled there soon after the war as a young science graduate, married Benjamin's mother and took responsibility for the 200 hectares that today is divided among Benjamin and his brothers. With the encouragement of a group of similarly minded young producers he made two profound changes: he replaced the white grapes with red, and imported a revolutionary system of vineyard management from Austria, the so called *vignes hautes*, or 'high-wire' system.

High-wire training is a distant descendant of the ancient practice of running vines up trees. It means taking out every other row of vines, and doubling the height of those that are left to compensate. As devised by Austria's largest producer, Lenz Moser, it opens up the vineyard for mechanization. When replanting after phylloxera, the French allowed enough space for the horse-plough. The Lenz Moser system creates broad avenues, grassed over rather than ploughed, with weedkiller used to keep the ground clear immediately under the vines.

'It was thanks to this that the whole region survived,' says Benjamin. 'But now people are turning against the *vignes hautes*. There are the most terrible polemics between the two sides. It gets very heated – *ça fait beaucoup de bruit*.'

A plantation of *vignes hautes* allows easy access for mechanical harvesters, which shake the vines till the individual grapes fall off. These were first used in New York State in the 1960s to harvest Concord grapes (one of the varieties derived from the American wild vines that till recently have been the mainstay of the wine industry of the Eastern states). This is much cheaper than using human grape pickers, but the machines tend to break the grapes' skins, allowing oxidation, and to introduce such detritus as leaves, stalks and insects. The *vignes hautes* also allow for mechanical pruning, with saws that zip through the last year's growth, leaving a spur of wood along the lower wire of the cordon from which the next year's shoots will burst.

For traditionalists mechanical pruning is a heresy. Pruning by hand takes most of the winter months, and growers say that it's the single most important operation in determining the quality of next year's crop. Charlie Lea of the London wine-merchants Lea and Sandeman jokes that when he's at a wine fair looking for new producers, he makes a point of looking for 'growers' hands', toughened and thickened by work on thousands of vines.

Growers recognize their handiwork – in an apparently continuous vineyard at Moulin-à-Vent in Beaujolais, Maurice Gay was immediately able to say he was among his own vines rather than his neighbour's by looking at the way he'd placed the cuts.

The vital thing is to restrict the number of growth points, but not to prune so hard as to overstimulate the vine. And in a hand-trimmed vineyard pruning is just the first of many operations. After the vines have flowered the leaf-bearing shoots need to be prevented from sprouting too luxuriously; they are usually pinned between wires and excess growth is removed. In some years yields will have been reduced by frost at the time of flowering or by hail. If the vineyard survives these hazards it may run the opposite risk of overcropping and hence producing underflavoured grapes. One solution, pioneered by the *négociants* and vineyard owners J-P Moueix, is a so-called 'green harvest', removing a proportion of the bunches while they are still immature. And even right up to the time of the grape harvest the dedicated *vigneron* will still be in the vineyard, this time picking off faded leaves that might harbour grey rot and mould.

In the Entre Deux Mers the tide of opinion is flowing against the *vignes hautes*. Even at the Australian-managed Château Carsin, the wine-maker Mandy Jones favours the traditional planting densities. The main French objection is founded in the national belief, enshrined in the rules of the *appellation controllée* system, that you must have low yields to make great wine. *Vignes hautes* vineyards have half as many vines as conventional ones, but do not have half the yields: therefore each vine must be bearing much more fruit than usual. I worked this out while Benjamin Mazeau was taking me along a row of Merlot (after a brief pause to look at the horses in a nearby paddock – his equal passion is going out riding with his wife). As soon as I reached my conclusion I blurted it out, then regretted it. 'Ah,' said Benjamin, ruefully. 'That's exactly the point our opponents make.' Arguments among French growers recall the doctrinal struggles of the Communist Party or the Byzantine church, and I sensed the intolerance directed at those who have not yet signed up for the new orthodoxy. Are they taking a hammer to crack a nut? 'All we're trying to do is to make easy-to-drink wines at an attractive price,' he pleads. 'And they age pretty well.'

During the 1960s, when the fashion for the *vignes hautes* was in full swing, Australians and Californians alike would have said that the Europeans' obsession with manicuring their vineyards was pretty irrelevant to the quality of their wine. It was during this time that the nine square miles of Coonawarra in South Australia were first fully planted up with vines. According to James Halliday and Hugh Johnson in *The Art and Science of Wine*, until 1979 the Coonawarra vines were left completely unpruned during the winter, following a philosophy of minimal maintenance.

But today shaggy-looking vineyards are out of favour. Dr Tony Jordan, who as a consultant helped set up many if not most of Australia's new independent vineyards of the last two decades, welcomes the new fashion for neatness. He hails this as an instance of science unearthing the logic underlying a traditional practice.

At Wynn's Coonawarra Estate, the largest of the properties in the area, they haven't brought back hand pruning; Paula Benson, the assistant vineyard manager, points out that in a region four hours by car from Melbourne or Adelaide they couldn't get the labour. 'We're right out in a country area, with only small towns surrounding us, so we don't have a strong community.' But if she could hand prune, she would. 'We've got a lot of dead wood that can inhibit air flow and act as a source for spores. My personal opinion is that we could really produce some outstanding quality and possibly reduce the risk of disease if we could go back to hand pruning.'

Old World growers should pause before they feel too flattered that their vineyard practices are now being imitated. The most influential New World viticulturalist says that if they were right it was for the wrong reasons. This guru is Dr Richard Smart, a former lecturer at Roseworthy Agricultural College, South Australia, and author of the manual *Sunlight into Wine*. He appears in his book photographed in a T-shirt saying 'canopy management rules OK' and with a trim beard that bears witness to conscientious pruning.

Other photographs show the best and worst possible vineyard practice. The ideal is represented by neat vines at Château Haut-Brion, the first-growth Bordeaux estate. The examples of the vineyards at their nadir come from California and South Australia: huge eruptions of leaves and tendrils, recalling the Thompson detectives' uncontrollably growing hair in the Tintin story *Explorers on the Moon*.

Dr Smart gives credit to the wisdom of centuries that has bequeathed growers a model of the ideal vine. Its leaves will be well exposed and there will be plenty of them in relation to the number of grape clusters; a high relative proportion of leaves is essential if the grapes are to ripen fully.

But this is the prelude to a debunking of tradition. Low yields, he suggests, are not necessary to make great wine. Low-yielding vines, old vines, vines on poor soil will all tend to have open leaf canopies and a high ratio of leaf to fruit. It is this that makes their grapes taste so good, not their low yields. Low yields are a cause and not an effect.

'Does high yield cause decreased quality,' he asks, 'or is there little or no effect?' In answer there are pages of endorsements from Australian growers testifying to the benefits of the innovative training and trellising systems which, Smart believes, can square the circle and unite quality with quantity. John Cassegrain from the Hunter Valley has doubled his yields. Vanya Cullen in the Margaret River, Western Australia had seen crops decline to uneconomic levels; she installed the Scott-Henry trellising system and was rewarded with Chardonnay production at up to 4 tons an acre (70–80 hectolitres of juice per hectare) with no loss in quality.

Conspicuously absent from this roll-call are Stephen and Pru Henschke, the proprietors of Australia's most celebrated vineyard: Hill of Grace in the Barossa, planted probably in the 1850s.

Hill of Grace makes a Shiraz wine that comes equal first with Penfolds Grange in any Australian roll of honour. The wines are both based on Barossa Shiraz, but come out of such different stables as to be excused from a head-to-head contest. Hill of Grace is produced from a single vineyard; Grange is a blend, not only of vineyards but of grape varieties: mainly Barossa old vine Shiraz, but with a small addition of Cabernet Sauvignon.

The Henschkes no longer see eye to eye with Richard Smart after collaborating with him in experiments on their property: in particular restructuring a less historic vineyard in their ownership along the lines he recommended. His offence was to declare the Hill of Grace vineyard ripe for improvement, as currently uneconomic, and to urge that it should be retrellised and irrigated to give higher yields (something he has not yet, as far as I know, urged on the proprietors of Château Haut-Brion). Pru Henschke was unenthusiastic. 'Would we see an improvement in quality?' she asks, rhetorically. 'It would destroy that vineyard.'

When the couple dug their heels in he went public. 'We got some very derogatory comments from him,' says Pru. 'He criticizes us for not having economic vineyards. It's very annoying when he goes and writes things in the local rag about our lack of response to his ideas. He doesn't like the old vine theory, the low-yielding theory. He thinks people should rip out their old vines and look for more economical grape production.'

The clash between the Henschkes and Richard Smart has reson-ances that travel beyond the Barossa Valley, South Australia. Growers are farmers whose income depends on the size of the harvest. As well they are often wine nuts with a self-imposed mission to extract the best possible quality from their parcel of land, and let economics go hang. With the prices they get for their wine Stephen and Pru Henschke manage to win both ways.

Irrigation comes into the controversy over yields and trellising; a water supply is essential to nourish the big high-yielding vines espoused by Richard Smart. Pru Henschke thinks it's better to do without it where possible, for the sake both of the quality of the grapes and of the Australian environment.

'He's developed these theories in New Zealand where water isn't an issue. But in Australia these resources are so restricted that the viticultural industry needs to screw its head on. To get high yields we'd be asking the government to bring in Murray River water at a huge cost to soils and the environment.'

Richard Smart's message that high yields can make good wine is one that the Australian industry, as opposed to a minority of 'dry vine' farmers, would dearly like to hear. Since 1950 the country has trebled production without increasing the total vineyard area.[1] Lost within the global figures, some Australian grape farmers are producing crops at levels that must be near a world record.[2] Rob Gibson, the grape supply manager for the Southcorp group's Pen-folds operation, talks of yields of 16 tons to the acre, the equivalent of some 280–320 hectolitres per hectare.[3] These he says are 'generally associated with poor quality' – and indeed it's hard to imagine any trellis on earth that could support a vine with a large enough leaf canopy to bring such a monstrous weight of fruit to proper maturity.

Rob Gibson features in *Sunlight into Wine*, praising the scientific yardsticks devised by Richard Smart for determining the condition of a crop. He writes: 'Vineyard assessment has been a useful tool for selection and isolation of premium grape bunches.'

After reading the book I had a question for him. If Smart is right in arguing that yield and quality are not linked, why does Penfolds, Rob Gibson's employer, pay top whack for Shiraz fruit from ancient low-yielding Barossa vines in order to make Grange Hermitage?

When his call came in from Nuriootpa, the little town in the Barossa that's dominated by various Southcorp installations and subsidiaries, I felt a little disorientated. This was partly because I'd got up before 7am to ring Australia but more because, using the jargon of his special field, he seemed to be saying that low yields *do* make better wine.

Point one: 'If you're talking about premium wine production, the higher value products are associated with the low end of yields. My "low end of yield" is something below 8 tons per hectare, say 5–8 tons per hectare.'

(These are highish yields in the context of the best European wines, but nothing out of the way, translating as 40–64 hectolitres per hectare. Champagne growers make some of the most expensive juice in the world, getting prices of more than £3 a litre even though their yields are over 70 hectolitres per hectare.)

Point two: The old vineyards, as far as Penfolds are concerned, produce grapes with a quality which derives from something more mysterious than the balance of leaf canopy to fruit load. 'The whole style and structure of Grange Hermitage, like many of the classic wines of the world, is built around low yields.'

In Australia this philosophy is gaining rather than losing ground. The Mitchelton estate in the Goulburn region of Victoria has always managed to ripen its fruit, even though irrigation has helped to make it extremely productive. But now they've decided to turn the taps off and cut yields. The wine-maker Don Lewis says: 'We've decided on a complete change in our viticultural approach. We're changing the trellising, using a sward between the vines to drive the roots down, getting more intensity into the grapes. I've been here for twenty-five years but until recently I haven't had much control over the vineyard; but I've known all along it was possible. I've known some other vineyards in Victoria produce some fantastic, really deeply characterful Cabernet and Shiraz.'

When Colin Preece planned Mitchelton thirty years ago he stocked it with unfashionable varieties but envisaged the same regime as had been introduced in the Coonawarra properties: irrigation, mechanization and unrestricted yields. Don Lewis comments: 'In the 1960s they did the best they could; it was up-to-date as far as technology was concerned.'

Indeed Mitchelton is continuing to use partial mechanical pruning, while bringing in vineyard workers with secateurs to make the final cut to control the number of growth points and so help determine how much fruit each vine will produce. I ask Don for his comments on the theory that high yields don't affect quality. 'I don't agree with it at all, not for one minute. The vine can ripen fruit at ten tons to the acre if there's enough leaf to fruit ratio. But the vine can only give you a certain amount of character, whether it's Marsanne or Shiraz. Above a certain level it just becomes dilute. The sugars will get there but not the flavours.'

Even if the realities of the market in Richard Smart's home country don't always sustain his theory, I do sympathize with his scientist's impatience to understand just why low yields should make wine better. What is the mechanism? If it isn't just about the leaf canopy, then what? Rob Gibson says he asked a visiting British professor of horticulture what the secret was of getting the best flavour in fruit. 'He said: "The same way that I get the best out of the tomatoes in my back yard – I neglect them." '

If, like me, you've been drip-fed the idea that science is successfully and relentlessly laying bare the secrets of the vineyard, it's disappointing to receive an answer that could come straight out of any issue of *Practical Gardening*. But if science can't explain the low yield/old vine effect it can at least measure it: Patrick Iland at the Waite Research Institute in South Australia has measured anthocyanin, the colour component in grapes, from vines producing every sort of yield. The results suggest different conclusions on the cut-off point for quality wines to those reached by Rob Gb1son. At between 6 and 20 tons per hectare (48–160 hectolitres per hectare) there was little difference. But below six tons every reduction in yield created an exponential increase in anthocyanins.

A discussion of yields is never complete without an obligatory quotation from Pliny the Elder, the naturalist and admiral of the Roman fleet, on the subject of the wine of Falernum. These vineyards were fifty miles to the north of the bay of Naples, both his home and the scene of his death in AD79 while observing the great eruption of Vesuvius that destroyed Pompeii. He wrote in Book XIV of his *Natural History* that 'Second in reputation [in Italy] is the district of Falernum and in particular the vineyard of Faustinius, due to the care and attention he has paid to it; this reputation is fading through the fault of paying more attention to quantity than quality.'⁴

It's a pity the old boy hadn't added some comments on the age of the vines as well. Elsewhere he quotes one scathing comment on a primitive piece of high-training, on elm trees: 'It's said that Cineas, the ambassador of King Pyrrhus, was astonished at the height of the vines at La Riccia [in northern Apulia] and joked that given the roughness of the wine, its parent vine thoroughly deserved to be punished by being strung up.'⁵

Wines of the Ancient World

No one knows quite what Roman wine tasted like; however ampelographers – that is, scientists specializing in identifying grapes and their origins – have made some tentative moves to say which of the grapes found in European vineyards since time immemorial can be identified with varieties described by Pliny and other classical writers.

Pierre Galet, the doyen of French ampelographers, detects the following traces of antiquity in his *Cépages et Vignobles de France* (Grape varieties and vineyards of France).

Cabernet Franc and **Cabernet Sauvignon** are both locally known as the *Bidure*. Many authors link this name with the *Biturica*, the vine grown by the *Bituriges Vibusci*, a Gallic tribe living near modern Bordeaux during the reign of Augustus, the first emperor who ruled at the time of the birth of Christ.

César – Pierre Galet says this was brought to Yonne (the *département* of Chablis) by the Roman legions, hence its name. It gives a 'hard', highly coloured wine. Only 2 hectares are left in cultivation.

Elbling – a high-producing, mediocre variety largely found in the

Mosel. One writer quoted by Galet, an A. Berget, derives its name from the great German river the Elbe (Latin: *Albis*), with the 'pejorative' suffix 'ling' (as in 'Earthling') to carry the sense of both the place of origin and inferiority.

The **Muscat** family (Muscat Blanc à Petits Grains AKA Muscat de Frontignan, Muscat d'Alexandrie and Muscat de Hamburg) The name is connected with the latin for a fly – *mosca*, which becomes *mouche* in French. The word covers all sorts of flying insects and the reference is to the appeal of these ultra-scented berries to bees and wasps, not houseflies.

Galet identifies Muscat grapes with the varieties called the *anathelicon moschaton* by the ancient Greeks and the *apianae* by the Romans. Muscat Blanc was brought to the Languedoc by the Romans, if not the Greeks, and began to be the basis of a widely exported wine by the time of Charlemagne.

Pinot Noir – Galet identifies this with one variety referred to by the Roman agronomist Columella. Some claim to see its characteristically rounded leaf in a Gallo-Roman bas-relief.

Riesling – some authors identify the great Rhine grape with the Roman *Argitis Minor*.

Syrah – Galet quotes both the view that this variety (the Australian 'Shiraz') arrived in the Rhône in the third century, when the emperor Probus relaxed a ban on vineyards outside Italy, and the legend that it was introduced by the crusading Chevalier de Sterimbourg who brought plants from either Shiraz in Iran or from Cyprus to set up the vineyard on the hill overlooking Tain l'Hermitage. Still other historians think it comes from Syracuse in Sicily. Oddly it isn't found in any of its supposed places of origin.

Trebbiano – Pliny talks about *Vinum Trebulanum* grown in the region of Naples. It arrived in France in the fourteenth century during the period when the papacy was based in Avignon. Under the name of Ugni Blanc, it's the main grape variety of Cognac, a major source of neutral Italian white wine, and the fourth most widely planted variety in the world.

While it's enjoyable to speculate, Sr Jaime Rodriguez, author of a work in progress on the 'Lost vines of Spain', points out that there isn't a shred of real evidence. Some grape pips have survived from antiquity; what would clinch the matter would be some traces of Roman pollen – these would be as good as a fingerprint or a DNA test result.

If you want to taste the grapes the Romans tasted, the surest bet is to stick to the Italian peninsula. The grape of Falernum was the *Vitis Hellenica* (Greek Vine) and it makes a very good modern wine in the form of the sexy, rugged **Aglianico del Vulture d'Angelo** from Basilicata in Southern Italy, imported by Alivini of North London (0181 880 2525) and sold, among others, by Lay and Wheeler of Colchester (01206 764446).

1 *A History of the Australian Wine Industry 1949–94* James Halliday, pub: The Australian Wine and Brandy Corporation.
2 There's little scope or incentive to bring these yields down. The industry's target, set out in the '2020' discussion document is, officially, to march steadily forward to supply 10 per cent of the world's wine, from the present level of 4 per cent. This will require a lot more water, in a country whose main rivers, the Murray and the Darling, have already been reduced to a trickle by the time they reach the sea. Most of the new water, it's hoped, can be found by diverting irrigation from declining industries like cotton and rice; but the industry envisaged in 2020 would make a significant claim on previously untapped water resources.
3 The top legal limit for even the cheapest French wine is around 90 hectolitres to the hectare.
4 *Natural History* Book XIV VIII 62: '*Secunda nobilitas Falerno agro erat et ex eo maxime Faustiano; cura culturaque id coegerat; exolescit haec quoque culpa copiae potius quam bonitati studentium.*'
5 *Natural History*, Book XIV III 12: '*mirant altitudinem earum Ariciae ferunt legatum regis Pyrrhi Cineam facete lusisse in austeriorem gustum vini, merito matrem eius pendere in tam alta cruce.*'

4
THE STATE OF THE ART

Real mystics don't hide mysteries, they reveal them. They set a thing up in broad daylight, and when you've seen it, it's still a mystery.

G. K. Chesterton. *The Incredulity of Father Brown*

Making wine used to mean employing simple techniques to steer and guide a complex and mysterious process. In the twentieth century the technology has become much more complicated and science has supplied a large number of chemical and biological agents with the aim of taking the unpredictability out of winemaking. Many small producers say 'No Thanks'. Is it just sour grapes because they can't afford the latest equipment?

18

When Two Worlds Collide

The two wineries are in the same region but they appear to belong to different eras. From visiting them you'd hardly believe that they make, fundamentally, the same product: red Bordeaux wine.

One was equipped in the early 1990s by a Finnish publishing millionaire. Money was no object. It was designed by the most in-demand Australian expert on winery layout, and boasts doubly-insulated stainless-steel fermentation tanks, plus rotary fermenters that turn slowly, ensuring constant gentle contact between the juice and the skins and pips. It looks terrific as well. An architect lined up the tanks in facing, symmetrical rows and swathed the interior with clean, varnished, new wood, giving a sauna-like impression.

The other dates from the 1960s, but could have been built decades earlier. On the right as you go in there is a vertical press of a type no longer manufactured. The fermentation tanks are made of concrete and, contrary to modern practice, are unlined. After a minute or two people who come to visit – and of these there are a fair number – run out of anything to look at. Although the place might belong to any unprosperous French peasant wine-maker, this is Château Pétrus. For most of recent times it has made the most expensive wine in the world, although it has been pipped for the last year or so by its tiny neighbour in Pomerol, Château Le Pin. Château Carsin, by contrast, sells for around £6 a bottle in Sainsbury's.

In the cellars of Château Pétrus, unlike at Château Carsin, it still appears that 'the art of wine-making is, in comparison with the manufacture of beer or spirits, a relatively simple operation', to quote the 1926 edition of the *Encyclopaedia Britannica*.

This is not the picture given by modern wine laws which give scope for the addition of a large number of unfamiliar substances, as shown, for example, by New Zealand's regulations.

Giving it all they've got?

This is a list of permitted additives in New Zealand wine. The difference between New Zealand and Europe is that the EU doesn't permit Ion Exchange, the use of Isoascorbic Acid or Oak Chips or Extractives. This doesn't make the list of EU-permitted additives significantly shorter.

Ascorbic acid
Calcium and ammonium phosphates
Calcium, sodium and potassium carbonates and bicarbonates
Citric acid
Copper as ions
Dimethylpolysiloxane
Specified enzymes
Fumaric acid
Grape anthocyanins
Isoascorbic acid
Lactic acid

Lactic acid bacteria
Malic acid
Metatartaric and tartaric acid and all their potassium salts
Oak chips
Oak extractives
Polyoxyethylene (40) monostearate
Potable spirit
Silicon dioxide
Silver as ions
Sorbitan monostearate
Yeast

The following fining and stabilizing agents:

Acacia
Activated carbon
Agar
Albumin
Bentonite
Casein
Cellulose fibre filtering aids
Diatomaceous earth
Gelatin
Polyvinylpolypyrrolidine

Ion exchange resins
Isinglass
Kaolin
Milk solids
Phytates
Silica sol
Spanish clay
Tannin
White of egg

The propellant carbon dioxide

The following preservatives:

Sulphur dioxide and sulphites
Sorbic acid and its sodium,

> potassium and calcium salts;
> and Dimethylicarbonate
> The following sweeteners:
>
> Fructose   Glucose syrup
> Glucose   Sugar

Nor are all the unfamiliar chemicals added during wine-making. New Zealand's fashionable white wines are also apt to show measurable levels of fungicide residues, especially in damp vintages. In 1996 the laboratory of the Liquor Control Board of Ontario found traces of Rovral in some of this wine. Rovral is listed by the United States Environmental Protection Agency as a 'probable carcinogen', its highest level of classification. Some of the samples from New Zealand's 1995 vintage represented the highest levels the lab had ever seen for any agricultural chemical, according to its head, Alex Karumanchiri. Although they were still at least a factor of ten below the permitted guidelines, Mr Karumanchiri said he was not satisfied. 'Grapes are permitted the highest levels as a seasonal fruit, but wine drinkers may consume wine every day. Vegetables consumed every day have more stringent limits.'

> *Iprodione levels in 1995 New Zealand white wine*
>
> The Liquor Control Board of Canada tested eighteen New Zealand wines, sixteen white and two red. Of these the average Iprodione level was 0.262 parts per million. Four wines had levels above this average, of 0.328 ppm, 0.681 ppm, 0.781 ppm and 0.971. It is rare to find any detectable Iprodione in wine, according to Mr Karumanchiri.

In the past wine was either adulterated or, by modern standards, very natural. The only vineyard treatments were sulphur and copper sulphate, and the latter, according to Alex Karumanchiri, drops entirely out during maturation leaving no residue in finished wine.

Many growers have reacted to the host of new products on offer for use in the vineyard and cellars by trying to work even without sugar and sulphur.

Sulphur has been used at least since Roman times, and is permitted in both organic and bio-dynamic wine-making. This doesn't mean, though, that everyone's happy about it. As we saw in the first chapter, in Beaujolais there is a circle of disciples of the late Jules Chauvet who make wine without it, although they use a little when bottling.

Sulphur certainly can spoil wine, either through a reaction that creates hydrogen sulphide, the rotten egg gas, or in its raw form creating a burning, ammonia-like sensation at the back of the nose. Some people are actually allergic to it. On the other hand grapes naturally contain some sulphur, and that can deceive tasters into unfounded complaints.

There are growers who go all the way and bottle wine with no sulphur. At the Domaine Gramenon in the hills above Valreas in the Southern Rhône there is a stack of labels saying *Vin issu de Raisins*: wine made from grapes. This sounds uncontentious. In fact it is a statement fraught with legal consequences. To claim your wine is made *only* from grapes is going pretty far even by the standards of the property's owner, Philippe Laurent, a natural rebel (his beard and billowing shirt make him look like an American backwoods wacko – misleadingly in view of his twinkly charm and gentleness of manner). Rather than face having to prove his claim in court, Laurent will probably have to get a fresh set printed.

Some, though not all, of Laurent's *cuvées* are bottled without any sulphur at all. These he warns should be stored at low temperatures. He doesn't add any before fermentation because he wants to keep all the yeasts and microflora alive. He is incredibly solicitous of the welfare of these little creatures. The wine descends with only the aid of gravity into tanks in the cellars he singlehandedly hewed from the rock with a pneumatic drill. To use a pump, he believes, 'stresses the yeasts'.

But his concerns extend to the human race as well. 'By avoiding chemicals I can work without my conscience bothering me. I know I'm not poisoning my customers.'

Laurent's love of his micro-organisms may sound eccentric, but his wines are serious. They were sold to the top Rhône *négociants* in the days before he went fully independent; today all the critics who matter rave about him. And his appeal isn't confined to Europe; Jason Conti, the son of Western Australian wine-maker Paul Conti, returned inspired after working on a vintage with him.

Jean-René Dard and François Ribo, who own a total of 6 hectares near Tain l'Hermitage, have moved away from the
conventional training they had at Beaune University where they
met in the early 1980s. Since the late 1980s they have used no
sulphur at all – for exactly the same reasons of purity as Philippe
Laurent: 'After all, sometimes you feel like drinking quite a bit,'
says Ribo.

The Dard-Ribo cellars close to the Paris–Lyons motorway have
a bit of magic about them. Fermentation takes place in vessels of
all shapes and sizes; all the barrels are ancient. The wines are the
opposite of the dense, dark, oaky concoctions that win prizes in
competitive tasting. They're vibrant, subtle and delicious, reflecting
their makers' taste for young wines that are 'gourmand' – straightforwardly enjoyable. 'Making unfiltered, unsulphured wines is a
whole different art,' according to François Ribo, who gave me
three bottles to take back to London. On the drive back the car
got so hot that the screen of my lap-top computer stopped working,
going a sick-looking yellow when powered up. The wines fared no
better: when opened in London they were more than halfway to
vinegar. Till recently the challenge of keeping these wines deterred
importers; recently though they've been taken on by Yapp Brothers
of Mere, Wiltshire.

One thing that's surprising is the number of growers who impose
a rigorously chemical-free regime on themselves without joining
any official group and without declaring it on the bottle. Jean-
Gérard Guillot is a case in point. He not only cultivates his vines
organically; he also uses the calender published by the French
Biodynamic group, the *Mouvement de Culture Biodynamique*, to
determine when he should carry out vineyard operations.

The idea of the influence of the planets is one of the many hard-
to-swallow aspects of the Biodynamic system, the most extreme
version of organic farming. Biodynamics is regarded as the creation
of the Austrian philosopher, mystic and educationalist Rudolph
Steiner (1861–1925), and the product of his lectures at a week-
long conference on agriculture in 1924. It was elaborated into a
practical system, however, by a German disciple, Maria Thun.

Frau Thun believed, from her observation of the behaviour of
seedlings and rapidly growing vegetables like lettuce and radishes,
that planets influenced plants. According to the state of the zodiac

they might put their energies into the roots, leaves, flowers or fruit. It followed, for example, that planting should only be done on 'root' days.

Organic, Biodynamic, Vegetarian and Vegan

Buried cows' horns play a big part in biodynamic agriculture; so can you call these wines vegetarian, even if they avoid the fining agents (gelatin from bones, isinglass from fish guts or casein from milk) which would disqualify them from Vegetarian or Vegan status?

Yes, according to the Vegetarian Society 'otherwise we'd have to ban vegetables grown with fish and bone meal, and that simply wouldn't be practical'.

There are many more organic, vegetarian etc. wines than are certified as such: plenty of the growers in this book avoid chemical sprays and wine-making treatments. For example, one of the Wine Society's cheaper champagnes, a grower's £13.50 **Fleury Brut**, is biodynamic (contact the Wine Society: 01438 741177).

The following importers specialize in these categories: Bottle Green/Vinceremos of Leeds (0113 257 7545) and Vintage Roots of Wargrave, Berkshire (01734 401222). Bottle Green, who sell to supermarkets, get Vegetarian Society certification; Vintage Roots don't (a fee is involved), but say they carry out thorough checks. One of the most extensive range of organic wines is carried by Planet Organic, 42 Westbourne Grove, London W2 (0171 221 7171).

Other contacts:

The Biodynamic Agriculture Association, Stourbridge, West Midlands 015628 84933

The Soil Association, Bristol 0117 929 0661

The Vegetarian Society, Altringham, Greater Manchester 0161 928 0793

Biodynamics sounds extremely dippy and is hard to reconcile with the robust leathery figure of Jean-Gérard. Indeed, he says, we are not *en biodynamie*. 'Even so,' his wife Jacqueline cuts in, 'any peasant knows there are days when you do things and days when you don't.' Jean-Gérard continues: 'Today isn't good on the planetary level.' (Just as well, I think, considering that it's Saturday lunchtime.) Three weeks ago he finished ploughing between the vines, and did it on a bad day, because he had wanted to get shot of the job. 'The result: the leaves are yellow, the sap's cut off, they're not breathing properly . . .'

I must look sceptical as the conversation takes a combative turn that's familiar in rural France. 'No one can dominate nature; you're paying the price in England, with your mad cows.'

The couple put astrological farming in the context of the ancestral beliefs of the area. 'Everyone knows that the grapes are ready to harvest a hundred days after the flowering of the *fleur-de-lys* – it always works.' When Jean-Gérard worked in Meursault, the wine would only be 'racked' (siphoned into a new barrel off the debris of dead yeast) exactly eight days before a new moon. And wines 'opened' and 'closed' in bottle, became more or less expressive when sniffed, according to atmospheric pressure which in turn corresponded to the phases of the moon.

So why did the Guillots' labels give no hint of their beliefs and practices? 'Lots of people aren't interested in all that. I've no reason to force it on them. Recently I was at a reception given by the wine buyer at a major Paris store with fifteen growers from all over France. It was called *Les Createurs du Vin*. When I got talking I found that thirteen of us were organic without using the word. But the person who'd organized the function was against organic viticulture. I never spoke up. *C'est une question de liberté*. I have the necessary paperwork to go organic. But in some cases it's a racket, anyway. Let's face it, either people like the wine or they don't. The whole philosophy is *in* the wine, not *on* the label.'

I admire the wines made by Jean-Gérard and Jacqueline and liked them as people, but took a suspect pleasure in the conversation. Their beliefs about the moon seemed to qualify them as *bona fide* rustics, and the source of a good anecdote to shock Australians with.

But eventually I discovered that the Guillots' views weren't unrepresentative. Telmo Rodriguez of the Remelluri Estate in Rioja told me that they pruned their young wines at the time of a waxing moon, their old vines at the time of a waning one. This was nothing to do with Biodynamics – Rodriguez had had a two-hour phone call from this movement's chief apostle, Nicholas Joly, without succumbing to his proselytizing – but was simply a traditional local practice.

Soon I realized that the only reason I had not heard more about the moon was that I hadn't asked. The next time the subject came up was quite unexpected. It was in the tasting room of Vintex, a Bordeaux company created by Bill Blatch, a former employee of the Bordeaux subsidiary of Allied Lyons. While Bill was on and off the phone to various big-league customers – Sainsburys and various American importers – I took a look at the eight typed pages of his report on the 1995 vintage.

It was a dramatic story, describing a 'terrible period' from 14 to 20 September, with pickers spending their time cutting out rotten grapes rather than harvesting them, three-quarters of the crop hanging on the vine while water came down in sheets all round. Then the weather cleared in Sauternes and: 'With the New Moon on the 25th there was an invasion of the most beautiful *Botrytis* we had seen for years.' Just in case anyone had overlooked this tribute to the moon, Bill repeated it in a footnote: 'This same co-incidence between the moon and the weather was also presumably [presumably?] responsible for a fantastic crop of "cèpes", the local fleshy boletus mushroom, that occurred during this week in all the woodlands of the region.'

When taxed with being an adept of Biodynamism, Bill replied that, on the contrary, the effects of the moon were widely under-stood and studied in France, and recommended that I looked in Bordeaux's main bookshop for a particular book, whose title he couldn't remember. The shop turned out to stock not one but three books on the moon and gardening.

The next day I raised the subject with Patrick Doche, the pro-prietor of Château Cayla, a small property in the Entre Deux Mers. At once he was up and running. 'The moon has such a big influence on wine,' he declared. 'It's absolutely correct that you shouldn't rack either on a full moon or a new moon. If you do you destroy the wine. They understand this better in Burgundy than here. Let me tell you some other things. A countrywoman in the past would never put the washing out during a full moon if she wanted it to keep its colour. Or something that glaziers know: you can't re-use sheet glass from a shop window. Why? Because with all the light of all those full moons on it it shatters so easily. Or with psychologi-cally disturbed people – anyone who's worked with them will tell you what a devastating effect a full moon has on them.'

M. Cayla had made a botrytized sweet white wine in 1995, taking the *appellation* of the nearby town of Cadillac. 'It was one of the three great vintages of the century,' he said, '1929, 1947 and now 1995. I've never made anything like it before. Nectar. I'll have to put it on the market for the millennium.'

He gave me a glass of it; he hadn't exaggerated. 'A pity though that it's a full moon – not right for tasting.'[1]

Here are two rationalist explanations, offered by Mandy Jones, who at Château Carsin is M. Doche's neighbour. On racking: the moon affects the atmospheric pressure, altering the level of the wine in its permeable wooden barrel. If you fill when pressure is low it will burst out later. *Botrytis*: full moons supply extra light at night, so starting the growth of both mushrooms and noble rot, which is then apparent by the time of the new moon.

Both explanations are quite plausible. There obviously is an effect which could be studied and, in time, explained. A few decades ago ageing wine in barrels and stirring up the spent yeast lees also appeared to be irrational practices inherited from the past.

Full-blown Biodynamics is taken seriously by serious people: the Domaine Leflaive at Puligny Montrachet in the Côte d'Or; the *Société Huet* at Vouvray and *Château de la Roche aux Moines*, Nicholas Joly's property, also on the Loire; James Millton in New Zealand, like Joly and Huet also a maker of great Chenin Blanc. It's hard too to argue with the underlying philosophy that emphasizes the interconnectedness of the universe or its targets: pollution, agribusiness and systemic poisons.

But horn dung? This is dung, placed in a cow's horn that is buried in the ground over winter where it fills up with 'vitalizing energy'. 'Horn silica' by contrast, is 'silica' placed in a cow's horn and buried during summer where it 'remains exposed to the sun's live forces'.

Noel Pinguet of Huet spelt out the reasoning in a paper prepared for Richards Walford, his British importers. 'Cows' horns, natural energy captors, are frequently used in Biodynamics. After all, the Egyptians represented the bullock Apis with a sun between its horns. [I like 'after all'] We also talk of the "horn of plenty".'

Pinguet admits not understanding Biodynamics, but says he finds it works. What's striking to the outsider is that, like all apparently effective belief systems, it serves not as a substitute to practical action but as a framework for it. An article he wrote in 1991 is littered with suggestive clues. Pinguet piously declares that the buried horns are 'essential for harmony and balance in the soil and plant', but concedes that they're not sufficient in themselves. Fertilizer is still required, whether plant compost or animal manure, as is spraying, either with herbal extracts or good old copper sulphate (Bordeaux mixture), against mildew, and with powdered sulphur against oidium.

His conclusion: 'A much closer follow-up of the vineyard is required, and this can only be a good thing, calling on the wine grower to be available with respect to the Seedling Calendar irrespective of long weekends or holidays.' In other words Biodynamics provides an excuse for the dedicated Pinguet to put in yet longer hours in the vineyard.

Biodynamic growers are set apart by their views and their practices both in France and New Zealand. It's hard to imagine New World colleagues being as rude as some French producers. For Olivier Merlin: 'It's easy to be ultra-concerned with nature when you've inherited your estate and don't have to worry about making a living.' Daniel Domergue laughed till tears ran down his face as he described the importance biodynamicists attach to the question of whether the cow's horn for burial should be a left- or a right-hand one. As a believer (Protestant), Domergue has much more time for Christian rites such as the late Jacques Reynaud of Château Rayas's annual Rogation service in the vineyard, to which the neighbourhood was invited, but at which Reynaud and the curé formed the major part of the congregation.

But for small-scale French growers, what they call 'chemical' or 'technological' wines are far from being a joke. In 1995 Simon Loftus of Adnams, the East Anglian brewers-cum-wine-merchants, organized a seminar on the theme of 'the classic prototype: old vines, low yields, barren hill slopes'. Invited to Adnams' home town of Southwold were Di Cullen, the Western Australian winemaker, Patricia Domergue, Aimé Guibert of Mas de Daumas Gassac, Charlie Melton from the Barossa and John Forrest from New Zealand.

It was a two-day session: the first asked whether old vines were really better, the second debated the merits of keeping the wines from individual vineyards separate or blending them. But by the second day Guibert had packed his bags and stormed off while

Mme Domergue was in a state of shocked distress, still apparent when she recalled the visit several months later.

'It hadn't been planned as a punch-up,' insists Loftus. Indeed, you might expect to have seen an outbreak of fellow feeling and hands-across-the-sea given a certain similarity in approach between most of these small-scale growers and wine-makers; the only wild card was played by the New Zealanders, with their belief that good wine can be made from young, high-yielding vines.

'I felt as if I'd walked into a trap,' said Mme Domergue, who found herself alone and, with her lack of English, uncomprehending, after Guibert's walk-out. 'England is a country with a long history, and I'd have expected them to understand and accept wines that express *un terroir*. I have a real sense of being betrayed, though Simon Loftus did try and stand up for me.'

Di Cullen, who recently handed over wine-making responsibilities to her daughter Vanya, had struck her as 'a really distinguished person'. Other members of the Antipodean contingent had been '*très insultants*'. (Loftus strongly denies this and it's not clear what might have constituted any such insults.) But the real wound had been left by the guests' apparent preference for the New Zealand wine.

Like her husband, Patricia Domergue can't believe that her competitors aren't cheating. 'I presented two wines: one is a blend of grape varieties, another is pure Cinsault. I was wrong: I put forward something that isn't oaked, that doesn't have flavourings, that doesn't have glycerol. We're just too "boy-scout"; we know that what we're trying to do is completely mad.'

Think Again, Domergues!

You can see why Daniel and Patricia Domergue, as exponents of subtlety and refinement, would find the British enthusiasm for New Zealand wines annoying. It's easy to get a taste for that country's Sauvignon Blanc – and just as easy to get sick of it. But there is more to New Zealand, even if, as so often in New World countries, the growers' wines are painfully dear. The best of New Zealand would include:

1 The Alsace fanatic Neil McCallum of **Dry River Wines**, Martinborough. Imported by Raeburn Fine Wines, Edinburgh. 0131 554

2652. Expensive if available at all.

2 Isabel Estate, Marlborough. The **Sauvignon Blanc** used to be sold to the pioneers Cloudy Bay. High planting densities create something with an elegance and complexity that's often missing. The 1996 was £10.60 from Morris and Verdin, London SE1 (0171 357 8866).

3 The Millton Estate. Wines from New Zealand's only biodynamic grower. The **Chenin Blanc** is James Millton's favoured child, at around £8.00 from Adnams, Southwold (01502 727222) and Planet Organic, London W2 (0171 221 7171). The 1996, tasted in spring 1997, had lots of flavours but they hadn't (yet) come together convincingly: £7.99 from Waitrose mail order, 0800 413331, and perhaps also in the 20 Waitrose stores with the 'inner cellar' special range. Milton's Chardonnay-based wines in Safeway are OK but more ordinary.

There is a real gulf here: one that in Britain it's considered good manners to tiptoe delicately around, with talk about 'reconciling technology and tradition'. Our wine trade can see that the New World expands the total market and attracts new wine drinkers. Why knock it?

Both sides can't be right. According to mainstream opinion in Australia and New Zealand, wine-makers like the Domergues are simply reactionaries, making unnecessarily expensive wines by out-dated means for reasons of pure dogma. Many Europeans, on the other hand, find the 'modern' style simply nasty; Jean Foillard from Beaujolais claims not to have been able to find anything drinkable among the 'tarted-up' ('*putassier*') examples at London's annual Australia Day tasting.

I thought one approach might be to try to find out who the new wine-makers are and what they actually do. Their exponents say they just apply hygiene and common sense. The other side take an apocalyptic view. Patricia Domergue says of the widespread New World use of oak shavings as flavouring: 'To do it means to lose your soul.' Her husband Daniel swears their rivals use synthetic aroma essences, an assertion for which I have no evidence but which I have heard elsewhere on impressive authority. He is adamant; it's common knowledge, he says. 'It's like taking a shit in the countryside [he mimes the necessary posture], someone always comes along and sees you.'

New World versus Old World. This is not a fresh theme; in fact it's eye-glazingly overfamiliar. But one bonus of doing a little research is discovering that Australia is not after all the original home of high-tech wine-making. The Australian role has been mainly that of transmitters rather than originators of new technology. The real story begins in Germany and Austria, with developments coming rapidly just before and just after the Second World War.[2]

1 Pliny: XIV XXVII 135: *Bruma aperiri vetant nisi sereno die, vetant austro flante lunave plena.*

2 At the wine school of Klosterneuberg in Austria work continued uninterrupted. The war years saw, in particular, the breeding of the red Zweigelt variety by the institute's director of that name, which is now, Jancis Robinson tells us in *Vines, Grapes and Wines*, the country's third most widely planted red variety. Dr Zweigelt was sacked after the war for collaboration with the Nazi authorities.

19

Vorsprung Durch Technik

Wolf Blass, the showman and wine-maker whose oaky Cabernets all carry his reproduced signature, is, like many of his fellow Australians, of German origin; he went to his adopted country for the first time in 1961 on contract to make wine for the Kaiser Stuhl company. Earlier he'd trained in Germany and worked in Britain. Just twelve years later he won Australia's top wine award, the Jimmy Watson Trophy: recognition that this small man had become one of the biggest forces in the industry and an important technical innovator.

He dates the start of the Australian wine boom to an event a few years before his arrival. In 1953, G. Gramp and Sons (the predecessor of Orlando, of Jacobs Creek fame) company imported pressure fermentation tanks from Seitz Werke of Bad Kreuznach on the River Nahe. These tanks enabled Colin Gramp to make a sweetish *petillant* white wine called Barossa Pearl: 'And it was Barossa Pearl which got people off beer and mixed drinks and on to the wine habit,' according to Blass, who had been hired by Kaiser Stuhl to work on a 'me too' product.

The airtight tanks had two main purposes: they made it possible to control how fast a fermentation ran by regulating the pressure of carbon dioxide; and by fermenting under pressure the wine-makers could retain some dissolved CO_2 in the wine, thus creating the 'spritz' that was to be characteristic of Barossa Pearl and its imitators. It was with these tanks, too, that Australia moved over to the modern practice of fermenting in vessels made of stainless steel rather than cement.

In the early 1950s pressurized fermentation and its inventor Wilhelm Geitz brought the wine world beating a path to the little town of Bad Kreuznach. But this success was nothing new. During the First World War the Seitz company had perfected the 'sterilizing filter', making it possible to remove all living micro-organisms from wine without heating it and so changing its flavours, as happens with pasteurization. The technology migrated from wine to the chemical and pharmaceutical industry; without it, for example, there would be no way of removing bacteria from blood products, which coagulate if pasteurized.

The filter worked by mixing the liquid to be sterilized with tiny strands and forcing it through a screen. Today asbestos is no longer used, but Fritz Neradt of Seitz's marketing department assured me that the company is not bracing itself for a blizzard of writs: 'All the evidence shows that if asbestos is ingested rather than inhaled it is completely harmless.'

It's to Seitz that Australia owes its most celebrated dry white wine: the Chenin Blanc based 'Houghtons White Burgundy' (imported to Britain as 'HWB' in deference to EU rules). Jack Mann, the former cricketer who made Houghton's wines, was able to make the first vintage in 1937, shortly after persuading his employers to import the Seitz filter. Only with this technique could he be confident that the wine would not spoil or referment.

Interestingly, Mann was to develop strong misgivings about the technology-led direction taken by the Australian industry. At the Houghtons 150th anniversary celebrations he spoke of modern 'thin wines' made in wineries 'more like dairies or small oil refineries'. He described temperature-controlled fermentation as 'the cold castration of grape juice'. The problem, he said, lay in overcropped grapes being picked before they were fully mature. In fact, like other great Australian industry figures, his philosophy turns out to have been that of a traditionalist. One of his pet dislikes was the term wine-maker. He said: 'It is wrong, and improper, to describe any man as a wine-maker. Nature makes the wine and man, if he is skilled, gives nature the opportunity to perform to the best advantage.'

Another technique that has transformed wine-making is the use of single yeast strains. The Australian-trained 'flying wine-makers' would be lost without them, but they are a German invention.

Until recently all wine was made by naturally occurring yeasts. The fermentation either just started or growers used the technique called *pied de cuve* (you pick a few of the ripest grapes you can find a little in advance of the main harvest and get those fermenting to create a starter culture). But it was not until Louis Pasteur started his investigations into wine and wine spoilage in the 1860s that the role of yeast was fully understood. Twenty years later the Swiss Professor Hermann Müller, working at the Geisenheim Research Institute in the Rheingau, began isolating single yeast strains, starting the collection still kept at Geisenheim.

Although he was a microbiologist, Prof. Müller's greatest interest was in grape varieties (in 1883 he created the Riesling Sylvaner cross later named Müller Thurgau after him, Thurgau being his native region of Switzerland). According to Ralph Kunkee, emeritus professor at the University of California's Davis Institute, Pasteur believed that yeast shaped the taste of wine, while Müller thought that the choice of grape variety had the greatest influence; this debate has rumbled on ever since, with Müller's point of view generally dominant.

Wine institutes and research stations began to build up holdings of selected strains which they made available to growers; in Champagne, for example, members go to the technical department of their *Comité Interprofessionelle*. Similarly, big firms like Gallo in California and Penfolds in South Australia made their own yeast cultures in-house from the 1950s. The idea was to have fermentations that would start and finish predictably, without the danger of introducing off flavours. Professor Ann Noble of the Davis Institute thinks it's simple common sense: 'It's like saying "Do you use a condom in San Francisco?" You may argue that the wine has more complexity without cultured yeasts, but it's a totally unacceptable balance of risk.'

In the 1960s big firms came on the scene. Redstar, a huge company making baking and brewing yeast started a wine division. Currently the world's biggest supplier of dried yeasts is a Canadian firm, Lallemand, with brands like Prise de Mousse, (also known by its European Union number EC 1118) favoured by Hugh Ryman, the flying wine-maker, whether he's at work in Chile or Moldova. 'It's something we strongly encouraged,' says Ralph Kunkee of Davis. 'Now people are saying, maybe we shouldn't have.'

Another piece of the jigsaw is temperature control of fermentation; this reached Australia from Austria in the 1950s. Wine-makers

have artificially *raised* temperatures since at least the nineteenth century; this is an alternative to seeding the juice with yeast – by heating some of it you give the naturally occurring yeasts a flying start.

If on the other hand the vat gets overheated by the fermentation reaction the yeasts can no longer multiply, the process stops or 'sticks', and there's a danger that bacteria will take over and turn everything to vinegar. This danger is greater when working on a large scale, in a hot climate or both.

The first large-scale cooling techniques were developed in the nineteenth century in Algeria when production there was stepped up to compensate for the loss of the French vineyards through phylloxera.

The Germain family were among the pioneers of industrial scale wine-making. From their 800-hectare domaine at Kamdouri, west of Algiers and numerous other estates they were responsible for a volume greater than that of the whole modern Corbières *appellation*. Their cooling method relied on the surprisingly ample water supplies of Algeria's coastal plain. They built open-sided sheds with vents positioned to catch any breezes; inside the fermenting wine circulated through *serpentins* (bronze coils covered with jute cloth, continually drenched in running water and positioned so that the air drawn through the shed passed over them). When the family moved to France in the 1950s, buying the Château de Caraguilhes in Corbières, they brought with them *serpentins*, so introducing temperature-controlled fermentation to mainland France.[1]

These days Caraguilhes uses more conventional temperature control, with refrigerated coils in the tanks. Modern heat pumps were developed at the Klosterneuberg Wine School in Austria by Professor W. Saller soon after the war. Max Schubert of Penfolds went to visit him there in 1957 and soon afterwards the Australian industry invested heavily in the new refrigeration technology.

Coke-Fra Classics

I've always liked the proud-to-be-industrial look of the labels on Martini bottles with their inset engraving of the way the factory looked a hundred years ago, topped with belching chimneys. It's a pity it's out of fashion, otherwise big producers could go in for futuristic designs showing off the high-tech gear used to tailor the various styles of modern wine.

Liebfraumilch, according to the German producer Wolfgang Siben,[2] was a product aimed at the GIs stationed in Germany after the war, with their ready-formed taste for sweet drinks like Coke. The label might pay tribute to the Seitz filter: filtration is the main method used in sterilizing grape juice to make the so-called *Süssreserve*, which sweetens Lieb; if it wasn't sterile the juice would risk setting off a second fermentation in the bottle.

Beaujolais Nouveau comes from putting the Gamay grape together with a yeast strain called 71b, temperature-controlled fermentation and, frequently, heat-extraction to obtain juice low in tannin, high in colour and fruit.

The same combination of cold fermentation and a selected yeast strain goes to make **Vin de Pays des Côtes de Gascogne**, but with the normally quite neutral-flavoured Ugni Blanc and Colombard grapes, previously grown in the region to make Cognac. Robert Parker loves it. I'm less sure.

Inexpensive '**Chardonnay**' from anywhere is a fashion product. In the 80s it was as dark yellow as possible with a strong vanilla smell from being fermented with oak chips. The style has been tweaked and freshened but the essentials are the same: enzymes and ascorbic acid to boost the fruit, skin contact for extra colour and flavour, oak chips or essence for more flavour.

Many **New Zealand Sauvignons** owe their big, strange aromas of gooseberries and green peppers to a proprietory yeast; a genetically-engineered variety of *Saccharomyces banaticus* rather than the more usual *Saccharomyces cerevisiae*.

The flow of expertise from Germany continued during the 1970s. Dr Tony Jordan[3] spent two years in Europe before starting the Enotech consultancy with Brian Croser, the fount and origin of 'Australian high technology' who, with Tony Laithwaite, loosed off the first wave of flying wine-makers into Europe. Dr Jordan did a sabbatical year at Geisenheim in 1977 as a visiting research scientist followed by a period touring with Helmut Becker of the Institute for Vine Breeding and Vine Propagation.

Tony Jordan describes Becker as: 'A real scientist cum entre-preneur for world wine – a real character. He took me under his wing and instead of me just sitting in Geisenheim he showed me all over the wine areas of Europe to look at what was going on at the cutting edge of research – everywhere where there was something interesting. I wasn't just a graduate: I was a research scientist. I was at their level. It gave me a very rapid insight into colloidal chemistry, aroma chemistry, a whole lot of areas.'

It's formidably impressive stuff. But do wine-makers really need such a high-powered scientific training? This question hits a nerve. 'It frustrates me. It's assumed that if you have a chemistry background you're only a technocrat. It's so much fucking crap. It drives me mad.'

You don't have to talk to Tony Jordan for long to realize that he's nice, super-bright and with a short fuse that adds to his charm. What would Patricia Domergue have made of him had he also been a guest at Southwold? In a sense he's public enemy number one of the traditionalists: as consultant to the leading Australian wine writer James Halliday he has an ultimate responsibility for many of the ideas in the book Halliday co-wrote with Hugh Johnson[4] that so infuriated Robert Parker, a champion of back-to-basics wine-making. But I suspect P. Domergue and T. Jordan would have got on rather well.

Because of the partnership in the 1980s between Tony Jordan and Tony Laithwaite of the *Sunday Times* Wine Club, flying wine-makers, many of them Croser- and Jordan-trained, are now at work in most wine regions of the world, Germany included.

Gerhardt Brauer of the Ruppertsberg co-operative in the Rheinpfalz worked with the best-known flying wine-maker, Hugh Ryman, on vintages in the early 1990s, but has not taken up his suggestions wholesale. A technique he likes and has adopted is the protracted settling of the grape juice to clarify it rather than the violent alternative of using a centrifuge. But the co-operative is no longer adding enzymes to speed the settling process, or the anti-oxidant ascorbic acid (vitamin C). Both these additives contribute to the 'up-front fruit' so loved by British journalists. But Brauer says: 'We don't have a problem of lack of fruit in our Riesling.' They have also drastically cut down the levels of sulphur dioxide Hugh Ryman insisted on. 'He's doing it because it's part of his concept and it's necessary in all the other regions where he works. He's doing his schema.'

A common accusation levelled at the flying wine-makers is that they put the same formula to work wherever they go. When they pack before setting off on their travels their check-list is likely to include sulphur dioxide, ascorbic acid, wood chips – and a book called *Making Good Wine* by Dr Bryce Rankine, the former head of the School of Viticulture and Oenology at Roseworthy Agricultural College.

Peter Taylor, the chief red wine-maker for Penfolds, lent me his personal copy. With his years of experience, the book's recommendations struck him as a bit basic: 'He does rather tend to spell things out.' Dr Tony Jordan is in turn less complimentary about the work, but it does at least give an insight into what young Australians are taught at college.

I tried it out on Olivier Merlin, as a French grower with a know-ledge of the New World from his time in the Napa Valley. The book is more than 350 pages long and Olivier's grasp of English had slipped, so we concentrated on the three pages dealing with dry white table wine-making, something Olivier can be allowed to know something about.

He thought the idea of a set of step-by-step instructions was fine: 'Just like a recipe book.' It fitted with his experience of the un-Burgundian practice of laying down rules and following them to the letter.

But right away he was pulled up by a reference to harvesting by machine. 'What is the book called – *Making Good Wine*? You cannot make good wine and machine harvest. Well, it depends what you mean by "good wine". All modern wines are "good" if all that means is not being actually bad.' Nor was the next sentence plain sailing, advising the addition of 50–75 milligrams per litre of sulphur dioxide as potassium or sodium metabisulphite, together with 50–100 milligrams per litre of ascorbic acid (vitamin C), either as the acid itself or as its isomer sodium erythorbate.

Wrong, said Merlin. In a good year you would add no sulphur or virtually none. Nor would he use ascorbic acid. It was wrong too to destem white grapes before pressing them (they get automatically destemmed by the harvester) or to adjust their acidity with tartaric acid. We had by now covered less than half a page without the slightest sign of consensus. Merlin had gone from mild interest to exasperation. 'I just hope the Australians carry on exactly like this. It's in my interests that they do.'

Almost all the recommendations, in Merlin's view, boiled down to attempts to overcome the bad effects of mechanical harvesting.

The machines, which shake the grapes loose by agitating the vines, tend to break the skins and so make them more likely to go off. With intact grapes, freshly harvested, you should need no ascorbic acid and only minimal sulphur.

The only reasons he could find not to hand harvest were economic. 'Mechanical harvesting is extremely lucrative. To do it by hand costs up to 10,000 francs a hectare. If you hire a machine it costs half that and if you buy one you'll pay 3,000 francs a year for the first few years and then nothing.'

He rapidly disposed of the need to use tartaric acid to correct the grapes' acid balance: this was a question of choosing varieties suited to your climate. Later we came to commercial yeast strains and enzymes to clarify juice, both of which he has used 'if there's a problem, if there's something that's gone out of control'. But his theme was that the better the job you did in the vineyard the less you needed to correct when it came to making the wine. 'Science keeps coming up with "better solutions"; but that tends to mean giving people an easier life rather than producing better grapes.

'Wine isn't information technology, and I'm not really interested in technology for its own sake. What science can't do is replace twenty centuries' worth of human observation. Science can analyse and explain, but that's all.' He gave an example: the ancient Burgundian practice of leaving white wine on its 'lees', the spent yeast cells left after fermentation. Till quite recently modern wine-makers filtered these off to create a clean, bright wine. But wine left on its lees in a barrel was actually better protected against the effects of oxygen than by having sulphur added; lees naturally mop up spare oxygen. And science was only just starting to explain why you improve your wine if you go in for *batonnage* (putting a stick in the barrel and stirring up the lees). This practice creates complex flavours and a silky texture by breaking up the cells and liberating amino acids. 'But people have been doing it for centuries. Wine is still very empirical.'

From the opposite perspective, the modernist Tony Jordan isn't against such peasant wine-making but sees it as only one approach among many. He talks about keeping clean fruit flavours in the wine, then having choices at the stage of blending, including 'building in complexity'. For traditionalists this is like making flour fit for Mothers Pride or Wonderloaf and then trying to blend back in flavour and roughage. Merlin *et al* argue that complexity of flavour isn't something you add but discover, a gift of the potential latent in your grapes and their attendant micro-organisms, brought to fruition, but not created, by the skill of the wine-maker.

The other theme of Olivier Merlin is that work in the vineyard means that a grower does not need to rely on an endless treadmill of chemical treatments to correct imbalances in the wine. Here are some widely practised winery manipulations and the reasons growers feel they can dispense with them.

Yeast Enrichment Grapes grown at high yields tend to be low on sugar, colour, acidity and nitrogen. The last is particularly a problem if a lot of sulphur is added at the time of the harvest as nitrogen-deficient grapes are likely to produce hydrogen sulphide, the 'rotten egg' gas, when the fermentation gets going. What's more, the same deficiency may cause the yeasts to give up before the fermentation is completed. The answer is another chemical: the ammonium salt diammonium phosphate.

So diammonium phosphate is required only to compensate for avoidable states of affairs: the presence of sulphur and the poor nutritional state of the grapes. The answer is to grow well-balanced grapes.

Chaptalization Chaptalization is the addition of sugar to raise alcohol levels. The raw materials of alcohol are the sugars: glucose, sucrose and fructose. With the growth of the sugar cane industry, built on slave labour in the eighteenth century, grapes stopped being the cheapest source of this raw material. Sugar's potential to replace grapes altogether was revealed at the end of the nineteenth century in the phylloxera crisis. With the vineyards devastated, merchants offered 'piquette', fermented sugar-water flavoured with grape skins. This product had such a price advantage over wine made from grapes that it caused almost as much harm to grape growers as phylloxera itself.

The fake wines sound disgraceful, but it's taken for granted that sugar will be used in the English country wines listed in Dorothy Hartley's classic *Food in England*: birch, bread, burnet, cowslip, dandelion, maidenhair, parsnip and potato; most are really flavoured sugar wines. Similarly the Biddenden Vineyards in Kent make a 'Special Reserve Cider' at 13 degrees of alcohol that owes more than half its strength to sugar.

In Europe, sugar has in fact become an essential part of the mainstream drinks industry; this now needs the Champagne region almost as much for its endless fields of sugar beet as for its better-known product. The beet makes the raw material of 'neutral spirit', which is the basis of cheap gin and vodka and fortifies a vast range of products, from vermouth to liqueurs to alcopops. The sugar also goes in huge quantities into the table wines of Northern France and Germany to boost alcohol levels. In the EU around 70,000 tonnes are used annually to boost alcohol levels in wine, compared to the 60,000 tonnes used in small-scale *patisseries* of the sort you see by the dozen in every French town. Champagne producers chaptalize with beet sugar, but prefer cane sugar for the two further additions that are special to Champagne and sparkling wines: as fuel to make the bubbles and as the *liqueur d'expédition*, put in at the time of the final corking to take the edge off the dryness of the wine.

Adding sugar to grape juice before or during fermentation is called chaptalization after Jean-Louis Chaptal. Chaptal, later to become Napoleon's minister of agriculture, trained as a chemist at Montpellier in the Languedoc before coming to Paris in 1793. In the book he published eight years later. *L'Art de Faire le Vin* (The Art of Wine Making), he addressed the greatest problem facing Northern French growers: that the grapes all too often rotted on the stem before ever ripening. His advice was 'to intervene to make good the sugar levels which would have been arrived at had conditions that year been more favourable'.

This idea was not widely acted on until the mid-nineteenth century; by this time the French had, in sugar beet, a new domestic source of cheap sugar (the result of another initiative of the Napoleonic era, aimed at countering the effects of the British blockade of French ports). Even so chaptalization wasn't universal until well into this century. Jules Chauvet told Kermit Lynch that in his youth, that is in the 1920s, Beaujolais in light years might be sold with only 9 or 10 degrees of alcohol rather than the 13 degrees that's normal today with the help of sugar.

Today what Chaptal intended to be a way of rescuing an exceptionally poor harvest has become a standby year in and year out. In Burgundy in particular it has been used to mask the drop in natural sugars created by the majority of the growers' pursuit of higher yields. Fertilizers and more productive clones have pushed these up from 29.02 hectolitres per hectare in 1960 to 45.74 hectolitres per hectare thirty years later. While low by New World standards, vines in Burgundy cropped at these levels barely get to the 10.5–11 degrees required if they are to get up to 13–13.5 degrees after chaptalization.

Before the practice came in, natural sugar levels were routinely much higher. Research by M de Vergnette of the *Societé d'Agriculture de Lyons* shows that in 1845–46 Pommards were coming in with 10.6–13.3 degrees of natural alcohol and Meursaults at 11.5–14.6 degrees.

Sugar has become part of the formula for most modern Beaujolais and Burgundy, widely added at levels above the legally permitted 2 degrees. This is not just because it's an undemanding way of raising alcohol levels but because of its contribution to texture and mouth feel. Kermit Lynch writes of his dislike of this characteristic but in general it adds to the wine's saleability.

Jules Chauvet, as described earlier, described how hard work in the vineyard could produce enough natural alcohol and his followers in Beaujolais try to adopt the practices he recommended while giving greater emphasis to his campaign against sulphur. Another, somewhat isolated, opponent of excessive chaptalization is the Dijon lawyer Hubert de Montille who has small-holdings in various vineyards mainly around Volnay. In 1960 he chaptalized the light wines of that vintage to the same level as his neighbours and found he had produced an unbalanced wine. Now adds only the minimal sugar required to take his red wines to 12 degrees – none if they get to 12 degrees naturally – and finds that they develop all the better in bottle for this restraint.

There's also a possibility that chaptalization may be bad for you. The sugar goes in as syrup, that is dissolved in water, which releases nitrates in the grapes. Alex Karumanchiri is concerned that these liberated nitrates may come into contact with a class of substances called biogenic amines and create nitrosoamines, which are carcinogens. He has found nitrosoamines in beer, and is about to begin looking for them specifically in wine.

Acidification At least one wine has had its acidity artificially boosted since time immemorial. The *Lancet* in 1898 published the findings of a committee investigating Sherry. It looked at the practice of dusting the grapes with gypsum (the raw material of plaster of paris) in order to prevent cloudiness in the wine and raise acidity, and concluded that it had 'no deleterious effect'. The team were told that adding gypsum had been inspired by the discovery, centuries earlier, that grapes with a dusting of the chalky soil called *albariza* made better Sherry.

Gypsum raises acidity through a reaction which converts potassium bitartrate in the grapes into free tartaric acid. In the 1930s the Australians began adding tartaric acid to their wines (at that date they were mainly fortified). They had discovered that by pushing the acidity up they could stop bacteria spoiling their 'ports' and 'sherries' by creating the taste and smell known as 'mousiness'.

But acidification was more important once the fashion for table wines took off. With a few exceptions wine-makers want ripe grapes, for their full flavours and soft tannins, but don't want the drop in acidity that comes with full maturity. Tartaric acid offers a way of squaring the circle. It's a solution that's restricted in the European Union. Growers are not allowed to add both tartaric acid and sugar to wine. (However the rule is widely circumvented by acidifying one vat, chaptalizing another and blending the two together.)

The solution that appeals to more committed growers is to try to combine maturity with ripeness by getting things right in the vineyard. What is important, according to this school, is to plant appropriate grape varieties, restrict yields and, in particular, to avoid using potassium fertilizers, notorious for their destructive effect on the acidity of grapes.

Other acids can be added after fermentation simply to make the wine taste better. Hugh Suter of Victoria Wines, formerly responsible for bottling wines imported in bulk by Grants of St James, remembers using citric acid, the basis of artificial lemonade, when bottling flabby-tasting bulk wine, 'just to tickle it up a little'. Lactic acid, as found in milk, is a short-cut to the 'buttery' quality of some white wines; traditionally this would be spontaneously created by the bacterial malolactic fermentation.

The converse in Northern Europe, especially in England and Germany, is the practice of adding chalk or other chemicals to make wine less green and acidic. The effect is like using Dolby noise reduction on your stereo: certain nuances get lost along with the offending elements. Dr Peter Jordan of the Weingut Jordan & Jordan in the Saar says with practice he can identify a particular taste with de-acidified wines. The answer, unsurprisingly, is to restrict crops and pick late.

Ion Exchange The trouble about acidifying with tartaric acid (a natural constituent of grape juice) is that it creates tartrate crystals in even greater quantities than would naturally occur. These are harmless but are thought to be off-putting to consumers.

A process called ion-exchange came into use in Australia in the 1950s. It stops wine throwing off potassium bitartrate crystals and raises the acidity into the bargain. The technique involves replacing positively charged potassium ions in the wine with a mixture of sodium ions and hydrogen ions.

This is not desirable for people on a low sodium diet as it makes wine rich in sodium rather than potassium, without creating a taste (salty, for example) that would act as a warning. This is a shame as red wine in moderation is otherwise positively helpful in reducing the risk of circulatory disease.

Ion exchange is banned in the European Union but as a special concession is permitted in imports from Australia, where this technique is in decline and used mainly on cheaper stuff.

The majority of the processes described in this chapter were either invented in Germany or have been essential in selling German wine to a mass market. As Fritz Neradt of Seize Werke and formerly of Geisenheim explained: 'Being so far north we often have very poor grapes and the cellar-masters had to have these technologies in order to make wine at all.'

These days there is no longer any shortage of wine and consumers increasingly recognize, and reject, attempts to make a silk purse out of a sow's ear. The more successful wine-makers either wear the cost of such ancestral techniques as barrel fermentation, or use science to work out and adapt the principles behind them.

1 Thanks to Galatée Faivre, the current head of the family for these details. In fact the waif-like Galatée sent a detailed description, in immaculate English, plus what looked like her own hand-drawn sketch of the Algerian vinification

cellars with a section of one of the *serpentins*, and an apology for not having answered by return of post!

2 Quoted in *Life Beyond Liebfraumilch*, Stuart Piggott, Sidgwick & Jackson Ltd, 1988.

3 The doctorate is a PhD in physical chemistry from University College, London.

4 *The Art and Science of Wine.*

20

Message in a Barrel

Germany may be a prime source of new technologies, but to learn to make fine red wine you go to Bordeaux, either as a student to take the university's famous oenology course or, as Max Schubert of Penfolds did in 1950, as a working wine-maker looking for tips. It is from the various pilgrims to the banks of the Garonne that the world has learned about Cabernet Sauvignon, the malolactic fermentation and the ageing of wine in new *barriques bordelaises* (220-litre casks). Not to mention one of the most puzzling ideas to have migrated from France to Australia: adding tannin to red wine.

An English Master of Wine found this practice hard to credit: 'You'd think in Australia they'd have too much tannin in their grapes, let alone want to add it.'

Tannin is the substance that you taste in overstewed tea. While there are no more than traces in white wine, it's present in red in varying quantities. There's less in pale, cold-climate reds, for example from the Loire or Alsace, or in Beaujolais, where the local technique is designed to remove them.

Wine-makers want tannin for various reasons. One is that it produces wines that make their presence felt in the mouth and mesh with the proteins in meat, cheese and beans. It is also a preservative: this role is intensely controversial, some experts claiming that tannic young wine just turns into tannic old wine, others that this substance holds the wine together until it reaches a perfect state of maturity. The much-argued-over reference point is the 1986 vintage in Bordeaux, initially very hard going, but which has apparently bloomed.

Tannins have their own wine vocabulary (for some reason they're plural in wine, unlike in tea). They can be 'rustic', 'coarse' or 'unripe'. They can also be 'dense' which is neither good nor bad. More positively they can be 'fine', 'ripe', 'well-integrated' or 'soft'.

Wine gets tannin from the skins, the pips and the stalks of grapes. It also comes from the wood of new oak barrels. And, surprisingly, it's also added as a concentrate derived from the galls insects make on the bark of oak trees.

For Australians this practice goes back to 1950 and Max Schubert's visit to Bordeaux that inspired him to create Penfold's Grange Hermitage. According to Huon Hooke, Schubert's biographer, he was taught about tannin addition by his host in the city, Christian Cruse, head of the family firm of *négociants*. The secret apparently was not to add the tannin all at one go but to 'feed' the wine with it steadily during fermentation and maturation. Tannin is added not only to Grange but also to other members of the Penfolds family of red wines.

But why? No one I met in Bordeaux had heard of the practice. An English source thought it had been done in the past, in light vintages, but was now obsolete. And why should a dodge used to beef up lighter vintages in Bordeaux have been exported to Australia where the vintages are all beefy enough anyway?

Seeking guidance I rang Richard Gibson, the group technical manager of Southcorp, Penfold's parent company. One of the pleasures of talking to Australian wine-makers is their candour in discussing tricks of the trade. This time, though, I felt I sensed a certain defensiveness.

Yes, Richard told me, Penfolds, like other Australian wine companies, added tannin in 'very small amounts'. The main aim was to stabilize the colour in red wine, so that it lasted for longer without showing the general browning and loss of intensity associated with age. It made old wine look less old and, coincidentally, young wine look less young, without the characteristic bright purpleness.

I told Richard that I'd found no French growers who said they used tannins in red wines. He wasn't surprised: 'The French don't always admit to things.' But the main suppliers of wine tannins were French and, what's more, the practice was written up in full in the 'bible' of French scientific wine-making: the *Traité d'Oenologie* by Ribéreau-Gayon and Peynaud. He'd fax all the relevant documents across to me.

It was an impressive bundle: seven pages including a photocopy from a learned journal, the pages from Ribéreau-Gayon and Peynaud and a letter from Groupe Oeno France offering to supply this essential substance, and everything, as Richard Gibson pointed out in his covering letter, in French. He rang to ensure everything had arrived safely just as I'd started, dictionary in hand, to wrestle with Ribéreau-Gayon and Peynaud.

Fifteen minutes later I was slightly shocked. The 'bible' of French wine-making, far from recommending the addition of tannin, turned out to advise explicitly against this practice. The learned pair recommended including the stems and pips rather than using artificial tannin, and conceded a role for this additive only when clarifying protein-rich white grape juice, as when making Champagne.

For help I turned to the French firm who had offered to supply Southcorp with tannin. Marie Madeleine Caillet their technical manager was in a meeting, but helped me out with a few quick answers. I quoted the *Traité d'Oenologie*. She chuckled in apparent agreement. So where was the main market for tannin additives? France or Australia? 'Overwhelmingly Australia.' Why? 'Because it contributes to the taste of the Anglo-Saxon market, for very oaky-tasting wine.'[1]

According to Marie Madeleine Caillet, you add tannin partly to stabilize the colour of red wine, as mentioned by Richard Gibson, but also partly to fatten it up and create a big, brooding character. The point is not simply to add tannin, but to set in motion reactions between the tannin and oxygen. At the end of this process you are left with physically bigger molecules, that are both resistant to colour change and that give a full, dense mouth feel.

The moral? The house of Cruse were hardly an ideal role model. In one of the wine world's periodic scandals the company collapsed twenty years after Max Schubert's visit after being caught out mislabelling wine. You might bracket *tanisation* with other hopefully extinct practices of the old French merchant houses, such as mislabelling and illicit blending.

But what if it works? Penfolds make a consistent product that is widely admired. Most of Bordeaux doesn't. Richard Gibson asks: 'When are consumers going to get the message about a region that turns out poor wine three times out of five?' But it's also worth asking whether customers value consistency above authenticity. A technique may 'work', for example the once widespread practice of improving a barrel of Burgundy with a bottle of Port, but it has to be something the producer can unashamedly own up to.

Of course the best known technique that Max Schubert took back to Australia was that of wood ageing; to create Grange he made the inspired substitution of old vine Barossa Shiraz for old Cabernet and the sweeter and more vanilla-flavoured American oak for the French oak barrels used in Bordeaux. The wine was denounced as undrinkable, but he continued making it in secret, hiding the stocks behind false walls in the Penfolds cellars. He was finally vindicated as the wines matured and softened.

Bordeaux's own consultants, notably Prof. Peynaud, have now taken the doctrine of ageing the best red wine in small new oak barrels to every corner of the globe. However it's a costly exercise, that appeals more in the first instance to Hollywood lawyers and Greek shipping tycoons than to the sons and daughters of long-established growers' families (unless they happen to be in Barolo or the Côte de Nuits). These are more likely to tell you that they don't like new oak. In Portugal, Spain and Italy wood-ageing is a long-established custom; the division is between traditionalists who continue to use huge barrels that allow gradual aeration but add neither tannin nor vanilla flavours, and the modernists who follow the same practices as in Bordeaux.

In cheaper wines today it's unlikely that the taste of oak has come from a barrel. In the 1970s oak essence was widely used in California but has gone out of favour. Should you want to try the effect for yourself, for under a tenner a UK-based winery supplies company[2] will send a kilo of oak chips designed to be included during fermentation (although you could always try the effect of an overnight soak before a dinner party).

But the taste of oak is only part of the picture: what's more important in wine maturation is the slow exposure to oxygen, preferably in contact with tannin.

The importance of air contact gets surprisingly little notice in the literature of wine. 'Oxidization' (more fogeyishly, 'oxidation') is not a flattering term in modern wine-speak. It is used in the same breath as 'tired', 'old-fashioned' and 'flabby'. In her *Oxford Companion to Wine*, Jancis Robinson defines oxidation, simply, as 'a wine fault', which, of course, it can be if the effect is out of place or unintentional.

The omission is probably because the flying wine-makers have emphasized the enormous effort they put into keeping grapes, juice and wine free from air contact. This continues after harvest in the refrigerated winery. A protective blanket of carbon dioxide is spread to keep oxygen at bay during fermentation followed by nitrogen bubbled, or 'sparged', through the finished wine.

But the Australians have known about and made use of exposure to air at least since Max Schubert's Bordeaux visit of 1950; and it's linked to the use of added tannin. More recently Patrick Ducornau, a grower at Madiran in South West France, has invented a system he calls *microbulles* (microbubbles) in which a tiny amount of oxygen is injected into the tannic local red wine as it matures on 'fine lees' (spent yeast) in tank; to be precise, 2 cubic centimetres per month per litre of wine. The idea is to mimic precisely the very gentle air contact undergone by wine during maturation in wooden casks but at less cost.

Give Me Air – Wines the Better for Oxidation

Exposing developing wines to air affects them in different ways. It can remove compounds from white wine – polyphenols – that would later cause browning. It can create richness and smoothness in red wines: the technique used for most reds in the Australian Penfolds range. The most controversial effect is to create acetic acid or volatile acidity. Are these wines 'faulty'? Do we care? Some examples:

1 Madeiras: **Sainsbury's Madeira Dry Sercial 5 Years Old**, £8.99. A touch of sweetness doesn't mask the fact that this is pickled in volatile acidity. With a scorched, salty quality this seems an appropriate product for a volcanic island whose modern history began when settlers put a torch to its forest cover. Odd: 5/5 Niceness 0/5. But try it.

2 Dry Amontillado and Oloroso Sherries: widely available.

3 **Marques de Murrieta Riojas**. The reds have a slight acidic tang but it's in Murrieta white that you really experience the old-fashioned rather refreshing sourness of an oxidized white wine. Till recently there was also a 'rosé' – actually turned pale orange with air contact. Murrieta wines are widely available – Oddbins,

---

Threshers, Majestic, Sainsbury's and many independents, priced at the time of writing between £7 and £9. To get the full experience choose the oldest vintage. Whites: Odd: 4/5 Niceness: 3/5.

4 **Château Musar.** Even if you never look at wine in the glass, the extremely unfashionable hue of the great wine of the Lebanon's Bekaa Valley makes it worth a quick glance: it's pale and a bit orangey-brown from oxidation. The flavours change from vintage to vintage, but you could say the core component was spicy and cedary (appropriate given its Lebanese provenance). For the 1989 vintage I tasted an animal note, virginia tobacco, and, bizarrely, a hint of jasmine. Sainsbury's and Waitrose usually have Musar – just under £9 at the time of writing – and specialist merchants may have older vintages. For example at Justerini and Brooks, London SW1 (0171 493 8721) 1988 (£8.90); 1982 (£12.50) and 1979 (£17.50). Tanners, Shrewsbury (01743 232400) 1989 (£9.20); 1986 (£9.60); 1980 (£13.85); 1977 (£23.75).

Stefan Defraisne has rigged up the necessary equipment at Château de Fontenille, his 25-hectare property in the Entre Deux Mers, a little south-east of Bordeaux. Ducornau's work has explained some of the chemistry that, he says, gives barrel-matured wine ' . . . more finesse, more of an impression of sweetness (though not being sweet), more fruit. It's a reaction between the oxygen, the alcohol and the tannin that produces these new substances.'

Oxygen is not, however, an additive permitted by the European Union and someone (presumably a friendly neighbour, after all this is the French countryside) sent the *Répression de Fraude* around to Defraisne's cellars to investigate. He managed to persuade the officers that this was not an essentially fraudulent exercise, since oxygen also enters wine during normal barrel maturation. 'These are the rules, and yet it's so natural. This really is a rule against progress.'

But why is wine in some cases improved and in others spoiled by contact with oxygen, which in compounds is the most common and most reactive of the elements in the earth's crust? It's partly a question of style: at the two extremes are 'modern' white wines, made with no air contact at all, and Madeira which has had so much it's halfway to vinegar. Somewhere between the two are traditional table wines. These get a little exposure to air, which strips out a class of bitter substances called polyphenols and gives some immunity to darkening and deterioration while the wine is maturing. At the same time contact with the lees, or spent yeast, counters the effect of oxidation and keeps the wine fresh tasting.

When red wines are matured in wood and racked from barrel to barrel they oxidize gently and gain complexity. This complexity of flavours and smells can come from tiny quantities of substances that in their pure form are highly offensive, for example, hydrogen sulphide, the 'rotten egg' gas, or the vinegary acetic acid, known to wine chemists as 'volatile acidity' or VA.

There are different opinions about volatile acidity. You might, wrongly, expect the French to tolerate it but the Australians to regard it as anathema. In fact Professor Emile Peynaud has a declared policy of zero tolerance of VA, writing that those who would like to allow it a place ' . . . are bad tasters who are talking nonsense. Either they lack sensitivity or they don't know how to tell good from bad.'[3]

But oxidation, and consequently high levels of VA, are trademark features not only of Madeira, Tawny Port and Oloroso and Amontillado sherries, but also of such celebrated table wines as Château Musar from the Lebanon and Grange itself. 'Do you know, Max, that this wine of yours is full of VA?' Grange's creator is said to have been told. 'I know it is,' was Schubert's perhaps apocryphal reply. 'And if it wasn't, we'd put it in.'

1 In France the main use of tannin is as a fining agent used in white wines, especially those with dense, protein-rich juices such as Champagne. It's added with sulphur dioxide to newly pressed juice, to help it clear, and again when the wine is bottled to undergo the secondary fermentation which makes Champagne fizzy. In the bottle it helps to collect the spent yeasts so that they can be removed before the bottle is finally corked. Much more of this fining mixture known as *colle* (glue) is required if the spent yeast is sent down into the neck of the bottle by machine, the *giropalette*, than if the champagne maker employs the older, slower method of inverting the bottles by hand over a period of weeks.
2 Vigo Vineyard Supplies, Hemyock, Devon, 01823 680230.
3 *Le Gout du Vin*, Emile Peynaud, tr. Michael Schuster, Macdonald, London, 1987.

21

Back to the Future

You wouldn't expect an unorganized assortment of peasants, small-holders and back-to-nature enthusiasts to have much influence on the international wine industry. Without winery equipment to sell or consultancies to offer they'd seem to be destined to stay on the margins.

Yet Europe's small wine-makers have become a source of ideas and inspiration to rival the established centres. There are various ways in which their philosophies get around. One is by being sought out by wine-makers who are impressed, for example, by artisanal Burgundies or Rhône wines and want to know how their makers go about their work. Another is through writers such as Kermit Lynch or Robert Parker who draw attention to practices such as leaving wines unfiltered or fermenting with wild yeasts. And then there are local innovations and initiatives, either to preserve threatened local traditions or to find ways of extending and enhancing them.

One thing that is absolutely lacking is a textbook on 'how to be a traditionalist producer'. As I went around growers clutching my copy of *Making Good Wine* I detected that there was a resistance, not just to this book, but to the very idea of a 'how to' guide. I didn't find people had much to add to Olivier Merlin. However when I found myself seated beside the grower/consultant/*négociant*/ oenologist Jean-Luc Colombo at his annual PR do at the 'Pic' in Valence, I bellowed a brief synopsis into his ear. 'You can write that Jean-Luc Colombo says that it's bullshit (*c'est de la connerie*),' he roared back.

In the classic tradition, wine-making is not something you can learn in college. Jean-Michel Vache, the leading producer of Vacqueras in the Southern Rhône, says that after taking the two year course at Montpellier he still had everything to learn from his father. 'When you study you get a superficial knowledge of a lot of things, but no real knowledge of anything; but when you leave you still have everything to learn. It's the difference between opening a door and going through it.'

Jean-Gérard Guillot, as we've seen, was one of the two children ostracized because his father, a Parisian lawyer, had come to a village in the Mâconnais to make wine, but refused to use the chemicals his neighbours regarded as essential.

Later, Jean-Gérard picked up enough expertise in the region's wine-making practices to make a career as number two with the Domaine Michelot, one of the most important properties in Meursault in the Côte d'Or. He did it by going south to Beaujolais and finding work in the named *cru* village of Brouilly.

It was his elderly neighbour rather than his employer whose secrets he wanted to discover. The old vigneron saw him coming and going and finally made an apparently friendly gesture.

'One day I got an invitation to come and taste with him. He gave me a glass of something. I said: "That's not good." ' Guillot had given evidence of a palate and of independent-mindedness. From then on the neighbour shared his secrets with him. 'What I learned was how to achieve a style of wine without resorting to formulas: this brand of yeast or that fermentation temperature.

'The way knowledge is transmitted goes back to the Celts and their civilization. It's that old, uncodified, oral culture. All it depends on is having someone with knowledge and someone who knows how to listen (*"celui qui sait et celui qui sait écouter"*).'

This view is shared in areas with a more recent history. 'Rocky' O'Callaghan, the bearded defender of the Barossa, takes the same dim view of book-learning and colleges. 'When you come out you can't make a single gallon of wine. An apprenticeship system is more appropriate than a scientific degree. The science anyway isn't that scientific. It's about timing and judgement: "Is that the flavour I want?" "Are those grapes ready to pick?"

'You can make wine by a formula and it's the right way to do it for something selling up to £4.99. But premium wines aren't made like that, they depend on an endless series of judgements.'

Philippe Colotte, a young producer in Marsannay, at the northern end of the Côte d'Or, relies on little more than his senses and his limbs. For refrigeration he uses a small milk tank; though it will take only a small proportion of the fermenting wine it is enough, when mixed back in, to drop the temperature two or three degrees. He uses no added yeasts; if a fermentation fails to start spontaneously he uses a resistor to warm slightly the contents of the tank. Once a fermentation gets going in one open *cuve* it spreads to the neighbouring ones.

'There are no secrets, just certain essential steps. First you must care for your vines very, very well. Don't allow too much growth on them and don't let them overcrop. Then the three rules when making the wine are to be clean, meticulous and courageous. Say for example you have a tank in danger of overheating. If that means you have to get up twice in the night to deal with it, that's what you have to do. When it needs *pigeage* it needs it right there and then.'

Hey Hey Marsannay

Marsannay, near Dijon, was only given an *appellation* in its own right as recently as 1987. In the past this village from the northern end of the Côte d'Or was mainly known for rosé, and to start with the new name appeared synonymous with wishy-washy under-flavoured reds. But no longer. Following sleuthing by Adam Bancroft and Jasper Morris there are now Marsannay growers available in Britain who deliver on the promise of the red Burgundy experience at a reasonable price.

Charles Audoin; Marsannay Rouge 1993, £9 per bottle (estimate), Adam Bancroft Associates, London SW8, 0171 793 1902.

Domaine Collotte; Marsannay Rouge 1995, £7.50 per bottle (estimate), Morris and Verdin, London SE1, 0171 357 8866.

Bruno Clair; Marsannay Rouge 'Les Langeroies' 1994, £9.90, Justerini and Brooks, London SW1, 0171 493 8721; 'Les Vaudenelles' 1995, £11.80, Tanners, Shrewsbury, 01743 232400.

This approach can only be taught by practical example. Gary Farr learned at first hand from Jacques Seysses at Domaine Dujac in Morey St Denis. But Farr isn't creating his own circle of disciples in the state of Victoria in South Eastern Australia. This is partly because he doesn't think his fellow countrymen and women would be receptive. 'Australians haven't been there and done it and they find it all fairly unbelievable. You've got to have a feeling for the whole thing.' But he doesn't in any case think that there's enough of a market for what he's doing to be happy about creating competitors: 'I don't necessarily want to give it up. Why should I give it up to anybody who wants to learn it?'

If the art of traditional wine-making is in the details, there are certain externals that the outside world can pick up on. One is an appreciation of procedures and technologies that college students are taught are obsolete.

PRESSING CONCERNS

Portuguese grapes' destiny has not in the past been to be mechanically 'crushed', in the brutal-sounding New World phrase. At worst they've faced being sprinkled with fag-ash as the cellar workers liberate their juices with the pressure of their feet.

Today one of the keenest advocates of the practice of treading grapes by foot in *lagares* is Dirk Niepoort. He says that the weight of the body as transmitted through bare feet has a perfect synergy with the structure and texture of grapes. 'The pressure isn't so strong as to hurt the fruit, the stems or the pips. With treading you make sure that all the liquid gets out of the skins and that you get everything out of the skins.'

To make Port or red table wines the grapes stay in the *lagar* for between two to seven days. 'The way it's done is very simple. In the evening we fill the *lagar* with grapes and spend four hours making a *corte*. It's very military and it's done without singing except for calling "up up": everybody stands side by side and they just go very slowly back and forth. The next day we do the same thing but in a more loose way and there's singing and dancing. Smoking – it seems to be an "in" thing to do and it was very hard to forbid them to do it. They still seem to want it.' Despite this threat to the fermenting wine Dirk has no doubts about the practice: 'I've no question that it's better for Port. The great thing too is that the temperature during fermentation is self-regulating. If you've got too much heat it immediately leaves the *lagars* instead of concentrating like in a tank. If you still need to control the temperature you just open the windows of the building and that way it escapes. But it does cost a lot more and you've got to do it properly. They have been putting fewer people into the *lagars* but you don't get any sort of extraction; it's still a very expensive way of doing things and you end up making a bad wine at half the cost.'

One piece of equipment you'd think technology could easily improve is the vertical wine press. Compared to the simplified lines of the programmable, horizontal version, the old up-and-down one looks like a medieval contraption for torturing grapes. Why on earth don't Château Pétrus get rid of theirs? They can afford to after all.

But contrary to appearances the old monsters are more controllable. Château Reynella in McLaren Vale, South Australia, and Robert O'Callaghan in the Barossa both boast on their labels of 'basket-pressed Shiraz', referring to their antique presses. According to O'Callaghan their big advantage is that they press without agitating the mass of fruit – unlike horizontal ones which perform a turn between each squeeze. This means gentler extraction and, he says, the mass of skins acts as a filter, removing rough tannins.

It's the same story in Champagne. At harvest time the old Coquard presses will be in service from the grandest Grande Marques to small village press houses. You can see why almost everyone else gave up on the up-and-down machines: in the absence of any other means of redistributing the skins, four workers have to be employed piling up the mass with pitchforks between each pressing. But in Champagne, where the majority of the wine comes from black grapes, it's more important to ensure a light pressing, and white juice, than to scrimp on labour costs.

The very newest machines, that use an inflated bag to squeeze the grapes, are held to be an improvement on the first generation of horizontal presses. Christophe Garnotel, who makes Champagne in the village of Rilly-la-Montagne, now has both a Coquard vertical press and one of the latest kind; he had to replace the previous horizontal press as it gave him pink juice. His presses service both his own needs and those of clients; he was careful to ensure that the Champagne sold under his family label of Adam-Garnotel came exclusively from the old-fashioned vertical press.

TANKS FOR THE MEMORY

My visit to the Remelluri estate in Rioja coincided with that of a group of wine tourists from England guided by Richard Mayson, who is an expert on the wines of Portugal and Spain. Telmo Rodriguez took us around, showing a natural pride in the thrilling setting of the vineyards, and in the mellow forms of the huge wooden matu-ration vats. Richard was impressed by the surroundings and by the wines we tasted, but retained a certain Anglo-Saxon scepticism. 'You see those doors that are kept locked,' he confided. 'Behind there I'm told it's all high tech, stainless steel. Nothing wrong with that at all, but it's funny that they don't want to show it to us.'

There's nothing like a hint of forbidden science to arouse your curiosity: Frankenstein, yokels muttering 'tes flyin' in the face o' nature' etc. Or was Richard Mayson simply implying that what we'd seen had been a Potemkin village, and that the real work was done in a state-of-the-art setting?

Telmo had slept atrociously and it was mean of me to ask him to open up an extra section of the *bodega*. The locked room mystery was revealed: a double row of big stainless-steel fermen-tation tanks, dating from the 1960s, not startling either for being especially old or especially new. They were off the Remelluri itin-erary because they were a bit boring. At the far end, though, there was something unusual: three open fermentation vats of the kind that's traditional in Burgundy. Remelluri is inching back to the past, away from stainless steel (*inox* to the Bordeaux oenologists who popularized it a quarter of a century ago) and back to the techniques of the Cistercian monks of the Clos Vougeot.

In the last century the Bordeaux châteaux used vast wooden fermentation vats, identical to those that at Remelluri are used for settling and storing wine prior to siphoning it into barrels for maturation. In the 1930s wood gave way to concrete, which was in turn replaced by steel fermentation tanks.

Stainless steel is easy to clean and easy to keep cool, either by incorporating refrigeration coils or simply by running water down the outside during fermentation. Yet, despite its advocacy by Pro-fessor Peynaud, the *inox* revolution is incomplete. Though other first growths now use *inox*, Château Mouton Rothschild has never given up its wooden *cuves*; Château Pétrus has stayed with concrete and so has Kanonkop, one of the best South African estates;

Château Léoville-Lascases, one of Prof. Peynaud's clients, bought a set of stainless-steel tanks, but in the event has gone on using concrete for fermentation . . .

There is no great mystery as to why wood and concrete give such good results, even if the conclusions are not given much publicity (something which may not be unconnected with the fact that there's no longer much money to be made from constructing tanks in these materials). The essential concept is the 'temperature gradient', the speed with which a material transmits a change in temperature. Anyone who cooks is familiar with this: it's the reason why it's easier to make a white sauce in a heavy cast-iron saucepan than in a flimsy aluminium one. Wine-makers of the old school believe that wine should have as few shocks as possible, whether these involve violent handling or violent changes of temperature. Mme Christine Courrian is quoted in the 1996 Adnams wine list on the reason she prefers to make wine in concrete at her Médoc property, Château Chantelys: 'I prefer vessels with some substance; I think they work better for me. The shape is better and they hold the temperature better. But ideally I should like to make wine in a sphere!'

Tankies

People can use cement tanks for the best or the worst of reasons: because they believe they are better and are prepared to do the fiddly cleaning required, even though with stainless steel it's much less bother – or because they're only going to do a cursory cleaning job anyway. Christine Courrian of **Château Chantelys** from the Médoc in Bordeaux is obviously in the former camp. Her 1994 (£6.95 from Adnams, Southwold, Suffolk 01502 727222) is rich and concentrated but not expressive at the time of tasting. Odd: 0/5 Niceness: 3/5.

Beyers Truter in Stellenbosch, South Africa, is famous for his advocacy of concrete tanks which, because they are open-topped and only 1½ metres high, are quite like the *lagares* of Northern Portugal, with the wine circulated with poles rather than feet. Wines from his **Kanonkop Estate** are imported by Raisin Social of London SW12 (0181 673 3040) and are found in Tesco and many independents. He also makes, as a *négociant*, the inexpensive **Beyers Truter Pinotage** – £4.99 in about half Tesco stores – in identical conditions.

YEAST STRAINS

It seems appropriate that yeast should be a live issue, as well as a living culture. How much influence does it have on the taste of wine, and are commercial yeasts standardizing wine and robbing it of its variety?

In France at any rate, growers who have stayed with the old-style 'natural' fermentations, using only the wild yeasts on the grape skin, smile happily when you raise the subject, glad to share their opinions. Those who've gone for cultured strains look about as comfortable as Labour Party members discussing their children's private education. They tell you that they really have no choice, that wild fermentations are an unacceptable risk, that they use strains which leave no mark on the wine . . . It's like talking about filtration. I sometimes feel that I'd physically embrace any grower who'd say 'yes, we give the wine a really uncompromising filtering to make it nice and bright, and centrifuge it and fine it into the bargain – it's fun' instead of the inevitable, shifty 'well yes, we do give it just a very light filtration.'

This is wandering off the subject. For clarity's sake, the yeast story should be taken up where it begins, at the dawn of time.

Wine goes back a long way: the earliest archaeological evidence of it has been dated to between 5,400 and 5,000 BC, or more than 2,000 years before the first recorded civilizations in ancient Egypt or China. It comes from a Stone Age site in the Zagros mountains of north-east Iran, a region whose natural vegetation is known to include a concentration of wild wine grapes.

But why wine and not beer, say, or the fermented juice of cherries, guavas or blackberries? The reason has nothing to do with the taste of grapes or their availability: it's simply that grapes are the most complete food for yeasts. Yeasts, not vines, are the plants essential for making alcoholic drinks, and they come in thousands upon thousands of different species and varieties.

Though they are plants yeasts are not, admittedly, very imposing ones. They're single celled, and a subdivision of fungi; as they lack chlorophyll they have to turn their immediate environment into food, rather than relying on photosynthesis. They're found in soil, water, our bodies and on the leaves and stems and flowers of plants. Above all they're associated with sugars. Dr Paul Henschke of the Australian Wine Research Institute suggests that they turn sugar into alcohol mainly to keep out competitors: most microorganisms eat sugars and excrete acids, as when bacteria turn milk sour. But almost no living things can survive in an alcoholic environment (it's one thing to ingest alcohol, but to have alcohol concentrations in blood equivalent to those in wine would be fatal).

When yeasts attack fruit they don't lessen its attractiveness to wildlife. Dr Henschke asked if I'd seen in one of the David Attenborough programmes a classic sequence of birds picking eagerly at partially fermented fruit, not put off by visibly becoming drunk on it.

The use of cultured yeasts started in California. Now a return to wild yeast fermentation has become fashionable at the top Californian estates, started as an experiment by francophile winemakers and celebrated on the labels with names like the Franciscan Estate's 'Cuvée Sauvage' or Peter Michael's 'Cuvée Indigene'. It's spread to Australia and even to the classiest sort of flying winemaker, if Paul Hobbs, responsible for the Catena range in Argentina, can be so described.

There are two issues. Does cultured yeast alter the taste of wine? If so is that a good or a bad thing? In Beaujolais one strain, '71b', is part of the formula for making the modern, sometimes rather bananaey, style of the wine. The commercial yeast suppliers credit themselves with impressive powers. One catalogue claims that its products will 'enhance fruit character and contribute to complexity and mouthfeel'. Other strains are offered as Burgundy or Côte du Rhône isolates, offering to create, for example, 'high Burgundy identification'.

'Bullshit' is how Ann Noble of the Davis Institute describes all this. Experimental tastings lead her to conclude that after wine has been kept for a relatively short time the aromas associated with fermentation completely disappear.

Peter Vinding-Diers claims to know differently. In the early 1990s this Danish-born wine-maker showed Master of Wine students two wines he had made at Château Rahoul in the Graves, using identical grape must and with otherwise identical fermentations, but with different yeast strains, one isolated at Château d'Angludet in Margaux, the other coming from Lynch-Bages in Pauillac. The point he wants to make is that yeast is an extension of the idea of *terroir*. Places lucky enough to have a population of exceptional yeasts will also make exceptional wine. Of the two Rahoul wines, he reports, 'Most people were surprised at just how different they were.' I told him of Ann Noble's opposite conclusions. 'Bullshit,' he snorted, unconsciously echoing her.

Yeast is Vinding-Diers's big thing. At the Australian-owned Château Rahoul in the Graves where he went to work in the late 1970s he refused to ferment with a selected strain; instead he isolated a culture from the property's own cellars. Later the consultant Brian Croser, who had worked with him on the second white wine vintage made this strain, 'R2', widely available throughout Australia.

(This summary of events at Château Rahoul hardly does justice to their significance; the property, dating from 1646, became a sort of forward camp for the penetration of Europe by Australian winemakers after its purchase in 1977 by Len Evans and Peter Fox. If you drew a diagram in the style of a Rock Family Tree, it would be at the centre of a spider's web of connecting lines.)

But why is yeast so often a sore point? When I mentioned the work done by Vinding-Diers at Rahoul to Len Evans, the estate's former owner became a bit heated. This was only partly because this creative partnership ended, as so many do, in less than perfect harmony, but also because he thought the fuss about cultured yeast was overdone. 'It has nothing to do with the quality of the wine,' he was saying in a raised voice when Don McWilliam, chairman of the big family-owned wine firm, overheard him and interjected, cruelly: 'Except when Mr Croser uses it to make all wines taste the same!'

Don McWilliam can't be quite right. Yeast isn't a magic substance which, when dusted on, transforms what it touches. To make a wine taste as if the Enotech team of Brian Croser and Tony Jordan have been your consultants you need the whole package. Even at the bargain basement level, Hugh Ryman told me, yeast is only one of the flying wine-maker's five essentials, along with enzymes, wood chips, sulphur and ascorbic acid.

But cultured yeast has come to be a symbol of the way in which wine-making has evolved from a mystery to a formula. Instead of making do with an unknown cocktail of yeast strains, which may create intriguingly complex flavours, but equally may turn your production to vinegar, you follow the instructions and get guaranteed results.

And for small growers, wild yeast is one trick up their sleeves that their big industrial competitors can't match. So many of the things they do have been first dismissed as old-fashioned unhygienic dogma, then analysed, then replicated. This applies to ageing in the barrel, to deliberate oxidation, to maturation on the lees of spent yeast . . . Some of the big producers are wild-fermenting small batches, experimentally, with a view to blending in complexity, but you sense a certain tokenism. With small vats, in contrast to a big producer with huge quantities at stake and a need to make winery operations reasonably predictable, a grower can afford to take risks. Wild yeast is rewarding; I believe, though I can't prove, that wines which use it have a living, multi-faceted quality denied to those using single strains; and it's irreducibly difficult and dangerous, which is no less a part of its appeal.

COLD AND SOAKING

Some small growers, especially in Alsace, are opposed to all new technologies. Many others make an exception for refrigeration, especially as they see it as giving them more of a chance to cut down on the use of sulphur or get rid of it altogether.

Alain Graillot in Crozes-Hermitage is one of these, while remaining opposed to other tickets to an easier life, such as using herbicides instead of ploughing his vineyards or fermenting with cultured yeast strains. This former chemical industry salesman calls the use of dried yeasts 'a criminal action; as bad as putting an oil refinery next to the vineyard'. Refrigeration is a different matter; he routinely chills the crushed grapes and holds them at a temperature too low for fermentation to start for between three to five days. The effect is to extract masses of colour and flavour, helping make his wines some of the most impressive of the *appellation* (though he insists 'you can't make that much difference with your method of vinification'). He discovered the technique by accident on his second-ever vintage, in 1986.

'I had to use some refrigeration as the temperatures had risen too far in 1985 and it was very hot again that year. I'd borrowed a cooling system from a friend in Burgundy [where the harvest is a little later than the Rhône]. However he asked for it back. So instead of controlling the fermentation from end to end I chilled the must right down, then returned the equipment to him, and let the fermentation go at its own temperature from there on in.'

It may have been a fluke rather than the result of an experiment, but as a result Graillot joined ranks with the very best Burgundy growers, such as Henri Jayer, who macerate their grapes before fermentation in precisely the same way. In *Burgundy,* Anthony Hanson suggests that this is a return to the past when fermentation happened in open sheds, the weather at the time of the vintage was cool and the yeasts would have taken three days or so to get going.[1]

Jean Foillard in Beaujolais, one of Jules Chauvet's disciples, is another enthusiast for the same blend of the old and the new.

Beaujolais is a region in which people tend to do things by the book; Foillard by contrast gets restless and feels a compulsion to experiment: 'If I found I knew everything there was to know I'd go and get another job.' He's based in an austere, rather stripped-looking house dating from 1780 just outside Villié-Morgon, in the centre of the Beaujolais *crus,* has longish hair, a slight look of Richard Gere around the eyes and you feel he would never, while he had his liberty, grow one of those Beaujolais moustaches. He's the son of a grower, but by his late adolescence detested wine; he trained as a motor mechanic and started making wine only because in 1981 his father was too ill to do the job and there were 11 hectares' worth of harvested grapes to vinify. He'd never learnt how to do it but ' . . . you find you've picked things up unconsciously. What happens here is that fathers pass on their methods. So, as a reaction, you try something different.'

His approach, developed with Jacques Neoport around Chauvet's teaching, looks, on the face of it, highly technological. The whole bunches of grapes from his vineyards (which include a much prized holding on the Mont du Py, according to some the only Morgon vineyard worth the name) are put in a freezer and chilled right down before being blanketed with carbon dioxide. CO_2 plays a part in conventional Beaujolais wine-making, but it is generated spontaneously as the whole grapes start to ferment, rather than coming hissing from a gas cylinder. After the juice starts running the temperature is kept down with the kind of refrigerator called a 'flag' (*drapeau*) that is dunked in the fermentation vat.

A Cold Soak

The Chauvet-Neoport disciples, most of whom go in for pre-fermentation maceration are listed on page 35. The following two also show how this technique can contribute a seductive immediate fruitiness to classic French wines.

Crozes-Hermitages 1994, Alain Graillot £9.75 Yapp Brothers, Mere, Wiltshire, 01747 860423

Château Le Charmail, Haut Médoc 1994, £7.82, Lay and Wheeler, Colchester, 01206 764446

The point of it all, though, is very Old World and French: to express that *terroir*'s naturally occurring yeasts which, without any added sulphur, are at full liberty to work their magic. The different vineyards' yeasts give quite different results: in one case primary aromas of red fruits, in another something not far from those infamous bananas. What they all share is silkiness, deep colour and long life, getting more complex in time without being taken over by farmyard smells. His wife Agnes has no doubts about the experiment. She calls their wine *le vin du futur*.

1 *Burgundy*, revised edition, Anthony Hanson, Faber, London, 1996.

5

BRINGING IT ALL BACK HOME

If these small producers make such great wines, why aren't they on sale in everyone's high street? With the glowing press that the supermarkets generally receive, some amount of explaining is required to justify scrabbling around a whole range of mail order clubs, wine merchants and off-licences as well as the names familiar from the weekly shop. In this section I try to dig below the surface of the wine trade and give credit to a cross-section of its real heroes: the people who have done the fieldwork necessary to bring the new wave of growers' wines back to this country.

22

Cutting out the Middle Men

The British drinks trade is the best in the world, we are always being told. Leaving aside alcopops, weak lager and designer ciders, I do have moments of pride. The business includes people who represent some of the best things about this country: curiosity, patience and the ability to get under the skin of another culture. Small-scale growers need allies if they are not to be hopelessly outgunned in our unsentimental retail arena. Even the supermarkets sometimes employ these paragons, though not sufficiently often.

One hazard of wine writing is being trapped at a tasting by a buyer who wants to tell you how he browbeat some cash-strapped co-operative until it accepted his miserable offer and at the same time agreed to ensure that what he bought was sufficiently bland and 'fruit-driven'. Have I ever heard someone use the phrase 'we went over there and kicked ass'? It seems likely, though I don't have the notes to prove it.

There is a happier side. In France especially, British and American merchants and brokers have helped to stimulate the rise of the independent growers just as their predecessors built the structure of the old wine trade, with its Bordeaux *négociants* and Port and Sherry houses shipping casks to the wine merchants of London and Bristol.

The earliest champions of estate-bottling in the 1930s were American, not British. However, the huge price hikes since then mean that the growers they worked with, who at the time were neither especially prosperous nor well rewarded, are now irrelevant in a book about affordable wine. Recently it has been the UK wine trade that has led the way in heading out beyond the long-established fine wine areas.

In the beginning there was Frank Schoonmaker, whom we've already met as the moving spirit behind American Sauvignon, Chardonnay and Cabernet. Eunice Fried, author of *Burgundy: the Country, the Wines, the People* also attests to his influence in persuading favourite growers to bottle their wines rather than sell them in bulk. His trademark phrase, used to win over sceptics during his explorations in Burgundy in the late 1930s was, apparently: 'Your wine will be yours. Your name will become famous.'

His successor in Burgundy was also an American, by naturalization: the late Alexis Lichine, a Russian *emigré* better known as the owner of Château Prieuré-Lichine in Margaux and founder of shipping and trading companies in Bordeaux and the USA. Lichine worked for Schoonmaker's importing firm for a few years before the war and like Schoonmaker he learnt about wine from Raymond Baudoin of the *Revue du Vin de France*.

In 1987 Eunice Fried interviewed Lichine, then in retirement. He told her: 'I was begging them in Burgundy to bottle. I was begging them in the States to buy. I was fighting to get people to understand what real Burgundy was all about, that it was a far cry from what most *négociant*-shippers were sending to them. In those years, many *négociants* had the habit of substituting one *appellation* for another in their blends. You can understand why the shippers began to resent me more and more.'

The Americans, after prohibition, were able to re-invent the wine business more or less from scratch. When they did so they collaborated with Baudoin's *Revue du Vin de France* to promote the grower at the expense of the old shipping houses.

The British trade imported estate-bottled Clarets and Burgundies but didn't go around actually encouraging this innovation. Instead it remained committed to the old order, and the bewildering number of intermediaries thought necessary to transmit wine from the producer to the consumer (*courtier*, *négociant*, shipper, wholesaler, retail wine merchant).

The old system was not only inefficient, but on occasions outright crooked. In 1972 Christopher Tatham, the general manager of the Wine Society, was headhunted to run the wholesale business of Barker and Dobson. He discovered that this company's main business was taking inferior *vin de table* and relabelling it as

Chablis, Pouilly-Fumé and other famous names. He recalls that he went to his boss and told him, 'I'd like to let you know that you haven't a decent bottle of wine in the place; every bottle is spurious *and* in bad condition.' Fortunately his employer, instead of sacking him, invited him to rebuild the operation from scratch.

One great innovator in the British trade has been Tony Laithwaite of Direct Wines (Bordeaux Direct and the *Sunday Times* Wine Club). He's not the type of wine-merchant you would automatically nominate as a champion of the small grower. Like Frank Schoonmaker with his American varietal wines, on first glance Tony Laithwaite owes his place in history to an innovation that does little for grass-roots wine-making: in 1987 he was the first to employ a 'flying wine-maker' to put an Australian gloss on a French co-operative wine, and then invented that term to convey what he was up to.

The 1980s was Australia's decade. By contrast, the 1960s, when Laithwaite set up in business, marked the high tide of Britain's post-war rediscovery of France. Elizabeth David had published *French Provincial Cooking*, and Terence Conran had opened Habitat stocked with Sabatier knives and Le Creuset cooking pots. Politically, Britain was putting its eggs in the European basket with its two unsuccessful applications for EEC membership. Both countries' technological prestige was at stake in the Concorde project, and there was talk of a Channel Tunnel.

Like thousands of other young Englishmen, Tony Laithwaite headed for France when he left college in 1965. After various jobs he found himself working as a cellar hand in the co-operative at Puisseguin in St Emilion, eighteen miles inland from Bordeaux.

'The director was someone who'd come in from outside, from the business world. He was semi-retired and took this job in his local co-op and he decided that he was going to bypass the *négoce* and sell directly. It helped that the place had its own bottling line, even though it was small and quite old. I'd tried to get jobs with various other people and failed, so I went back to my bottle-washing job. He said, "You could always sell our wine in England." We wrote a letter and sent it out – and that's how I got started in the mail-order business. It was all about being in the right place at the right time. It was a combination of changes in France and the abolition of Resale Price Maintenance in Britain. There had been such a strong cartel between the merchants in Bordeaux and in Britain. Small producers couldn't do much except sit and hope that the merchant would want to buy their wine.'

The next ingredient was that other phenomenon of the period: the Sunday colour supplement. In 1973 Laithwaite's company launched an offer in the *Sunday Times Magazine* and the *Sunday Times* Wine Club was born with the writer Hugh Johnson as its president. 'It worked very well because it was a bit of a change. We started to offer little country wines that hadn't previously been seen in Britain: Bergerac, Corbières, Cahors, Côtes de Duras, and they were direct from the source which was a bit unusual. Most people would still buy from a great list provided by the merchants.'

Laithwaite was first in with the flying wine-maker trend – and first out. The very first such vintage was made at the St Vivien co-op in the Dordogne by the Australian Nigel Sneyd, who now works for BRL Hardy's Domaine de la Baume in the Languedoc. 'We didn't tell people who had made the wine that year – we just said, here it is, it's from a really good cellar. To be frank, although the idea has got the wine trade excited it doesn't seem to do very much for the customer. We find that most of our customers still like the idea of a little old Frenchman making the wine.'

The next British mail-order business to start buying directly was the Wine Society, looking explicitly for growers' wines. Unlike Tony Laithwaite's operation this was a venerable institution: a co-operative run by its members for more than a century. The job of sleuthing round France was undertaken by Christopher Tatham with the authority of the society's then-chairman, Edmund Penning-Rowsell. These two forceful men formed a somewhat uneasy partnership but the growers they signed up then remain at the core of the society's list. Perhaps because of it's non-profit character, the Wine Society has gone on being an essential place to look for interesting wines.

Chris Tatham recalls: 'I used to spend seven weeks a year for the Wine Society. I went to the local INAO [*Institut National des Appellations d'Origine*] and asked them to give me addresses and reputations and of course they loved doing it. They're absolutely thrilled when someone wants to talk quality. I did it by simply going to a place and calling on every grower. I got the best in every single district.'

This may sound an optimistic self-assessment, but it would not have been as Herculean a task in the late 1960s as today; growers were only just starting to bottle their wine and sell directly. Christopher Tatham is nice about colleagues, such as Clive Coates, who worked with him at the Wine Society, and for many of those who have followed in his steps – though not all. 'There are lots of bright sparks, people who come down to wherever and say "the wine's awfully good" but it isn't – and they bring it back and flog it on, and it's a bit of a nonsense.'

Mail Order Standbys – Lathwaite and IECWS Long-term Suppliers

IECWS:
The Loire provided Christopher Tatham with rich pickings. The estates he signed in the 1960s are now in the hands of the next generation but the quality of these shows why the Society has stayed loyal all these years:

Pouilly Fumé 1995, Michel Bailly, £7.50. A lean impression of flinty minerals, but concentrated in the mouth. Sauvignon Blanc for people who thought they didn't like this grape. Odd: 2/5 Niceness: 2/5

Sancerre, La Reine Blanche 1995, Jean Vacheron, £8.60. More fruity with lemons and hedgerow flowers. Like the Pouilly Fumé, this will last and last. Odd: 2/5 Niceness 3/5

Vouvray Moelleux, Clos du Bourg 1986, Huet, £14.50. From a great estate (see pages 119 and 204). This year the sweet wines show little or no botrytis; they're pivoted around a honeyed quality and high acidity. Not a dessert wine, but try it with a fish in a cream-based sauce. Odd: 4/5 Niceness: 3/5

Bordeaux Direct/The Sunday Times Wine Club 017344 81713
The club sent me samples from three long-term suppliers. They were all good medium to high priced examples from regions that have acquired a reputation for reliability if not for surprises.

Domaine des Cassagnoles, Vin de Pays des Côtes de Gascogne 1996, £5.99. A single estate version of this modern classic, with pizazz and exotic fruit flavours.

Les Abeilles Cuvée André Roux Côtes du Rhône 1995, £6.75.
This *cuvée* from the Chusclan co-op is deep-coloured, sweet on
the palate with soft spicy tannins.

Bodegas Martinez Bujanda Rioja Gran Reserva 1986, £12.99.
Gran Reservas are sometimes exhausted by their long confine-
ment in American Oak barrels, but this is still pumping fruit.

Yapp Brothers of Mere in Somerset is the first port of call for
anyone interested in the growers of the Rhône and Loire. Its list
offers an enjoyable meander down these two wine regions at the
side of Robin Yapp, generous with facts and anecdotes, a little out
of breath under the sheer weight of adjectives. But as he makes
clear in his autobiography *Drilling for Wine* (Faber, 1988) the
business began in 1968 as a 'sort of wine clearing house', with
two-thirds of the stock coming from a single London wine merchant. For the first six months of the enterprise, he admits, 'I had
been busily and vociferously claiming the status of a, if not *the*,
leading specialist in the wines of the Loire and the Rhône, an
epithet to which my entitlement was extremely dubious indeed –
my field experience having consisted of that one day in the Loire
valley the previous year, and not so much as a single minute
anywhere in the Rhône.'

This was, he tells us, a gruelling period as endless Francophile
visitors rolled up, eager to swap anecdotes about the producers on
his list: ' . . . my sense of being fraudulent, a veritable charlatan,
mounted with each encounter.' Early in 1969, though, Robin Yapp
made his first field-trip to the Rhône *négociants* Vidal-Fleury and
there encountered local wines – Lirac, Gigondas, Muscat de
Beames-de-Venises – that the London agents weren't bothering to
ship. He insisted they did and found they sold well. 'The main
lesson for me was that such esoteric wines truly existed out there
in the vineyard areas, and reconfirmed my earliest suspicion that
these delightful rarities might indeed be marketable.' Within the
next few years the firm evolved into an importer of growers' wines
in its own right, with star signings such as the legendary Gérard
Chave in Hermitage.

Those early years seem to have been like the immediate aftermath of a revolution: no one knew what new structures were going to replace the old ones. Roger Harris, now a Beaujolais shipper, formerly an automobile engineer, had an unlikely sounding distribution plan in mind when he began importing in 1974. His idea was to shift his first purchase, of ten cases from the Juliénas co-op ' . . . through something like a Tupperware party, with friends coming and tasting. I think we gave them cheese to eat.' But ' . . . pretty soon it was clear that was going to be a fairly slow way of building it up, so I wrote a mail-order list.' Out of this has come a business that is the automatic port of call for retailers who don't simply want to use the biggest name in Beaujolais, Georges Duboeuf; Harris's regular customers include Sainsbury's and Marks and Spencer.

Trevor Hughes, who began shipping for his company T&W wines in the early 1980s, takes a fundamentalist view of the ethics of being a small-scale shipper. He keeps the established importers at bay to the extent of buying Bollinger Champagne in France rather than using the company's London agents. 'It's a very hard and expensive way of doing things because I have to hold such large stocks. But it's a matter of principle. I want to be able to say "I ship this". That's what being a proper wine merchant is. So many other merchants in this country buy from other merchants and then stick a margin on. To be honest the majority of wine merchants are a fairly lazy bunch. It's a much easier way to do it. They find time to go to all the tastings and all the big lunches and dinners, but don't have the time to go and do the legwork. That was the reason I went to buy a house in France, in Burgundy, so I could be there on the spot. The things you learn from being there, how the co-operative system works, what producers do behind closed doors, the secret cellars . . . I've learned more by being there than you could by reading any book.'

Hughes is scornful of merchants who claim to be 'visiting their growers' when this involves nothing more than a single day in each region; he regards this as a junket at the suppliers' expense rather than serious work. 'Once you start staying with people you have dinner with them and leave after breakfast. I go out to work. I want to stay several days in the area and go and do visits. I want to be independent.'

You feel that merchants with such an austere stand are the ones to take seriously. The London equivalent are Lea and Sandeman, who refuse to buy through agents. You'd think France, their main area of interest, would already have been picked clean, but somehow they've contrived to fill their three shops to the ceiling with desirable bottles, without any recourse to mass-market make-weights.

It's unusual for a high-street chain to buy directly from growers: if they do it's often for the unedifying reason that they have elbowed out the agent who originally approached them with the samples. There is also the complication that many retailers have come to expect: that their suppliers will regularly contribute to the 'marketing budget', a practice that causes some surprise and concern to the more innocent growers.

But there are exceptions. Thresher say they are trying to build long-term relationships with a handful of small producers in the *Côtes*, the less expensive Bordeaux *appellations* where the red wines are mainly based on Merlot not Cabernet Sauvignon. And their buyer Julian Thwaites is adamant that the proprietors won't be asked to pay for the privilege. He tells me that Thresher can get all the 'support' they need from beer and spirits let alone branded wines: 'For us it isn't an important part of the wine business.'

It wasn't till this decade that the group decided to start buying directly in Bordeaux rather than through *négociants*. One reason was that the search for good wine after the bad vintages of the early 1990s required a wider trawl through the region that had to be undertaken in person. Now Julian Thwaites is looking towards the end of the decade, with good vintages in 1995 and 1996 and much more competition for red Bordeaux, and all but hugging himself with pleasure at his foresight in signing up a clutch of unknown names.

'We started it in June 1994 when we went out to one of the conventions – the Côtes convention held actually in Bordeaux. Ninety per cent of the people from the Côtes de Bourg, the Côtes de Blaye, and the Premières Côtes de Bordeaux were there. There was a lot of bad wine but there were also individual properties who made what we thought was really good wine.

'Now we're dealing directly with the owners and we're trying to build trust and come up with long-term arrangements: we're not going to dump them.' Julian Thwaites says these *petits châteaux* will now bottle a far greater proportion of each year's production than in the past and should have enough funds to reinvest, putting quality on an upwards spiral. 'We're paying a fair price.'

If it all sounds too good to be true, that's exactly the impression that the transaction made on one of the proprietors Julian Thwaites signed up, at Château Mercier in the Côtes de Bourg. When Thwaites ran out of the 1993 vintage and tried to re-order he found that the proprietor had already sold it off without contacting Threshers: 'He'd assumed that we'd have dropped it.'

Even though more than a quarter of a century has passed since Tony Laithwaite started Bordeaux Direct, there is still plenty of work for intermediaries, although these days they are more likely to invent their own jobs than join an old established firm. What changed rapidly, though, was the customers' expectations. There are very good wine-retailers who source all their own wine. There are others, every bit as good, who mainly don't, but who feel obliged to create the impression that they personally discovered every grower on their list.

It is a measure of the sophistication of Adnams Wine Merchants that they don't go in for this game. With their association agency Haughton Wines they are significant importers in their own right, but when they draw on local expertise, such as that of Nicholas Belfrage in Italy, Telmo Rodriguez in Spain or David Baverstock in Portugal, they acknowledge it.

Credit where credit is due is not a bad principle if diversity is the very essence of your business. Adnams' chairman Simon Loftus is the small growers' chief public advocate in Britain, as a writer, importer and retailer. He intended to be an architect, not a wine merchant, but chose to look after his family's interests in the Suffolk brewery after his father's death in a road accident in 1968. He went to learn the ropes in the small wine department, whose main function was to importing Sherry and dubious 'Claret' and 'Burgundy' in casks for sale in tied pubs and hotels. In between learning the art of bottling rum by hand he took a look at the accounts, and learned that the wine side was losing two shillings and twopence on every bottle it sold. In the intervening years he has turned it into a division with a £30 million turnover, an average size for an independent wine merchant.

'The point is though that our visibility and our influence is greater by far than our actual turnover suggests. I certainly think we've had some influence on the way other people do business.' He means, chiefly, the Adnams list which, since the early 1980s, has relied, not just on the traditional forms of wine-merchant-speak – 'rich and full-flavoured', 'attractively round with some finesse' etc – but also on trying to bring the customers into imaginative contact with the producers: 'I want people to be able to smell the vineyards and feel the heat of the sun and have an immediate, vivid sense of the producer's personality – because these are the things that have interested me.'

Now it's becoming accepted that this is what a wine list should be like. Perhaps the best of the rest is produced by Adnam's friendly rival, Lay and Wheeler in Colchester, where Simon Loftus spent some months in the late 1960s learning about the business.

'What keeps me going as a merchant isn't the product itself, interesting as it is – it's the circumstances, the combination of the producers and the place. We try to convey a very genuine enthusiasm, but in a completely unpretentious way. One of the things I try to remember is that wine's an agricultural product, and it's meant to be drunk. It isn't made for reverence, and I can't stand it when people start comparing wine to a fine art.'

Most of the names on the Adnams list are craft-scale wine-makers, putting Loftus in the opposite camp to what he groups together as '. . . homogenizing trends – flying wine-making, standardization, international grape varieties. We are absolutely obsessive about wine's diversity.' But Adnams shows a certain deftness in combating the contemporary world's drift towards sameness by using modern techniques. There are the lists and special offers that break with the fusty style of the wine trade of the old school. There's an understanding of brands: Adnams' wine from Navarra, made by Telmo Rodriguez of Remelluri, is called 'Baso' – this is the Spanish for the French *gobelet*, referring to the method by which old Grenache vines are pruned, but the reason for choosing the word is that it's as easy to pronounce in almost any country as 'Kodak' or 'Sony'.

And the company's great marketing triumph has been to find a way of selling the *idea* of diversity: this has been to tie it in with Loftus's personal style, which sits more in a broad category you could class as media/music business/fashion than as city/legal/professional like most of his colleagues and rivals. Once it acquires the label of 'one of Simon Loftus's enthusiasms,' all sorts of odd stuff makes sense to Adnams' customers, and by a kind of seepage to the UK trade in general.

Listings Guide: All Rounders

Wine lists have been becoming to merchants what Dreadnought-class battleships were to the pre-First World War major powers: expensive status symbols of unproved efficacy. As they're free (you can ignore the £2.50 nominal price Adnams purport to charge) it's a worrying trend for those who hope to persuade people to pay to read about wine. Here are some of the current blockbusters:

Adnams, Southwold. 100 literate and informative pages. 01502 727220. If you sent for only one list this might be it (though the prices are not the keenest).

Tanners, Shrewsbury. This Shrewsbury-based merchant is good on both its range and its prices. Useful 140-page smaller format list. 01743 232400.

The Wine Society, Stevenage. Another contender for the single essential list. Here the unique selling proposition is the stocks of affordable mature older vintages. You have to join (£20). 01438 741177.

Lay and Wheeler, Colchester. The mother of all wine lists: 130 or so pages and full colour printing. Their contents page reads like a list of their specialist strengths: Alsace, Australia, Austria, Beaujolais, Bordeaux . . . 01206 764446

Gelston Castle Fine Wines, Galloway, with an office in London SW1. A very good selection of growers and a list which reflects a generous desire to communicate enthusiasms. 01556 503012 (Galloway), 0171 821 6841 (London).

Raeburn Fine Wines, Edinburgh. Hand in glove with the great importers Richards Walford, among others. Crucial. 0131 554 2652.

Bibendum, London NW1. A catholic selection studded with great names. Recently this list was in a state of Trotskyist-style permanent graphic revolution; this year (1997) it has adopted a more conventional interest in small growers. 0171 722 5577.

Lea and Sandeman, London SW3. These shops are all about growers' wines; somehow this list doesn't capture the excitement of actually going and looking, but get it anyway. 0171 351 0275

T&W Wines. Thetford, Norfolk. Trevor Hughes's list isn't beautiful but it tops the scales at 140 A4 pages, full of personal discoveries. 01842 765646

Justerini and Brooks, London SW1. Of the two traditional St James' merchants, Justerini's, rather than Berry Brothers and Rudd, shows the greater commitment to small growers. A good straightforwardly presented list. 0171 493 8721.

One reason not to be dogmatic about only selling people you personally sign is that so little of France, at any rate, remains virgin territory. Anyone who goes there looking for new signings starts at a disadvantage to the Anglo-Saxons resident in all the major regions: Charles Sydney in the Loire, Bill Blatch and Christopher Carran in Bordeaux, Charles Blagden in the South, and the doyenne of expatriates, Becky Wasserman in Burgundy. Many of the top names will already have been trailed in front of the British wine trade by appearing on the lists of bars and restaurants managed by expats: Le Mimosa in St-Guiraud run by David Pugh and in Paris Willi's Wine Bar, opened in 1980 by Mark Williamson and Tim Johnstone. And the really coveted names are the most likely to be already on the books of an importer.

It is perfectly possible to make your own discoveries, Charles Sydney concedes, but the grower will ask for a steeper price than he would give the man on the spot and it will take a huge amount of legwork. 'The Loire is a region with about 50,000 hectares of vines and thousands of growers. You can reckon on seeing five growers a day. How long is it going to take you? It took me and my wife Philippa three years to find out whose wines we didn't want.'

When I met Charles Sydney I was on a three-day press trip/jaunt in the region. He appeared, bearded and hippyish-looking, and all but hi-jacked the minibus, taking it on an unscheduled diversion to the Bourgueil co-op, for whom he'd just struck a deal to supply a handful of supermarkets and high-street chains. He plotted this coup despite having only that day heard that we were in the region, possibly drawing on the training in tactics he gained from his university naval scholarship.

Sydney and his wife are former employees of Tony Laithwaite's *Sunday Times* Wine Club: Philippa was the wine manager and gave Charles his job. They got tired of working out of a London office and invented their present role by analogy with their wine-broker friends in Burgundy, Becky Wasserman, who is American, and her English husband Russell Hone. They chose, however, to base themselves in Chinon, an old stone-built town on the Loire whose wine already had a long history when Rabelais wrote about it. 'In Burgundy the discoveries have already been made,' says Charles.

In the Loire a new web of commercial relationships is still taking shape, replacing the former power of the *négociants*. New intermediaries like Charles Sydney are in the process of encouraging the growers to carve out an identity for themselves, where the old ones simply see their role as providers of blending material: 'the classic business of mixing it all up and stirring it with a spoon', as he describes it.

'We work on people to try and encourage them to sell a little bit less in bulk, though they often want to for their cash revenues. We had a lot of success in 1989 and 1990 and persuaded the growers to build up a rollover; it was a good thing as the 1991 vintage was lost to frost. If they hadn't had the stock they'd have lost all their markets.'

So who are the crucial names that the couple have brought to a wider audience? Charles names three growers, one in Muscadet, one in Saumur making sweet wine and one making Sancerre. None of them mean a thing to me. 'But what about Joguet and Druet? I thought you represented them?' He does, but the question is as on-the-ball as asking a young ragga fan if he likes Bob Marley. These names are established, get good prices and they're in the *Guide Hachette*, the French vineyard guide that's the standby of many English would-be importers.

He sees the point of his job as being to bring new talent to the attention of clients in England, something that needs stamina: 'When you go to taste in a village fair you can reckon on 10 per cent being good, 30 per cent average and the rest pretty bad. After a day of it you think "why do I do it?" '

The brokers, like Charles Sydney, often become good friends with the growers they represent, but they're in the odd position of having two clients with diametrically opposed interests: the British retailers who ask them to find growers and the producers who look for a good price. How does he cope? 'You just must behave and be seen to behave with complete integrity.'

Life is even more complicated for Bill Blatch of Vintex. This firm is one of the main ports of call for the British and American wine trade; sometimes Blatch works with the Bordeaux *négociants* and sometimes he bypasses them.

He laid on a tasting for me in an office far removed in spirit from the elegance of the eighteenth-century stone-faced buildings on Bordeaux's river frontage, the Quai des Chartrons, where the wine trade is supposed to congregate. Vintex instead is on the edge of town in an industrial wasteland so featureless I drove past the building, then past it again, distracted by the sight of a vast and windowless structure in old battered concrete. Finally I found directions at a filling station. The building that dwarfs the block housing Vintex turned out to be Bordeaux's U-boat base, the target of tragically inaccurate Allied bombing, and which more recently was used for the filming of the TV submarine epic, *Das Boot*.

Vintex's unassuming offices are where many supermarkets like to come when they decide they must do something about their Bordeaux range. It feels like an extension of their own world – the company was formed from the rump of Allied Breweries' own *négociant* business, Delors. But Bill Blatch, born an Australian, has also managed to get under the skin of Bordeaux.

This is the most formal of the French wine regions (though the Champagne houses of Epernay also go in for drawing rooms and uniformed servants). Bill calls it 'a bit suit and ties, though personally I don't wear a tie'. The top estates tend to have managers, not owners, the owners being insurance groups or Japanese drinks companies, and instead of tasting in the cellar with the winemakers, the châteaux like to usher guests into ritzy tasting rooms under the eye of a hostess. But after twenty-two years, Bill can take liberties. 'I refuse to taste in those places. I go into the cellar.'

Here, as in Burgundy and the Loire, more producers are bottling their own wine. 'A leap of faith into the future', Bill calls it. 'If they want to sell in bulk they just look up the going rate, get on the phone to their favourite *courtier*, he'll be there the next morning and the following day they'll have an order, if he's lucky. But for someone to snap out of that, have to wait for a whole year to be paid, in the end not getting much more if he bottles in than if he doesn't . . .'

Bill Blatch speaks the growers' language, but he is also, of course, equally fluent when he talks to his overseas clients. The phone rings endlessly and I sit, eavesdropping: 'I'll toss in a franc, you'll toss in a franc . . . don't make any waves . . . I'll have a word with Jean-Luc, just for this pallette . . . no don't worry, I'll see if I can work it back to twenty-one.'

Richards Walford are Bordeaux *négociants* but this is the minor part of their business. Their main significance is in being arguably the most influential British dealers in French growers' wines, (with an increasing interest in Italy). If earth tremors swallowed up their offices and cellars in the flat Rutland countryside there would be shortages in the fine wine business as catastrophic as those experienced in the computer industry in the wake of the Kobe earthquake of 1995. They've managed to sew up the top names, from Henri Jayer and his successors in Burgundy, to the Thienpont family in Bordeaux, whose properties include the world's most sought after estate as measured by price, Le Pin in Pomerol, to the Huet and Joly domaines in the Loire, to Paul Avril's Clos des Papes in the Rhône. What's more relevant is that they also have the pick of the affordable growers of the Languedoc-Roussillon.

There are plenty of excellent growers who haven't been netted by Roy Richards and Mark Walford. But their firm is the biggest single beneficiary of the move away from the *négociants*, and it all but scooped the pool in Burgundy in the early 1980s.

Why? And if this firm hadn't done the legwork would a rival have achieved an equivalent hit-rate? If they have a formula, its essential elements would include:

1 **Spotting Growers** It's annoying to suspect, as Roald Dahl said of the American wine guru Robert Parker, that 'the bugger's always right'. As far as I can tell the suppliers are chosen solely because of the way their wine tastes rather than because they share a philosophy. However, when you investigate they turn out to subscribe to the same approach: low yields, hard work in the vineyard and minimal intervention in the wine-making process.

2 **Hard Cash** buying their wines with hard cash, rather than offering to represent them. Britain's wine trade is notorious in France for not paying. In the absence of written contracts, hard cash cements relationships and makes it less likely that growers will be poached. Another buyer has described to me the long-term strategy he successfully used to woo a producer from a different rival – repeated visits, tastings, small gifts – but a similar approach failed to prise even a small allocation from one of Richards Walford's growers.

3 **Attitudes to UK Outlets** a robust approach with the UK wine trade and in particular the supermarkets and multiples. Richards Walford point-blank refuse to make payments towards marketing budgets: 'backhanders' as the firm's Charlie Allen bluntly calls them. They are prepared to bear grudges. 'Unfortunately there's a school of thought which thinks it smart or clever to force a grower to sell at a loss,' says Roy Richards. His response in one case has been to refuse ever to do business with one major UK chain, despite its potential importance as a customer. How do they get away with it? 'Simply because their stuff is extremely good,' according to Jo Standen, the boss of Wine Rack. 'There will always be a market for quality.'

That willingness to pay for quality can be relied on more, however, among the well-heeled. This is a pity. It must be more satisfying to get a wine like the Gilbert Alquier Faugères into a Lewisham off-licence than a Grand Cru Burgundy into the St James premises of Justerini and Brookes. In 1994 Threshers, Jo Standen's employer, did briefly take on an enviable range of South of France growers' wines. The Threshers' by-the-case subsidiary Bottoms Up did the new signings proud in its wine list with grainy photos of the assembled growers; most of these had never met before, but they'd been brought together from across the 200 kilometre expanse of the region for an outdoor meal and a photo session.

But it didn't last and most of the growers were retired from the Threshers list in little more than a year (though Roy Richards swears they sold in respectable quantities). Threshers' South of France range is now almost entirely restricted to a cheap selection from the large-scale suppliers.

Roy Richards is schoolmasterish, ironic, rather twitchy. He poses as a *Telegraph*-reading reactionary but has an un-élitist concern for the general quality of life. He believes that ordinary customers in Britain are short-changed because of the supermarkets' and multiples' liking for the convenience of buying from a handful of big suppliers and for the easy revenues generated by promotion moneys.

And he takes a serious view of his responsibilities to his suppliers. 'Think of what it means to a small farmer with only 2 or 3 hectares to sell you a whole year's work,' he once told me. 'It's a terrific responsibility. I think it's important that the wine-maker should be able to stay in business to sell to you the following year.'

23

The Whole Wide World

Till about the mid 1980s 'growers' wines' in Britain meant French growers' wines, even though Italy, for example, is a producer of about comparable size (together France and Italy make two-thirds of the world's wine) and the middle classes are almost as at home in Tuscany as the Dordogne. But now enthusiasts are starting to discover the same potential in the whole of the Mediterranean that an earlier generation of importers found in the French regions. The supermarkets are keen to explore widely, but this is not always a help; when Raymond Reynolds shows his Portuguese growers' wines he faces a preconception that the point of that country is to make wines to sell below a £2.99 price point.

ITALY

Nicholas Belfrage blames history and geography for the bias in favour of French wine, one that he has spent much of his life working to redress. In his first survey of Italian wine, *Life beyond Lambrusco*,[1] he describes how the international wine trade was based on coastal regions (Bordeaux, Oporto, Jerez and Funchal in Madeira) or those with access to rivers and hence to the open seas (Burgundy, Champagne, Northern Germany and the Loire). It was not till long after the development of trade based on the Atlantic and North Sea, he writes, that the Mediterranean was truly open to British shipping.

Belfrage's greatest achievement to date has been to make British retailers and restaurateurs feel happy about buying Italian wine. He wasn't the first importer to venture beyond the usual industrially produced stuff; that was Renato Trestini in the 1970s, with his advocacy of previously unseen artisanally made wines from such Piemontese *denominazione* as Sizzano and Carema. But Belfrage ought to be able to congratulate himself on being the man who achieved for Italy's small wine growers what his colleagues in the trade had done for their French counterparts; so far, though, he doesn't feel able to. Despite having the field largely to himself through fluency in Italian built on a degree at University College London, he feels his story has been one of hard grind rather than unqualified triumph.

'Britain has been slower than any other country to catch on to quality Italian wines, and that remains the case,' he sighs. 'The producers here are becoming less and less interested in us. They think the English are just interested in buying to price points, which the Italians think is absurd.'

You might think there was a natural entry point, since almost wherever you find yourself in Britain, the local restaurant will be Chinese, Indian – or a 'trattoria', complete with Alpine hunting-lodge decor and peppergrinder-wielding waiters.

But this hasn't helped at all. 'The wine in the restaurants was almost entirely industrial rubbish, and it's what gave Italy such a bad name. The situation is now so different to what it was twenty years ago. Now there are hundreds of thousands of little producers making very nice wines. The German, the Swiss, the Austrian markets are picking up on it, the US quite a lot – even Australia. Practically everybody is ahead of us.'

In 1994 Nicholas Belfrage ended one phase of his battle to shake us out of our prejudices. He sold Winecellars, the importers, wholesalers and retailers he had founded in the mid 1970s, and moved to 'halfway up a hill' called Monte Giovi near Rufina, where the best Chianti is made, twenty kilometres east of Florence. Winecellars continues trading under the ownership of Enotria, an old rival, with a roll call of top names assembled by Belfrage in the course of field-trips throughout the 1980s from Piemonte in the north-west to Puglia in the heel of Italy. Today he trades as Vinexus, one of those unmemorable wine-industry names; he works as a broker rather than a buyer in his own right and also continues to write.

In the heyday of Winecellars, its Wandsworth headquarters was a crucial institution if you wanted to find out about Italian wine. Most wine-producing countries do their PR on an official or semi-official basis. If as a journalist you express the slightest curiosity about the wines of France, Germany, Spain, California or, above all, Australia, you will find yourself invited to tastings, put on mailing lists, any questions answered and even air tickets to whisk you out at short notice. I have never penetrated the consciousness of any Italian equivalent (though my phone directory lists an 'Italian Wine Centre' in the West End – a cover for something?), but Winecellars seemed to employ any number of experts, mostly Masters of Wine like Belfrage himself, able to illustrate any question with reference to their encyclopaedially stocked cellars.

Even without Winecellars he would have a claim to a place in history. Sainsbury's may have been the first supermarket to sell wine, at its branch at Broadmead in Bristol in 1962, but Nick Belfrage claims that he was the first ever buyer to go out to France to strike deals directly with co-ops and growers. It was the early 1970s and he was working for a group called Vince's Foods, and some associated off-licences called Grapevine. Long after he'd started putting his energies into Italy he continued to be a supermarket owner, with the Europa Foods chain in London (until he told me this I'd never understood why the Europa store at the Highbury end of Upper Street, Islington, had such unexpectedly good wine).

GERMANY

In contrast to Italy there has never been a lack of importers for German estate wines; companies like Walter Siegel and O. W. Loeb were founded to carry on this business. Lately though their main interests have turned elsewhere, leaving individuals such as Freddy Price as carriers of the flame.

'Never trust a man in a bow tie,' is one piece of life's wisdom that the Hollywood script guru Robert McKee passes on in his courses for would-be screen writers along with his tips on story structure. If acted on, this advice could be disastrous for people's confidence in members of the wine trade (not to mention architects and the late Sir Winston Churchill). It's especially unfair when applied to Freddy Price, as decent a man as ever tried to align one of the wretched things in front of a mirror in a good light (I feel sure he wouldn't cheat by wearing a clip-on one).

Freddy Price is the agent for seven of the top German wine estates, which he markets as 'The Magnificent Seven'. These are traditional hand-made wines with lots of character and they're surprisingly affordable; in fact, despite a history of being some of the most coveted wines in the world, they now share the same price bracket as an aspiring but second-division region, like the Languedoc or the Mâconnais. Many of the other producers in this book are aspiring to greatness; the Germans have known it but now find themselves in somewhat reduced circumstances, mainly because of the collapse of confidence described in Chapter Seven.

Freddy Price has a nose for up-and-coming producers, like the young Jean Christophe Bott-Geyl in Alsace or Château Malraumé in Bordeaux. But looking after a clutch of German estates is more a task of consolidation, holding the line, keeping the flag flying and waiting for a change in the tide of fashion. He gets plenty of moral support: 'I think the press has been intensely helpful – Jancis [Robinson], Hugh [Johnson] and the other wine writers. It's beginning to translate into sales. I believe their wines are particularly good examples and they see the UK as being still a very important market because it's an entry to the Far East and the US. They're not yet doing really well in this country but they are in Japan and Scandinavia.'

The wine writers have been talking up a revival in Riesling for years. Hamish Wakes-Miller, still in his mid-twenties, thinks he sees signs of it among his own age group who've come to it not through Germany but Australia, where this long-established grape variety is getting a fresh wind, like the equally long-established Marsanne or Verdelho, as an alternative to Chardonnay. He works for Walter S. Siegel; like O. W. Loeb this is a long-established German-founded company which, true to its history, still represents some German producers. One of Hamish's jobs is to find customers for Ernie Loosen's Mosel wines, and, like Freddy Price, he sees glimmers of a revival: 'It's hard work but very fulfilling.'

AUSTRIA

If it's an uphill battle to sell the products of German or Italian growers at a profit, how does Noel Young manage to thrive – not, admittedly, in an overcrowded field – as the leading importer of hand-made Austrian wines?

The answer is that the profitability is not connected with his speciality. Noel Young, the bearded son of publican parents, has made a reputation on the basis of the five Austrian growers he imports, but the financial health of the enterprise depends on a large list of more conventional French and Australian names.

This independent merchant, importer and wholesaler went to work for Victoria Wines in 1988 after failing to find a job in a small brewery, his first career choice. Three years later he set up on his own. He is a product of his times; some years earlier he might well have made his whole career in one of the big brewing companies who dominated the wine trade: Allied Breweries with Victoria Wine and Delor in Bordeaux, the Bass Charrington counterparts Augustus Barnett with the Alexis Lichine *négociant* business or Whitbread's Thresher group. Today the whole scene has split open, among the importers as among the producers. For those who want customers to beat a path to their door in this changed landscape, it's useful, if not vital, to have something special to offer.

He discovered Austria through the London Wine Trade Fair. In 1991 he was just setting up on his own and decided to try the product on offer at the national Austrian stand. 'I didn't know anything about these wines but I was fairly taken aback by their quality.' Other wine merchants didn't appear to be interested, so he took the plunge. Although he speaks no German he showed up the following year at Winova, the Vienna wine fair, and made contact with Alois Kracher, who had no UK importer despite building up a passionate local following for his *botrytized* wines made, like those of his cousin Willi Opitz, on the shores of the Neuseidler See.

Like so many of their European neighbours, the Austrians have increasingly been putting their wines in bottle and sending them further afield than the traditional local markets. 'A lot of the wineries had an attached *heurige* [a tavern for drinking jug wine of the current vintage] or they sold it by the carafe. What we're now seeing is the younger generation taking over their parents' estates – a lot of them are under thirty – and aspiring to something greater.'

Austrian wines aren't especially Germanic. Noel Young compares the Rieslings to the fuller, drier style of Alsace and the reds to Burgundy, a region that like Austria saw vines introduced by the Romans and cultivated through the Middle Ages by the Cistercian Order of monks. Unfortunately like Burgundy it's close to the prosperous heart of *Mitteleuropa* and it's hard to uncover bargains in a country criss-crossed by prosperous German and Italian tourists. At least, though, the Americans are not yet major customers: Austria does not get a single line in either of the last two editions of Robert Parker's doorstopper *Wine Buyer's Guide*.

Noel Young is aware of the difficulty of building a mass market for a range of wines whose price starts at over £5. But he isn't at all sure that he wants to anyway, preferring to deal with restaurants and independent merchants than with national chains. 'These growers don't make wine that's dictated by market forces. If you've got a contract with a supermarket you're only in limited control. Rather than make the same style year in year out these people are free to experiment.'

GREECE

If for most people in Britain, a knowledge of Italian wine only requires you to hang on to the names Lambrusco, Chianti and Valpolicella, Greek wine can be summed up in two: Demestica and Retsina. But in Greece as elsewhere around the Mediterranean, there is a revolution in progress, at the fore of which, according to Jordanis Petridis of the Greek Wine Centre in Shrewsbury, are middle-class good-lifers. 'Quite often they've decided to give up their other profession to concentrate on their vineyards. A lot of people working in Athens still own land out in the country. It's all so sudden. Five years ago I probably knew every Greek wine-producer personally. Now there are so many. There's an explosion of new faces, new ideas, new people.'

He began his wine business in 1984 after spending ten years in Britain as an architect; he was on the team designing and planning the new town of Telford in the West Midlands, not far from his present home. Now he runs an import and wholesale business, selling cases of wine by mail order though not through a shop.

Greece may be one of the poorer members of the European Union, but at Jordanis's end of the market, there's no question of picking up wine for a song. 'The internal market is thirsty for good bottled wine, and that's one reason that they tend to be rather on the expensive side.' At best he can hope to lay his hands on smaller quantities, sold because the producers enjoy the status of exporters rather than because they need his business.

To date it is the supermarkets rather than the specialist merchants who are likely to stock Greek wines, and these stock the big producers – who are often extremely good value – rather than Jordanis Patridis's small producers. But he's in negotiation with several retailers and hopes for great things.

SPAIN

Laymont and Shaw of Truro have a number of important agencies for the big firms who have dominated Spanish wine for decades; but for small growers the most important outfit is Moreno, an importer who also has a couple of shops around Paddington. Both firms have been advised at some stage by different generations of the Read family, a fact that seems to put them at odds rather than inspire much common feeling.

Carlos Read signed up a clutch of important small-scale Spanish growers for Moreno in the late 1980s. His father Jan had worked with John Hawes on the Laymont and Shaw list a decade earlier, also writing some of the first books to make sense of Spanish wine for English readers.

Neither Jan Read nor Juan Moreno, who began his import business in the 1970s, have had lives that begin and end with the wine trade. Moreno commanded a tank brigade during the Spanish Civil War, slipping across to France after the final defeat of the Republic. He was interned, but escaped to Morocco from where, like the refugees milling around Bogart and Bergman in *Casablanca*, he aimed to get to the States, finally stowing away. When he was discovered he was returned to Gibraltar, and so Britain, rather than America, became his home in exile.

Jan Read started life as a research chemist, wrote scripts in Hollywood for Fritz Lang and in Britain for post-war classics like *The Blue Lamp* (which introduced Jack Warner in the precursor of his *Dixon of Dock Green* role). He then moved into TV to script episodes of *Dangerman* and *Dr Finlay's Casebook* before teaming up with his Spanish wife to explore Spanish culture and gastronomy.

This last subject is one taken incredibly seriously in Spain. 'It's almost too much, almost a religion here,' according to Señora Amaya Rodriguez at Remelluri. (The Rodriguez family lobbed a series of questions at me, in the course of a delicious meal in their kitchen, to try to discover if we were less food-obsessed in Britain, and if so why. They wanted to believe it was a puritan legacy of Protestantism.) When Carlos Read started looking for growers to sign for Moreno he had the benefit of at least fifteen food magazines with substantial wine sections. 'There were people I'd see constantly mentioned who were never exported, so it was just a question of getting out to see if the quality was up to scratch. Then, for two weeks in July 1988 I sent about thirty cases of samples[2] back to London so they could be tasted at Moreno to see if the wines would actually travel.'

Carlos is no fan of the mainstream wine made by the large *bodegas* – the 'crap big name Gran Reserva' – or the more internationally styled modern wines that have had such success in export markets. He was able to take a risk with some less-established names – 'it's a bit of a crusade' – because of the security given by new agencies in Chile secured by Juan Moreno's son Manuel, now in charge of the business. The growers' wines have taken off, and can be found in some chains as well as several independent wine merchants.

Carlos even sees an ally in the dreadful weather, which with drought and rain has ruined many recent Spanish vintages. 'Hundreds of co-ops who always sold everything in bulk, for example to the big Rioja houses, have declared their independence and are selling under their own names. This has left a shortage of wine for the big firms: their cheap wine isn't cheap any more. It gives us a great opportunity to pop in with really decent original wines that are now only a little bit more expensive.'

PORTUGAL

People from Southern Europe don't think of wine as separate from food; in an Italian deli wine sits next to dried pasta and the importers, if Italian, are likely to have both brought over as part of a single operation.

Similarly D&F, the importers who these days sell a lot of Portuguese wine to the supermarkets, started out in food. In the 1970s Dino Ventura and Fausto Ferraz opened one of London's first Portuguese restaurants, 'Arcos' in Victoria. 'They started selling wines there and they started importing small quantities,' says D&F's sales director José Leitão. 'One evening a very big group turned up and asked for this particular wine, and drank it, and one of the party asked if they imported it.

'Well it turned out that they were a group of buyers from Oddbins. This fellow said, "Can you turn up at my office at Wimbledon in the morning with some samples?" Till that time they'd been bringing in five pallets of this or that – now they suddenly found themselves shipping two container loads.'

D&F have a high profile these days, partly because of their relationship with the Australian David Baverstock, who makes wine at Esporão in the Alentejo, and Quinta de la Rosa and Quinto do Crasto in the Douro. Even more central to the operation financially are the co-operatives which D&F have guided away from their old export markets – Brazil and Portugal's African colonies – and towards Kwiksave, Somerfield and Waitrose. They also have single estates, such as the much-praised Dão of Alvaro Figueiredo e Castro, made with wild yeasts and, of course, indigenous grapes, but using presses, fermentation tanks and temperature control rather than an old-fashioned *lagar*. (He says: 'It looks nice for the tourists, but I think the tanks make better wine.')

If you want to find hard-core traditionalists, or more generally, very good single estates, the importer to go for is Raymond Reynolds, who knows both about wine and Portugal, where he grew up and where his family has been based for a century and a half, mainly trading in cork (half the world's corks come from Portugal). He studied chemistry at Leicester and oenology at Bordeaux under the legendary Professor Ribéreau-Gayon, the mentor of Emile Peynaud, before going to make the wine for Taylors Port. When in Oporto he met Dirk Niepoort, whose Ports and table wines he now imports, and he continues to team up with him to find and encourage 'wines which are characteristic of the areas they come from – we aren't into international wine styles even if, commercially, they make sense.'

One outstanding example is the wine of Antonia Gonçalves Faria in Bairrada, north of Coimbra in central Portugal. Gonçalves Faria, a technician in the local wine commission, owns just 12 hectares of Baga grapes and sells most of his deep sweet-scented old-fashioned wine to visitors and friends. His raw material is the same as that mainly used by Luis Pato, the modernizer of Bairrada: old *Baga* grapes. However, instead of modern presses he uses treading by foot and an old basket press, and instead of new French oak he puts the wine in well-used vats.

Raymond Reynolds and Dirk Niepoort have found plenty of scope in Portugal recently: 'In the last ten years there's been a genuine explosion; there have just been so many growers.' The most worthwhile, he finds, are those who have been making wine all along and are now beginning to put it into bottle themselves: 'people who make wine with the heart rather than the wallet'. Of considerably less interest are what he calls 'the magnates'. 'It's getting trendy to have your own winery: I'm not saying they shouldn't, but they're right down at the bottom of the league. A lot of people think "if we throw money at it we'll get great wine" but you go to these places and the wine comes out and you just think "oh dear".'

Listings Guide: Specialists

Some wine merchants are importers as well as retailers; conversely, importers have a tendency to break out of their core speciality to become more general wine merchants. All the following outfits are closely linked with one wine region, even if in some cases they've widened their horizons. Many of these sell mail order only by the case.

Austria – Noel Young Wines, 56 High Street, Trumpington, Cambridge CB2 2LS 01223 844744. Plus California and Australia's Barossa.

France, Beaujolais – Roger Harris Loke Farm, Weston Longville, Norfolk NR9 5LG, 01603 880171.

France, Bordeaux and Burgundy – Corney and Barrow 12 Helmet Row, London EC1V 3QJ, 0171 251 4051. Generally I have left out the most expensive merchants; C&B get in because of the cheaper wines that come in through their agencies for Moueix in Bordeaux and Olivier Leflaive in Burgundy.

France, Burgundy – Haynes, Hanson and Clarke, 25 Ecclestone Street, London SW1, 0171 259 0102.

France, Burgundy – Morris and Verdin Ltd, 10 The Leathermarket, Weston Street, London SE1 3ER, 0171 357 8866. Also strong on California.

France, Loire – RSJ Wine Company, 13a Coin Street, London SE1, 0171 633 0489.

France, Loire and Rhône – Yapp Brothers, Mere, Wiltshire, BA12 6DY, 01747 860423.

France, Languedoc – La Vigneronne, 105 Old Brompton Road, London SW7 3LE, 0171 589 6113.

Germany – Longford Wines, Great North Barn, Hamsey, Lewes, E Sussex BN8 5TB, 01273 480791. Longford Wines have Freddy Price's German 'Magnificient Seven' and other discoveries.

Greece – The Greek Wine Centre, 48 Underdale Road, Shrewsbury SY2 5DT, 01743 364636.

Italy – Alivini, Units 2 and 3, 199 Eade Road, London N4 1DN, 0181 880 2525.

Italy – Enotria Winecellars, Chandos Park East, Chandos Road, London NW10, 0181 961 4411.

Portugal – Raymond Reynolds Ltd, Furness Vale Industrial Estate, Station Road, Furness Vale, High Peak, SK23 7SW, 01663 742230.

Portugal – D&F Wineshippers, Centre House, Leonards Road, London NW10 6FT, 0181 838 4399.

Spain – Laymont and Shaw, The Old Chapel, Millpool, Truro, Cornwall TR1 1EX, 01872 70545.

Spain – Moreno Wine Importers, 2 Norfolk Place, London W2 1QN, 0171 723 6897.

If importers now look beyond France it owes as much to the opportunity to do business with the supermarkets as to a passion for a particular country's traditions. There is a potential contradiction between the two roles: third-world countries and Eastern European countries chiefly appeal to British multiples because they're cheap.

But novices at supplying supermarkets can be pleasantly surprised. When Safeway first expressed interest in the organic wines shipped by Bottle Green in Leeds, Jem Gardener feared the worst. 'We had the impression that they'd do the dirty on us, that we'd be eased out. But actually it was all refreshingly human and not that different to dealing with any large customer. We've got a lot of time for Liz Robertson [Safeway's chief buyer] and her approach.' The result of the relationship is that Safeway is unusually strong in organic wines from small growers, with a Chianti, the Millton Estate from New Zealand and a selection from the Loire and the South of France. I always wonder if organic wine is going to be good or just organic. Apparently French consumers suffer the same doubts – there are far more organic French wines than are admitted to on the label. However, says Jem Gardener, it helps to be explicitly organic when selling to Northern Europe: Britain, Germany and Scandinavia.

Bottle Green began life in 1985 as Vinceremos (still the name of the wholesale operation), memorable from that era for its ads in the back of *Marxism Today* for wines from Zimbabwe and the socialist bloc countries. It was the brainchild of Jerry Lockspeiser, a Leeds-based youth worker, who was impressed by the wines and spirits served on an Aeroflot flight to Singapore which he had taken because the fare was so cheap.

It seems paradoxical to go from being a supplier of socialist-bloc wines to their current role, ensuring that wines are made precisely to the supermarkets' specifications. Sometimes the brief might just be to make an oaked Chardonnay for £3.99, irrespective of country. 'It feels almost colonialist in some sense,' says Jem, 'being English and telling the locals what to do.' He also worries about authenticity – up to a point. 'If the wines aren't drinkable, as in some cases they weren't before we got Australians to give them some advice, then there's no point in being authentic. The other plus is that by supplying people with reliable versions of Chardonnay and Sauvignon, we've been able to build the local grapes, Kekfrankos, Furmint, Irsay Oliver . . .'

In general independent small growers see flying wine-makers as a threat. This is because they are able to put some of the features of good wine – fruit, oakiness, freshness – into stuff that hits the lowest supermarket price points. How do they do it?

To try to understand the economics I went in search of Hugh Ryman, the man who has French traditionalists waking up in their beds at night in a cold sweat (they pronounce him Yoog Reemann, which sounds extra sinister). I found him at the London Wine Trade Fair at Olympia in early May 1996 sitting behind his stand having a meeting with lots of fresh-faced young men in suits with mobile phones and pocket calculators. One reason, or consequence, of his being in such demand was immediately obvious: he works punishingly hard – his eyes were a deeper shade of pink than the colour of most of his rosé wines.

He told me that something priced, at that time, under £3 a bottle in a supermarket translated at a case price of £6, or 50p a bottle before duty and taxes. This had to be made in Eastern Europe, South America or South Africa: 'Undeveloped countries – the basic thing you look for is the cost, the price they buy grapes for.' This price would have to be about 2 French francs a kilo (about 12p a pound), which is about one-fifteenth of the price of the world's most expensive grapes, which are those grown in Champagne. The two ways of achieving these prices were low labour costs – he quoted $20 a *month* for a vineyard worker in Eastern Europe (he must have meant Moldova rather than the more prosperous countries further west like Hungary or the Czech Republic) – and high yields of up to 180 hectolitres per hectare. He quoted Richard Smart's theories on yields in justification (see Chapter Seventeen). By comparison 90–100 hectolitres per hectare would be the limit for French *vin ordinaire* and levels of 50 hectolitres per hectare in Burgundy would be thought excessive.

The supermarkets and their customers benefit from these deals. Do the suppliers? Mike Paul, who runs the London office of Southcorp, the biggest Australian wine group, has collaborated with Hugh Ryman's company in the former Soviet republic of Moldava; Southcorp pulled out in despair at the local absence of the work ethic. I asked if he thought Western involvement had done local people any good. He shrugged: 'It's like a guy standing with his hat out on a street corner. Do you do him more good by giving him some money or just passing by?'

Chile is often given as an example of an economic transformation through trade. Even so the story of one co-operative and its dealings with Sainsbury's shows ambiguities even in an apparent success story.

It has not one but two wine industries, one based on the Criolla grape variety introduced by the Jesuits, the other modelled on California's with a strong input from the Torres company from Spanish Catalonia. While the Chileans may not themselves consume produce of the type they send abroad, whether ultra-immaculate salad vegetables or 'fruit-driven' wines, most are proud of the economic growth the new agriculture has created.

In richer countries the last few decades have brought small producers increased opportunities for independence. The reverse happened in Chile under General Pinochet's dictatorship. Huge estates were built up partly, according to Marc Bontemps of Oxfam, by tricking smallholders out of their land. 'Most of the cases involved loans they had to take out, and the bank then sold the loan on to a big landowner. The big owners got the possibility to develop rather an industrial way of producing fruit and to force the people who'd had their own land into being temporary labourers who are employed for only three months of the year.'

The wine industry in Chile is now dominated by a few very large companies. Those growers who retained their independence during the dictatorship rarely make or bottle their own wine – something which in Europe depends on having a strong local market – and instead sell their grapes to the major concerns. But the real money is made by those who turn the grapes into wine.

A way out is through membership of a co-op, which will vinify the grapes and share out the returns. One of the most important of these is called Los Robles (The Oaks) based in the outskirts of Curico, a medium-sized town at the heart of the vineyard region of central Chile. A few years ago it was looking for export partners offering both a business opportunity and an opportunity, through 'fair trading' to redress social wrongs. (Jem Gardener of Vinceremos remembers being offered a bottle of Cabernet Sauvignon with a quaint label featuring a horse-drawn coach.) Soon afterwards Los Robles scored a big contract to supply Sainsbury's with their own-brand Chilean wine, both in bottle and bag-in-the-box. The deal was done though the agency of the importers Ehrmann's, who married Los Robles with the flying wine-maker services of Peter Bright, the Portugal-based Australian.

However the result of this apparent good fortune has been to split the co-op, leaving 120 of the original 180 members out in the cold and worse off than they were beforehand. Now Oxfam's Fair Trade office in Belgium has commissioned a report on the affair with a view to finding ways of helping the former co-op members.

I asked Allan Cheesman, the head of Sainsbury's wine department, to tell me about the story. When I spoke to him I understood that a million dollars of investment had been required by the supermarket as a condition for a one-year contract. The poorer members had not been able to shoulder the financial burden and had to leave.

Although I wasn't sure if the story had a moral, Allan Cheesman sensed one. He smiled a semi-wolfish, semi-winning smile. 'Ah,' he said, 'the slave labour stuff.' This tack was familiar to him from his years in charge of fruit and veg. But legally the company had to be seen to be acting with due diligence in maintaining adequate standards from its suppliers. What exactly were the improvements required? Surprisingly, since Allan Cheesman owes his place in history to bypassing the trade and dealing directly with suppliers, he suggested that this question would be better answered by Ehrmanns, who are Sainsbury's frequent partner in such ventures. 'Anyway,' he said, 'there's one word suppliers can always use: "No".'

Julian Eggar of Ehrmanns ferreted away in response to my request for information. Soon he had the details of the investment: a bottling machine which had anyway been planned, a new labelling machine, a bit of stainless steel and a dry goods store. He said that any splits in the co-op had nothing to do with Sainsbury's and related instead to a new policy that members had to give Los Robles first option on their grapes.

Back to Marc Bontemps of Oxfam in Belgium. He insisted that the members had been forced to contribute, albeit in an indirect way. The investment had put a big strain on the co-operative's resources that had been felt by the poorest members. In the past profits had been distributed at the end of the year; now everything had to be put back in the business. Another consequence was that there was now no cash to pre-pay the farmers for their wine and they had to wait several months for settlement.

'The situation is that the small farmer couldn't wait that long for his money, and he was forced to sell to private middle men. These middle men would give him far less money but at least they would pay cash. And therefore, as he wasn't any longer selling to the co-op, the co-op decided to chase him away. So the investment indirectly affected the small farmers.'

I couldn't see, though, that it could be other than a good thing for the co-op to invest. Marc Bontemps argued that the effect of the deal was to deny the farmers spare cash for investment in the vineyards. Oxfam was now considering offering loans to enable co-op members to replant with Merlot instead of the local Pais, which has no export potential. ('Very rustic, thin wine,' to quote Jancis Robinson.) The charity's objective was to help the poorer farmers to rejoin the co-op.

'Sainsbury's may not be interested in all this but I think they did create this problem. The farmers want to be in this very competitive market and there is no other way except investment. We are thinking of starting to give them credits in order to be able to invest in new vineyards, and we'd like to organize a pressure group, though that phrase is perhaps a bit too strong, to give the small farmers more opportunity to defend their rights in the co-op. In my eyes Sainsbury's should have offered them a contract of more than one year. What happens if Sainsbury's say "We've finished"? There they are with all their investments and no market, so I think Sainsbury's is putting them in a difficult situation.'

Germaine Greer has written about how our comfort in the West depends on driving down the value of commodities that were originally highly prized, even revered, in their countries of origin. She contrasts the ritual of making coffee in the highlands of Ethiopia – counting out the beans and crushing them by hand to create something that will be intensely appreciated – to our unnoticing way with instant coffee. French wine-growers are her only instance of primary producers who can still deal with their customers from a position of equality or even, if they are in Champagne, of advantage.

For suppliers, power depends on having something everyone wants that cannot be duplicated elsewhere. For traders the trick is to buy in a market that is oversupplied. Champagne can these days only come from the Champagne region of France; Chardonnay can come from anywhere. So although the Los Robles growers have the choice of saying 'yes' or 'no' to a European customer, they do not come to it from a position of strength. Given that the terms of world trade are, and are likely to stay, unequal, outright charity is sometimes the best we offer to cash-starved producers.

A spectacular instance of cross-cultural goodwill is the case of Heinrich Vollmer and the Indian community in Peru to whom he owes his life. In 1983 Vollmer was in his mid-thirties, a successful estate owner at Bad Durkheim in the Rheinpfaltz and a fanatical mountaineer. That year he set his sights on the Andes, but before starting on any real rock climbing he judged it wise to get accustomed to the climate and altitude and so stayed for a while, living at an altitude of 4,000 metres with a remote Indian community, working with them in the fields to bring in the grain harvest. The villagers told him of the hardship of their lives and their fears for their children, faced either with poverty in that barren hill region or with the uncertainty of life in the slums of Peru's large cities.

After a fortnight Vollmer set off into the mountains. Soon afterwards there was an earthquake and a series of avalanches. The bodies of a group of Yugoslav climbers were recovered and the authorities announced that Vollmer was one of the dead.

But the Indians didn't believe it. They could make out his tent on a distant slope and thought he might still be alive. Despite a strong cultural taboo against climbing the mountain they went and rescued him, carrying him more than forty miles to safety.

After he recovered his health Vollmer was determined to return to the Andes. He found a suitable property at Tunuyan, fifty miles south of Mendoza, one of the original sites of wine-growing in Argentina, and started planting in 1987. So far nine Peruvian families have travelled the many hundreds of miles to a new life on the estate. At the time of writing Vollmer is in negotiation with the Argentinian authorities to gain their right to emigrate to this most European of the South American states.

Vollmer has more influence than most foreigners, being an honorary captain in the Argentinian army. For liberals with memories of the lethal 'dirty war' fought by that army against its own people, this is not the happiest of honours. He won it though for the best of reasons. When climbing in the Argentinean Andes he came across two stranded soldiers, one dead and one near death, and carried the living soldier to safety.

Handy Andes

The South American wine industry comes in two non-matching halves: Chile and Argentina. Argentina is a wine-drinking nation, predominantly Italian in origin, whereas Chile is dominated by wine made to a price on a Californian model. I find Argentina much more interesting. The grand old name is **Bodegas y Cavas de Weinert**. Till recently they sold to the unappreciative customers of the supermarkets, meaning that in 1996 I found an eleven-year-old bottle of their top wine in Sainsbury's for *£3.50*. Now the importers are concentrating on independent merchants – even so the prices aren't too bad: for example, at the time of writing, Lea and Sandeman, London SW3 (0171 376 4767) had the range of Weinert reds at between £9 and £11 a bottle. Other sources: Corney and Barrow, London EC1 (0171 251 4051); Robersons, London W14 (0171 371 2072); Justerini and Brooks, London SW1 (0171 493 8721); Gelston Castle Fine Wines, Galloway (01556 503012) and London SW1 (0171 821 6841). The new name is **Catena**: good if owing less to regional tastes. Last year they brought out their first version of **Malbec** – the main grape of Cahors (see page 113) and Argentinian speciality, listed by the Fullers chain and Bibendum Wine Ltd, London NW1 (0171 916 7706) at £9.00.

---

1 Sidgwick & Jackson, 1985.
2 'Samples' in the wine trade means bottles of wine.

24
Off Their Trolleys

━━━━━

When Robin Yapp sells on to a supermarket he does so with a heavy heart. It's a sign that he's bought something he can't persuade his mail-order customers is worth their money. Unlike a high-street retailer he sticks with his growers vintage after vintage, buying the same allocation if it's a sensational year or a washout and denounced as such by the media.

'It's unfair because if they're hand picking and they're not large estates they can go to enormous lengths to get perfect fruit.' If he can't sell to clients he has no choice but to sell a vintage lock stock and barrel to a high-street chain or supermarket. 'Of course they're delighted to have growers' wines of the calibre of Chave or Clape, but they're terribly rigid about what they'll pay – very hard nosed. I don't enjoy dealing on those terms, but you have to face up to it.' The unfairness is that the 'off-vintages' are often fine: 'There are people out there with the 1987 Cornas and Hermitage. They should be hugging themselves.'

He isn't sure that his suppliers appreciate the sacrifices he makes in keeping faith with them, but finds it repaid in their loyalty to him in the face of attempted poaching. 'I went to see Auguste Clape and he had three or four letters from my dear colleagues – but hadn't replied to any – so I'd write slightly admonishing letters to those bastards. Friendship's very important indeed.

'I think it's something marvellous that these hairy-arsed people are surviving and making wine in the modern world. Compared to the *négociants*, individual growers are so much more worthwhile – what they're handcrafting is like something you'd put in the V&A.'

But not necessarily in M&S. The supermarkets, which have

squeezed the life out of so many small competitors, from bakers to fishmongers to dry cleaners, encounter greater resistance when it comes to hand-made wines. If as an importer you can set out your stall elsewhere you will. (The first choice will be the booming restaurant trade: Robin's son Jason has built up a profitable line supplying fashionable London, from the Groucho Club to the Atlantic Bar and Grill.)

Producers often share the same prejudice. The export manager of one of the most respected French *négociant* houses insisted on going off the record to say: 'We won't touch the big chains. It's not our image.' Why? He gave a blank look. Because they can pick you up and drop you? He nodded.

But growers' wines do get on the supermarket shelves – sometimes for the reasons that give Robin Yapp such pain – and when they do they tend to be bargains. Allan Cheesman of Sainsbury's finds it worthwhile to add a dusting to small growers' wines to his range, even if many of these appear only in the largest stores. 'Buying from small producers takes resources, it takes time and people, but it adds a dimension to our range which, I have to confess, is a little bit of icing on the cake. But it's part of us being a supermarket with a reputation for wine. I'm not saying that we're going to be Justerini and Brookes but that being said we are quite happy to deal with a small producer.'

In fact it's surprising that the high-street chains and supermarkets bother with growers at all. With their liking for large volume, continuity of supply and a manageably small number of industry contacts, the supermarkets have the same requirements as the old brewery-linked merchants. If there's a Burgundy on the shelves, it will almost certainly be from a *négociant* or a co-operative. In the South of France, buyers will look to the huge Val d'Orbieu confederation of co-operatives or a handful of competitors. Australia is dominated by four big concerns, which between them have most of the market: it's rare to find anything that doesn't come from Southcorp, BRL Hardy, Orlando or Mildara Blass (for Penfolds read Southcorp, ditto Lindemans, ditto Seaview, ditto Seppelt, ditto Wynn's Coonawarra estate). Germany equals Moselland and St Ursula, Austria Lenz Moser.

The downward pressure on prices, paradoxically, keeps many of the best bargains out of the reach of the consumer. Real value in wine is more likely to come from an £8 bottle of Muscadet than an £8 bottle of Meursault from the Côte d'Or. Cheap versions of wines that should be expensive are almost always disappointing. Expensive versions of underrated ones are usually a revelation.

You might think that there would be some public-relations benefit to multiples in offering growers' wines. It's true that the supermarkets, whose social and environmental impact is at least controversial, are drip-fed favourable publicity in the wine columns of newspapers. Yet this arrives come rain or shine and largely still celebrates the improvement in cheap wine, rather as if food correspondents still thought it was worth praising battery-raised chicken for its tenderness .

But a lot of good wine gets bought because buyers believe in it and because, as if to defy cynicism, there has proved to be a market for it.

Take Majestic, to whom Robin Yapp, in pain and grief, was compelled to sell some irreplaceable stocks of older vintages in the early 1990s. At present they are managing to be more adventurous than their rivals, with growers' wines from Spain, Italy, Germany and from parts of France without that much obvious appeal for customers, such as the red-wine-producing *appellations* of the Loire. And the group is visibly thriving, expanding and making money.

It isn't, you learn with a feeling of inevitability, the interesting wines that make the money. Instead the firm's secret is (a) that business of making customers buy a minimum of twelve bottles (something required by no licensing legislation) and (b) a shrewd and pessimistic understanding of our motives in buying what we do. Jeremy Palmer hasn't spent all his working life in the wine business; before he joined a branch of Majestic he edited a medical journal. He has a clear-eyed diagnosis of what will sell and why. 'Specific to the wine trade is that it's very, very usual to overestimate how interested our customers are in the whole thing, though obviously the more we can get who are interested, the better.

'People want to come in and buy wine that tastes nice. They don't care much where it comes from and most people aren't interested in who the grower is. So if you can find Chablis which is quite good for a fiver you'll sell seven to eight thousand cases. It isn't the best Chablis you'll ever drink, but it catches people's imagination, like when you can offer white Burgundy at £2.99. It keeps the punters coming in. But if that was all we did we might as well set up on an industrial estate in Calais. It means that we can go and add things like growers' wines and special bottlings. The volume stuff establishes our credibility as offering good value, so the customers will trust us, and it gives us cash flow.'

Jeremy Palmer is pleased with the rate at which Majestic's been adding new suppliers: 'Eight hundred now as against three hundred five years ago.' With this huge range, much will depend on the ability of the young and far-from-overpaid staff to persuade customers to broaden their horizons. 'My job as a buyer is to sell the wine to the staff, otherwise it doesn't matter how much I personally believe in it.'

Perhaps it's ambitious to expect the supermarkets to educate their customers to share the taste of the most sophisticated buyers. It is certainly true that today's imaginative purchase by the wine department is all too likely to end in tomorrow's clearance rack.

But there is, in effect, a continuous promotional effort by wine departments: special offers, 'gondolas' (separate displays at the end of the row to grab the customer's eye), leaflets, wines of the month . . . It would be nice to think that the only reason wines were pushed in this way was because the buyers felt they were unusually good value or because they had stood out in a comparative tasting. In fact it's often just a question of money. If you don't pay into the 'promotional budget' your wine, at best, will have to take its chances without an extra marketing push; at worst it won't be taken on at all.

The sums involved can run into millions of pounds. One importer was startled to be told that to have his inexpensive New World wine listed would cost a quarter of a million pounds, working out at a payment of £12 per case. The trick, I've been told, is to refuse point-blank to make any such payments; those who agree can expect an endless blizzard of invoices. The bigger producers can afford to go in for this kind of thing; for small growers and the shoestring outfits who import them, the cost will be disproportionate to any benefits.

At Majestic, as elsewhere, they promote by price-cutting and, like their competitors, they ask suppliers to put their hands in their pockets – after being pretty keen on prices in the first place. As I steered the interview on to this bumpy track Jeremy braced himself but remained cordial.

How much of Majestic's income came from its suppliers, in contributions to the marketing budget, rather than from its customers? On the company's £40 million turnover Jeremy admitted to some hundreds of thousands of pounds, though not to millions. 'It's an add-on to our business, but if we can get a supplier to price-promote his product we do. It doesn't just go in the kitty. But you have to promote during the year because everyone else is doing it.' He gives the example of the high-volume Chilean Chardonnays, which regularly cut their price from £4.99 to £4.49. An importer who refused ever to join in would get squeezed out of the market.

Majestic ask suppliers to give them what they call a 'retro discount'. If the exercise in price-cutting doesn't sell any bottles, then the supplier doesn't pay. But what do growers in, say, the more remote French regions make of this way of doing business?

'I try to persuade them. It doesn't mean that I won't buy their wine if I can't promote it, but it means they're less likely to become a core line, because core lines will get killed off if you don't promote them. It's a bit weird. I'd guess Britain has quite a sophisticated retail culture compared to France – corner shops over there haven't been driven out of business by the supermarkets. There are farmers who, when I speak to them about a promotion, don't know what I'm talking about.'

Like many people I have some doubts about our sophisticated retail culture. In particular much supermarket wine strikes me as window-dressing, creating an appearance of diversity rather than supplying it. If wines are made from the same clone of the same grape variety by the same wine-maker with the same yeasts, does it matter whether it's called Echo Hill, Chapel Hill or Badger Hill, or whether the grapes were grown in Chile, the Languedoc or Hungary?

At a posh tasting of grand Bordeaux dry whites I run into David Gill, a young Master of Wine with an intense look and close-cropped hair; at the time of our meeting he's one of several MWs in Waitrose's highly qualified buying department. He's far from overwhelmed by the occasion: 'We taste between twenty-five and seventy wines a day and I can tell you, absolutely guarantee, that I could show you wines at those tastings,' he glances round the room, 'that make some of these taste thin and dull.'

I liked most of the wines, but we agree, in a century-of-the-common-man sort of way, that wines made on a small scale by rich people will never be great value. He continues: 'If you've got expensive real estate, if you've got a bloody great mansion of a château too you've got to service that and your wine's going to be expensive.'

In fact David, who is spiky and articulate, turns out to be just the person to listen to and to answer my gripes, especially as Waitrose have a reputation for straight dealings with their suppliers. The case I want him to answer is that as a sector, supermarkets neglect small growers' wines because they are too much trouble and can't afford to pay towards 'promotion'.

His first point is that growers' wines are relatively expensive for their *appellation*. 'People have to want the stuff, otherwise there's no point in us buying it. We could get a Crozes Hermitage costing £10 a bottle but people wouldn't buy it. People need a commercial Crozes, not an expensive one at the expense of a Hermitage, or the expense of a Châteauneuf du Pape or a Côte Rotie'.

Second, supermarkets are there to provide what people expect. 'If you want to go out and buy a grower's wine you tend to go to a specialist.'

Third, there is a problem of logistics. 'We also need to buy in a certain quantity. You try finding a hundred cases of mature Bordeaux of the early 1980s. They're few and far between.'

Fourth, the wine they sell is good. 'The quality of wines has improved at every level in the past fifteen years. We aren't talking about super-concentrated wines that cost a lot of money; that's a different market. But the reason people are buying a lot of wine these days is that there's good quality.'

Quality is a term the supermarkets love, as do the people who write those business-school style 'mission statements' for every contemporary institution, from hospitals, to universities to the Church of England. It's defined as fitness for a purpose, and its meaning slithers around to accommodate the purpose in question. What if the qualities you are looking for in wine are the same ones Waitrose caters for with its artisanal olive oil and hand-made cheeses?

'It's a different market. There are lots of cheese producers who get our support. But people are much more fussy and knowledgeable about wine than they are about cheese. People will experiment with quirky cheeses, but a bottle of wine is going to cost £5 or £6.'

But hand-made oils and balsamic vinegars can cost much more than that. 'Absolutely, people are prepared to pay £20 for a bottle of oil.' David talks about a certain cachet or snobbism that's been built up around olive oil and balsamic vinegar and again talks about it being a different market. But why is it a different market? Why welcome in peasants who make oil while finding reasons to exclude those who make wine?

His answer is that the most important task in selling wine is to dispel the snobbishness surrounding it. 'In twenty years' time we'll probably be trying to create cachet in wine and to remove the cachet in olive oil.'

This answer muddled me by evoking those caterers' sachets of salad dressing (being muddled is an ever-present danger if you go for the lunch at a tasting and drink wine rather than spitting it out) and I never regained my grip on the argument. Perhaps this was a good thing, or we might still have been vying for the last word after they'd locked the doors and were clearing away the glasses.

This is what mine would have been. I would have conceded the persistence of wine snobbery. But growers making middle-priced wines are the victims of it rather than the cause of it. The main difficulty in getting people to give serious attention to wines from Germany, Sicily, the Languedoc or the Loire is not that they are too expensive; it's that for people who associate great wine with spending at least £30 a bottle they aren't nearly expensive enough.

Wine growers don't spend their winters pruning their vines with reddened hands or get up in the small hours to keep an eye on their fermentation for reasons of social prestige. They do it to express their passion for a place and a perfectionism felt by few of the workers who make the stuff that ends up on supermarket shelves.

They may not find the structures of our retail system a comfortable fit, but I suspect that those structures will have to change to accommodate them, rather than the reverse. For the moment they are an anachronism of the most hopeful kind. Can we have more of them, please?

Bibliography

Barr, Andrew, *Wine Snobbery: an Insider's Guide to the Booze Business*, Faber and Faber, 1990.

Belfrage, Nicolas, *Life Beyond Lambrusco*, Sidgewick and Jackson, 1985.

Broadbent, Michael, *Wine Tasting*, Mitchell Beazley, 1994.

Clarke, Oz, *Oz Clarke's Wine Guide 1997*, Webster/Mitchell Beazley.

Dion, Roger, *Histoire de la Vigne et du Vin en France*, Flammarion, Paris, 1959.

Fried, Eunice, *Burgundy, the Country, the People, the Wines*, Harper and Row, New York, 1986.

Galet, Pierre, *Cépages et Vignobles de France*, Charles Deham Montpellier France, 1990.

Halliday, James, *A History of the Australian Wine Industry, 1949–94*, The Australian Wine and Brandy Corporation in association with Winetitles Adelaide, 1994.

Halliday, James, *1995 Pocket Booklet Guide to the Wines of Australia and New Zealand*, Angus & Robertson.

Halliday, James, and Johnson, Hugh, *The Art and Science of Wine*, Mitchell Beazley, 1995.

Hanson, Anthony, *Burgundy*, Faber and Faber, 1995.

Hooke, Huon, *Max Schubert, Winemaker*, Kerr Publishing, Australia, 1994.

Jefford, Andrew, *Evening Standard Wine Guide 1997*, Evening Standard Books.

Jeffs, Julian, *Sherry*, Faber and Faber, 1992.

Johnson, Hugh, *The World Atlas of Wine*, Mitchell Beazley, 1995.

Jones, Frank, *The Save Your Heart Wine Guide*, Headline, 1995.

Loftus, Simon, *Puligny-Montrachet: Journal of a Village in Burgundy*, Penguin, 1995.

MacDonagh, Giles, *The Wine and Food of Austria*, Mitchell Beazley, 1992.

Mayson, Richard, *Portugal's Wine and Winemakers*, Ebury Press, 1992.

Norman, Remington, *Rhône Renaissance*, Mitchell Beazley, 1995.

Oliver, Jeremy, *Evans on Earth: the Story of Len Evans' Affair with Wine*, Lothian, Victoria, Australia, 1992.

Parker, Robert (ed). *The Wine Buyer's Guide*, Dorling Kindersley.

Platter, John, *South African Wine Guide*, Mitchell Beazley.

Rackham, H. (trsl.), *Pliny's Natural History*, *IV*, Harvard, Heinemann, 1995.

Rankine, Bryce, *Making Good Wine*, Sun Books, Macmillan, Australia, 1989.

Read, Jan, *Sherry and the Sherry Bodegas*, Sotheby's, 1988.

Robinson, Jancis, *Vines, Grapes and Wines*, Mitchell Beazley, 1986.

Smart, Richard, *Sunlight into Wine: a Manual of Viticultural Practice*, Wine Titles, South Australia, 1992.

Stevenson, Tom, *Champagne*, Sotheby's, 1986.

Yapp, Robin, *Drilling for Wine*, Faber and Faber, 1988.

Index of Wine Producers

———

Bold type indicates a page containing details of suppliers in the UK

Argentina

Australia

INDEX OF WINE PRODUCERS

INDEX OF WINE PRODUCERS

Alvear, Montilla, 132
Basa (Telmo Rodriguez/Adnams), Rueda, 46
Baso (Telmo Rodriguez/Adnams), Navarra, 46, 254
Barbadillo, Sanlocar de Barrameda, 124, 126
Bodegas Campo Viejo, Roija, 46
Gonzales Byass, Jerez, 125
Pedro Domecq, Jerez, 126
Bodegas Guelbenzu, 13, 47
Harveys, Jerez, 132
Hidalgo, Sanlocar de Barrameda, 125
Lustau, Jerez, 132
Bodegas Martinez Bujanda, Rioja, 250
Bodegas Masa Barril, Priorato, 17–20, 20
Bodegas Pazo de Barrantes, Rias Baixas, 12
Bodegas Marques de Murrieta, Rioja, 226–7
Bodegas Remelluri (Telmo Rodriguez), Rioja Alavesa, 44–6, 47, 60, 81, 202,
    234, 253, 269
Bodegas Rodi, Rioja, 46
Bodegas SMS, Rioja, 46
Sandeman, Jerez, 125, 127
Hermanos Scholtz, 134
Torrews, Catalonia, 275
Bodegas Valdesano, Rioja Alavesa, 47
Valdespino, Jerez, 125, 127–9, 131, 132

USA
Almadén Vineyards, Santa Clara, 155
Bonny Doon Vineyard (Randall Grahm), Santa Cruz, 164–9, 168, 173
Edmunds St John, Sonoma, 167–9, 169
Franciscan Vineyards, Napa Valley, 237
Jade Mountain (Doug Danielak), Napa Valley, 169
Louis Martini, Napa Valley, 154
Peter Michael Winery, Sonoma, 154
Ridge Vineyards (Paul Draper), Santa Cruz, 11, 166, 170
St Supery, Napa Valley, 159
Joseph Swan Vineyards, Sonoma, 42, 170
Wente Brothers, Livermore Valley, 153–5, 154

Index

Croser, Brian, 212, 213, 238
Crozes, 82–3
Crozes Hermitage, 59, 81, 239, 285
cru committees, 53, 54
Cruse, 223, 224
Cruse, Christian, 223
Cullen, Di, 204
Cullen, Vanya, 186, 205
Cuvée à l'Ancienne, 56
Cuvée Carignanissime, 50
Cuvée Indigene, 237
Cuvée Sauvage, 237
cuves, 234

D&F Wineshippers, 270, 272
Dahl, Roald, 259
Les Dames des Arts de la Table, 52
Daniel, Steve, 50
Dard, Jean-René, 198
David, Elizabeth, 247
Davis Institute, University of
   California, 164, 210, 237
debuttage, 181
Decanter magazine, 46
Defraisne, Stefan, 160, 227
Demestica, 267
Les Demoiselles de Chiroubles, 52
denominazione d'origine, 18, 66, 67
density of planting, 49
diammonium phosphate, 216
Dion, Prof. Roger, 142–3
Direct Wines, 247
distillation, 135
diversity, 8–9
Divina Pastora, 126
Doche, Patrick, 202
Domergue, Daniel, 48–51, 69, 75, 80,
   172–3, 178, 204, 206, 207
Domergue, Patricia, 48–51, 69–70, 75,
   171, 172–3, 178, 204–6, 207, 213
'Dr L. Riesling', 63, 66
drapeau, 240
Draper, Paul 11, 166, 170
Drilling for Wine (Yapp), 250
Duboeuf, Georges, 55, 251
Dubordieu, Denis, 79
Ducornau, Patrick, 177, 226

EARL (Enterprise à Responsibilité
   Limité), 88
Echo Hill, 98
Edmunds, Cornelia, 167
Edmunds, Steven, 167–8, 169
early picking, 68, 118
Eggar, Julian, 276
Ehrmann's, 276
Elbling, 191
'Elizabeth', 26, 27
Elizabeth II, Queen, 156
Emoryville, Berkeley, 167
en foule planting, 181, 182
English country wines, 216
English wine, 142–5
Enjalbert, Professeur Henri, 67
Enotech consultancy, 212, 238
Enotria Winecellars, 272
Entre Deux Mers, 137, 160, 182, 184,
   203, 227
enzymes, 11, 26, 213, 215
Epernay, 258
erzeugerabfüllung (bottled by the
   grower), 88
estate-bottling, 70, 72, 139, 245–6
Europa Foods chain, 264
European Union, 66, 150n, 155, 196,
   209, 217, 219, 220, 227, 247
Evans, Len, 107, 112, 238
extractives, 196P3 ('3PL'oo'Fadat,
   Sylvain, 114, 115, 173

Fair Trade (Oxfam), 276
Faivre, Galatée, 220n
Falernum, 190
Farr, Gary, 27–9, 34, 39, 165, 231–2
Faugères, 173
Faustinius, 190
Federaoes dos Vinicultores, 74
fermentation, 231, 232, 239, 286
   in the Dard-Ribo cellars, 199
   'malolactic', 11
   temperature control of, 210–11
at ultra-cold temperatures, 11, 41
fermentation tanks, 17–18, 29, 195,
   234–5, 270
   with built-in refrigeration, 33
   pressurized, 208